Worship AT THE Next Level

Worship AT THE
Next Level

INSIGHT FROM CONTEMPORARY VOICES

EDITED BY Tim A. Dearborn
AND Scott Coil

BakerBooks

Grand Rapids, Michigan

Published by Baker Books
a division of Baker Book House Company
P.O. Box 6287, Grand Rapids, MI 49516-6287
www.bakerbooks.com

Printed in the United States of America

Library of Congress Cataloging-in-Publication Data
Worship at the next level : insight from contemporary voices / edited by Tim A. Dearborn and Scott Coil.
    p.   cm.
Includes bibliographical references.
ISBN 0-8010-9167-5 (pbk.)
1. Worship. I. Dearborn, Tim. II. Coil, Scott, 1979-
BV10.3.W67 2004
264—dc22   2003027335

Contents

Foreword   7
Introduction   9

1. What Do We Mean by "Christian Worship"?   17
   JAMES F. WHITE

2. Worship as Adoration and Action: *Reflections on a Christian Way of Being-in-the-World*   30
   MIROSLAV VOLF

3. Liturgical Assembly as Locus of Mission   42
   THOMAS H. SCHATTAUER

4. On Starting with People   61
   JAMES F. WHITE

5. The Triumph of the Praise Songs: *How Guitars Beat Out the Organ in the Worship Wars*   74
   MICHAEL S. HAMILTON

6. The Crisis of Evangelical Worship: *Authentic Worship in a Changing World*   86
   ROBERT E. WEBBER

7. A New Reformation: *Re-creating Worship for a Postmodern World*   102
   LEONARD SWEET

8. Moshing for Jesus: *Adolescence as a Cultural Context for Worship*   116
   KENDA CREASY DEAN

9. Amplified Versions: *Worship Wars Come Down to Music and a Power Plug*   128
ANDY CROUCH

A Humbling Experience: *Contemporary Worship's Simple Aesthetic*   131
ANDY CROUCH

10. New Approaches to Worship   136
MIKE RIDDELL, MARK PIERSON, CATHY KIRKPATRICK

11. Missing God at Church?   147
GARY M. BURGE

12. Art for Faith's Sake   156
CLAYTON J. SCHMIT

13. Beyond Style: *Rethinking the Role of Music in Worship*   163
JOHN D. WITVLIET

14. A Matter of Taste?   180
FRANK BURCH BROWN

Notes   193
Contributors   205

Foreword

WHAT ABOUT 'ANSWERS' ? ARE THERE ANY?

Worship at the Next Level raises new and important questions about the church, its worship, and its relationship to culture. In this brief foreword I want to give a historical perspective on how this book is a direct response to the changing cultural situation that worship must address. There has always been a deep and abiding relationship between worship and culture. A quick overview of the history of the Christian church in the West makes this very clear.

In the first three centuries of the church, worship was countercultural. In the pagan setting of the Roman Empire, the worship of many gods was highly common. Every person could worship the gods of a variety of cults, or myths, so long as Caesar was acknowledged as God. The church's worship, however, proclaimed an exclusive worship when it affirmed in the earliest Christian creed "Jesus is Lord." For this confession ancient Christians could and would be put to death.

After Constantine the role was reversed. Only the Christian God of the Bible could be freely worshiped. Gradually as the church became the heir of the Roman empire it adapted the Roman ceremonials to its liturgy, making the institutional church and its worship the place where heaven was made present on earth. The drama of God's salvation was played out in the dance of the high mass as the people observed and paid homage to God through this great and wondrous portrayal of truth called worship. In Medieval Europe, culture reflected the church and its worship.

Then the invention of the Gutenberg Press, the rise of the Renaissance, and the emergence of the print world shifted worship from the enacted drama to the spoken word. The word was elevated in culture and in worship; the power of the verbal portrayal of God's drama of salvation was embraced; symbol, ceremony, and liturgy fell into decline in the rise and spread of Protestant worship. Both culture and worship were joined in the emphasis on verbal communication.

Then came modernity. As culture shifted into the Enlightenment, a new emphasis appeared in the church and its worship: explanation. The sermon and the teaching of Christian truth became the primary purpose of worship even as the culture of the Enlightenment bowed to the power of reason.

Meanwhile, in the nineteenth century the impact of the Romantic movement touched a sizeable number of Protestants. Revivalism was born. Worship reflected the rise of and became characterized by emotional singing, and fervent evangelistic preaching, which climaxed in the invitation.

In the 1960s a new revolution introduced another cultural revolution. The past was rejected in favor of the experience of the moment. Music became the primary form of communication. Folk songs and rock bands focused on the self and the existential moment. Once again worship changed. The genre of contemporary music was born as the church followed the curvature of culture, emphasizing the experience of God in music.

Alan Wolfe raises the same question about the culturalized form of twenty-first-century evangelicalism, which the writers of this book raise. He says, "The biggest challenge posed to American society by the popularity of the mega-churches and other forms of growth-oriented Protestantism is not bigotry, but bathos."[1]

Bathos means "the sudden appearance of the commonplace." I take this to mean that worship during the last thirty years has so enmeshed itself with culture that it has become weak, banal, and insipid.

I don't know that the authors of *Worship at the Next Level* would use these terms, but I do find within their writings a common concern over the "bathos" of worship. However, rather than merely critiquing worship catechized by culture, these writers cut a path that will lead the church out of the unholy union of worship and contemporary culture. Interestingly, a theme that recurs again and again is that the road to the future runs through the past.

Like the early church, we live once again in a pagan culture. Perhaps the future relationship of worship to culture is to become, once again, countercultural.

The argument is compelling.

Robert Webber
Myers Professor of Ministry
Northern Seminary

Introduction

Corporate worship today is suffering from a crisis of leadership. In spite of abundant conferences, seminars, books, magazines, websites, and courses devoted to worship, few worshiping communities have theologically and aesthetically educated leadership. Robb Redman writes in *Worship Leader Magazine*:

> The lack of training, support and networking among worship leaders is taking its toll. For every successful worship leader there are several others with stories of pain, heartache and disappointment. Many of the best and most talented are collapsing under the load of unfulfilled expectations from their churches, pastors, teams, families, and most of all, from themselves. The sad truth is that many worship leaders are having to learn on the job, and the lessons aren't being learned fast enough.[1]

In order to address this critical need we have compiled notable articles pertaining to current corporate worship leadership. These provide a resource to encourage the interdisciplinary reflection and creative innovation required for leading contemporary multidimensional worship.

Much has changed in corporate worship in recent decades. Worship today can involve an eclectic mix of liturgies, media, music, and artistic expressions. A clip from a recent movie along with praise choruses written last week can be integrated with eighteenth-century hymns. Afro-Caribbean rhythms accompany fourteenth-century prayer texts incorporated into a third-century liturgy, all illustrated with art from around the world projected on dual screens. Such a mix of expressions, historic and modern, is a common characteristic of the widespread renewal in corporate worship within the church. Increasingly, worship leaders need to be gifted with an understanding of historic Western wor-

9

IS IT THE "sign" OF RENEWAL

ship forms, global music, and the latest forms of electronic technology, plus be anointed with the skills of a choreographer and the wisdom of a diplomat. Worship leaders today are a combination of curator, hostess, artistic director, and composer.

Most of our churches have moved beyond the "worship wars" of the past decades. The polarities of "traditional" versus "contemporary" or "guitars and drums" versus "choirs and organs" are fading. While critics lament that these expressions of worship are too loud, too similar to rock concerts, or too sensual, this kind of contemporary worship practice is thriving. However, forsaking hymnals for choruses projected in Power-Point, replacing choir directors and organists with worship bands, or neglecting historic liturgical rites in favor of spontaneity and "relevance," deprive God's people of rich resources for worship. Contemporary worship leadership engages multifaceted skills and resources.

In spite of this renewal, however, it is becoming less likely that a person involved in leading multidimensional corporate worship is employed to do so on a full-time basis, has credentials of formal theological or musical education, or takes the time to engage fruitfully in any of the many conferences, seminars, magazines, books, and websites available. To be sure, there are plenty of worship leaders, but few have been resourced with the education needed to thoughtfully and effectively fuse different media, forms, and styles into a cohesive whole. Often these leaders are self-educated. They listen to CDs of worship music, attend one or more traveling seminars for worship leaders, or model everything after an experienced worship leader who is at best a mentor, at worst a mass-marketed, celebrity-type personality. Too often, these resources lack the benefit of rigorous theological, aesthetic, and conceptual reflection.

One solution is to train people to integrate all these diverse gifts of God's people: hymnals and choruses, organists and worship bands, historic rites and spontaneous expressions, art, drama, and dance into a multidimensional worship experience. Done well, this multidimensional approach will invite worshipers into rich encounters with the triune God that engage every aspect of their being and equip every aspect of their lives as disciples of Christ. The old polarities of traditional versus contemporary, or head versus heart, will disappear, leaving in their place an organic both/and synthesis, what could be called a dynamic, synergistic ritual.

Ritual, broadly defined, is simply that which is done in worship, whether formalized as in a written liturgy or completely extemporaneous. Ritual is composed of the words spoken, the songs sung, the people gathered, the context where they meet, and most importantly, the creative activity of the triune God. According to Craig Douglas Erickson, a synergistic ritual is a worship service in which all the parts work together: the words and music, the leaders, the worshipers, and the context unite to draw people into a dynamic encounter with God.

> When worshippers, by the power of the Spirit, participate knowingly, actively and fruitfully in the liturgy, the individual person, the church, and the liturgy are joined together in synergistic ritual. In synergistic ritual, each agent is mutually enriched: personal faith responses are confirmed in substance, upheld in solidarity, deepened in perception, and poised for action in the world. The church is strengthened as its individual members bear witness to their essential unity in the Spirit, grow in the prayer of the church, function more harmoniously as the body of Christ and prefigure the kingdom of God.[2]

Understanding how God, the ritual, the congregation, and those who lead the congregation participate together knowingly, actively, and fruitfully in any given worship service is therefore essential for effective worship leadership.

The articles selected for this reader underscore the centrality of trinitarian theology for a solid engagement in worship. *Participation* is a key word in all discussions of worship. However, it is not our participation in the rituals and forms of worship that are of such importance; but rather, as James Torrance says, "our participation through the Spirit in the Son's communion with the Father, in his vicarious life of worship and intercession."[3] All of creation was meant to praise and glorify God; yet as a result of sin, it is now unable adequately to do so. God in Christ fulfills the purpose for which we were created. As in the Old Testament, when the high priest would offer a sacrifice on behalf of the entire nation of Israel, so Christ came to offer the only acceptable actions of worship. Christ is our High Priest, and our worship is our participation by the Spirit in Christ's priestly life. Therefore, as Torrance says,

> Whatever else our worship is, it is our liturgical amen to the worship of Christ. This is the "wonderful exchange" . . . by which Christ takes what is ours (our broken lives and unworthy prayers), sanctifies them, offers them without spot or wrinkle to the Father, and gives it back to us, that we might "feed" upon him in thanksgiving. He takes our prayers and makes them his prayers, and he makes his prayers our prayers, and we know our prayers are heard "for Jesus' sake." . . . This is the Trinitarian nature of all true worship and communion.[4]

Because Christian worship, by definition, is our participation in the life of the triune God, worship simultaneously expresses our theology and shapes it. Therefore, our worship must be "intelligent"—using our minds (as well as our hearts, voices, and bodies). Worship leaders are some of the church's primary theological educators, and they need to work through the theological and cultural truths involved in worship. Torrance presses the point, saying,

> If our worship is to be intelligent, meaningful worship, offered joyfully in the freedom of the Spirit, we must look at the realities which inspire us and demand from us an intelligent, meaningful response. So the apostle says in Romans 12:1—after expounding the gospel of grace in the first eleven chapters—"With eyes wide open to the mercies of God, I beg you, my brothers (and sisters), as an act of intelligent worship (*logike latreia*), to give him your bodies as a living sacrifice, consecrated to him and acceptable by him" (J. B. Phillips).[5]

As theological educators, it is therefore essential that those leading in worship be theologically, culturally, and aesthetically educated.

Beginning from this trinitarian perspective raises the question, though, if Christ is always interceding on behalf of creation before the Father, and we in faith, by the work of the Spirit, are eternally participating in this divine communion, why worship corporately? Furthermore, if through faith anything we do is acceptable to God only insofar as the Spirit enables us to participate in the perfect life of Christ, is not all of life worship? Is there any difference between corporate worship and personal devotion? Is it the same thing to go to church on Sunday as it is to climb to a spectacular mountaintop view?

While we understand the trinitarian dynamic of worship in our own individual lives, we also realize this participation in community, as the body of Christ. Corporate worship is unique, irreplaceable, and essential for the Christian life. As D. A. Carson writes,

> The church in assembly not only approaches God, but it provides encouragement to its members. . . . This means that the purist model of addressing *only* God in our corporate worship is too restrictive. On the other hand, while one of the purposes of our singing should be mutual edification, that is rather different from making ourselves and our experience of worship the *topic* of our singing.[6]

Christian worship occurs both in the individual believer and in the community of the church, the body of believers. The body of Christ consists not merely of those members of a particular congregation, but believers of all times and places. Therefore, the corporate assembly of Christians when gathered for worship reveals a larger reality than one's own personal participation in the life of Christ. It signifies the gathering of the whole of creation throughout all time under the headship of Christ. Drawing upon historical and global liturgies and traditions is both appropriate and necessary, for when we worship we are participating in the worship of the body of believers from all time and all places. The other members of the body are in a very real sense present when one particular community gathers for worship!

Furthermore, corporate worship provides what solitary devotion cannot do: the revelation and proclamation of the presence of God at work in the world, in and through God's people, the church. Because the community gathered to *do* corporate worship is continually defined and shaped by the liturgy, F. Russell Mitman comments, careful attention to liturgy is essential for a community's spiritual formation. "Through the Spirit," explains Mitman,

> Christ is always present in his church; our doing does not make Christ any more present than he already is. Doing liturgy is a human action that opens the community to *knowing* God in Christ through God's own self-revelation. It is a posturing of the community to stand before the burning bush in the anticipation and on the promise that the burning-bush God will create a holy ground. . . . Liturgy is humanly orchestrated yet divinely directed . . . It is human words, yet it is God's Word.[7]

Obviously, the interaction between the human orchestration and the divine direction of corporate worship is its most controversial and unstable factor. Whenever there is too much stress on the human orchestration, or as Erickson describes it, the prevalence of ritualism over synergism, "the synergistic relationship among persons, church, and liturgy has become dysfunctional. Devotion to God is eclipsed by a sole recourse to ritual which thereby becomes excessive because the reality behind the ritual has 'fallen away.'"[8] To unleash the richness of the church's participation in the life of the triune God, the church needs to be freed to draw upon the rich diversity of liturgical practices of worship traditions throughout history and throughout the world. This openness is rooted in the conviction that "many paths lead to this goal, each of which is determined by a variety of cultural, theological, historical, pastoral and personal considerations."[9]

Participating in the Spirit of God's orchestration of worship creates what Michael Hawn aptly calls a "liturgical trilemma" for worship leaders. This trilemma is the challenge to: "(1) evaluate and embrace the best of the liturgical traditions that have taught us to pray; (2) celebrate liturgical plurality—the manifestations of the Incarnate One around the world . . . ; and (3) resist liturgical centrism by placing our personal concerns within the spectrum of prayer on behalf of the world."[10]

This trilemma rests in the reality that we worship as a community of distinct individuals for the sake of the world. Worship centers our lives and communities, drawing us to God and thwarting both our individualism and egotism, rooting us in the corporate nature of life. Rather than being a respite from the world and a distraction from the pressures of life, worship is central to the mission of God for people in the world. As we draw upon the church's "liturgical plurality," so also do we recognize that corporate worship is the expression of the hearts and minds of a particular people. It is socially and culturally specific. The Trinity as a communion of Persons draws us into worship that can be individually specific and corporately united at the same time. Furthermore, through our faith in the incarnate Christ, the mediator of all worship, we recognize that our worship is by definition vicarious—our participation by the Spirit in Christ's worship of the Father. Thus, our worship can also be mediated through other people. Though a particular liturgical form may not "move me" or satisfy my preferences, I can worship vicariously through other people's experience of worship.

Finally, because our worship is in the Spirit, worship is by nature highly creative. This collection of articles is not a "how-to" manual of techniques for worship. Rather, this book is intended to provide a resource that steps back and steps down—away from the urgent pressure to "come up with something for Sunday night" to explore more fully why and how we worship. O that the Creator Spirit would unleash in the church the full flowering of the artistic, aesthetic, and musical creativity of God's people for the glory of God, in anticipation of the ultimate celebration of worship in the redeemed and renewed creation! Our worship now is our anticipation of that ultimate worship service when we shall worship together in one grand and eternal synergistic ritual, as revealed to John:

> After this I looked, and there was a great multitude that no one could count, from every nation, from all tribes and peoples and languages, standing before the throne and before the Lamb, robed in white, with palm branches in their hands. They cried out in a loud voice, saying, "Salvation belongs to our God who is seated on the throne, and to the Lamb!" And all the angels stood around the throne and around the elders and the four living creatures, and they fell on their faces before the throne and worshipped God, singing, "Amen! Blessing and glory and wisdom and thanksgiving and honor and power and might be to our God forever and ever! Amen." (Rev. 7:9–12)

Acknowledgments

We would especially like to express our appreciation to John D. Witvliet, the director of the Calvin Institute of Christian Worship at Calvin College and Calvin Theological Seminary in Grand Rapids, Michigan, and to the staff of the Institute for their support and encouragement. The compilation of this Reader was made possible by a grant from the Institute.

Rev. Tim Dearborn, Ph.D.
Associate Director, Faith and Development: World Vision International
(former Dean of the Chapel, Seattle Pacific University)

Scott Coil
Music Director, St. Alban's Episcopal Church, Edmonds, Washington
(former Worship Research Assistant, Seattle Pacific University)

Pentecost 2003

1

What Do We Mean by "Christian Worship"?

James F. White

*Drawing from Protestant, Catholic, and Orthodox views,
James White introduces the language and actions of historic corporate worship.*

In order to speak intelligently about *Christian worship*, one must first
decide just what this term means. It is not an easy expression to define.
Yet until one reflects on what is distinctive about authentic Christian worship, it is all too easy to confuse such worship with irrelevant accretions
from present or past cultures in which Christians have worshiped.

First of all, *worship* itself is an exasperatingly difficult word to pin
down. What distinguishes worship from other human activities, particularly those noted for their frequent repetition? Why is worship a
different type of activity from daily chores or any habitual action? More
specifically, how does worship differ from other recurring activities

Reprinted from James F. White, *Introduction to Christian Worship*, 3rd ed. (Nashville:
Abingdon Press, 2000), 17–32, 305–6. © 2000 by Abingdon Press. Used by permission.

of the Christian community itself? What distinguishes worship from Christian education or works of charity, for instance? Is a "seeker service" meant to be worship?

And second, once we have made up our minds about what we mean by worship, how do we determine what makes such worship "Christian"? Our culture is full of various types of worship. A variety of oriental religions have made their advent in many communities. Many practice worship but obviously it is not Christian. What distinctive marks make some worship "Christian"? For that matter, is all worship offered by the Christian community always "Christian"?

None of these are easy questions to resolve but they certainly need to be probed. And they are not simply speculative matters of theoretical interest alone. Defining what is distinctive about Christian worship is a vital, practical tool for anyone who has responsibility for planning, preparing for, or leading Christian worship. The continuing appearance of new forms of worship has made this type of basic analysis even more crucial for those people charged with worship ministry. Such people are constantly involved in decision making as they serve the Christian community through worship leadership. The more practical the decision, the more necessary the theoretical foundations often become. Is a certain act, such as pledging one's allegiance to a national flag, appropriate in Christian worship? Or is that act out of place? Should other acts, such as celebrating the adoption of a child, which have not been customarily included in worship, find a place in the worship life of the church? Or is that not appropriate in Christian worship? Only if one has a working definition of Christian worship can one cope with such practical problems.

The Phenomenon of Christian Worship

One of the best ways to determine what we mean by Christian worship is to describe the outward and visible forms of worship by Christians. This approach looks at the whole phenomenon of Christian worship as it might appear to a detached or alien observer trying to grasp what it is Christians do when they come together.

Christian worship belongs to a wide category of human behavior known as ritual and is the subject of the academic discipline of ritual studies. The term *ritual* is used in a variety of ways but seems to have certain abiding characteristics. First, it is behavior; second, by its very nature ritual is repetitive. Third, it is social activity and serves some communal function. George Worgul describes it succinctly: "as a repeated interpersonal behavior, ritual is purposeful."[1] It is of great interest to anthropologists, sociologists, and psychologists. Various kinds of ritual are necessary to the cohesive existence of any human community. Whether it is the celebration of a national holiday, the opening of a new highway, or a college football weekend, ritual plays a vital role in making a proper observance. Family rituals include birthday parties, anniversary celebrations, and visits from grandchildren.

Christian worship, as a repeated social behavior with definite purposes, is probably the most common form of ritual in many Western societies. We can analyze it as a whole because, despite all the different cultures and historical epochs in which it occurs, Christian worship has employed remarkably stable and permanent forms. We shall speak of these as structures (such as a calendar for organizing a year's worship) or as services (such as the Lord's Supper). Despite constant adaptation, these prove to be remarkably durable. One way to describe Christian worship is simply to list these chief structures and services. . . .

In the late-twentieth century, liturgical scholars often speak of the essential structures and services collectively as an *ordo*, from the term used by the Russian Orthodox theologian Alexander Schmemann. Gordon W. Lathrop, a Lutheran theologian, describes the *ordo* as a "core Christian pattern" of worship which he identifies as consisting of Sunday and the week, the service of word and table, praise and beseeching, teaching and bath, and the year and Pascha (Easter).[2] United Methodist theologian Don E. Saliers prefers to speak of a "canon" of basic structures "that have endured the test of time."[3] He adds the "pastoral offices" to the list.

While useful in identifying historically central items, the limitation of such categories is that they suggest that the *ordo*, or canon, is limited and, presumably, closed. This method ignores ecstatic worship which has been around for centuries (1 Cor. 14:6–19), in which Paul himself excelled (v. 18), and which may have been the most prevalent form of Christian worship at mid-first century and may again be predominant at mid-twenty-first century. It overlooks the richness of recent centuries in developing new functions for worship and creating new forms to fulfill them. For example, early Methodist worship in England took on a new missional function which demanded new services (watch nights) and new components in familiar services (hymnody).

With these cautions in mind, we shall immediately do what Schmemann, Lathrop, and Saliers suggest: list the chief components of the perennial structures and services as a means of defining Christian worship. Even within the New Testament, we see indications of a weekly structure of time. This structure was soon elaborated in various annual calendars for commemorating events in the memory of the Christian community: Christ's death and resurrection, for example, and memorials of various local martyrs. Eventually daily schedules for public and private prayer were devised. Daily, weekly, and yearly schedules of time are still important components of Christian worship . . . . For our present purpose, however, one thing we can say about Christian worship is that it is a type of worship that relies heavily on the structuring of time to help it fulfill its purposes.

Just as they have found it necessary to arrange time, Christians have always found it convenient to organize a space to shelter and enable their worship. Though various forms have been tried by different cultures over the centuries, the requirements in terms of space and furnishings have remained remarkably consistent. . . . In addition, since early times, Christians have found music a vital means of expression for their acts of worship.

In ancient times and up through today, Christians have used a small number of basic services. The first of these is services of daily public prayer. . . . A second type of service focuses on the reading and preaching of Scripture and hence is often referred to as the "service of the word." It is familiar as the usual Protestant Sunday service; it also serves as the first portion of the Eucharist or Lord's Supper. . . . It provides a constant order, which many Christians identify as their prime experience of what Christian worship is.

Virtually every Christian community has some means of distinguishing those who belong within its body from outsiders. In terms of forms of worship, this designation takes place in various services of Christian initiation. Baptism is the most widely known of these rites but catechesis, confirmation, first communion, and various forms of renewal, affirmation, or reaffirmation of the baptismal covenant are important parts of the ritual process, too. Most Christian communities are currently rethinking their theology and practice for making one a Christian . . . .

Since New Testament times, we have testimony of Christians gathering to celebrate what Paul calls "the Lord's Supper" (1 Cor. 11:20). For many Christians, this is the archetypal form of Christian worship. Only a small minority avoid celebrating it in outward forms. In many churches, it is a weekly or even daily experience. . . .

Finally there are a variety of occasional services or pastoral rites common in one form or another to almost all worshiping Christian communities. Some of these mark steps in life's journey, which we may or may not repeat: services of forgiveness and reconciliation or services for healing and blessing the sick and dying. Others are one-time rites of passage such as weddings, ordinations, religious profession or commissioning, or funerals. Many of these are called for only as the occasion demands. Many of life's stages and experiences are common to all people, Christian or not. Occasional services to mark some of these journeys or passages have evolved into permanent types of Christian worship. . . .

Obviously, these basic structures and services do not cover all the possibilities in Christian worship, but they do describe the vast majority of instances of such worship. Various prayer meetings, sacred concerts, revivals, novenas, and a wide range of devotions may be added to them. But, for most Christians, all of these are clearly subsidiary to the items we have listed above and are, to a certain degree, dispensable. Accordingly, our discussion in this book will be chiefly concerned with the basic structures and services with only occasional mention of other possibilities.

Thus our first answer to the question, What is Christian worship? is simply to list and describe the basic forms Christian worship takes and to say these define it best. Nonetheless, we must also investigate other approaches.

Definitions of Christian Worship

Our purpose in looking at the various ways different Christian thinkers have spoken about Christian worship is not to compare practices but to stimulate reflection. The best way to grasp the meaning of any term is to observe it in use rather than to give a simple definition. So we shall look over the shoulders of several Protestant, Orthodox, and Roman Catholic thinkers to see how they use the term. None of these varying uses of the term excludes the others. Frequently they overlap, but each application adds new insights and dimensions, thus complementing the rest. This effort to "say what we mean and to mean what we say" is a continuing one that is subject to revision as our understanding of Christian worship matures and deepens.

Luther

One of the most attractive definitions of Christian worship can be found in a sermon preached by Martin Luther at the dedication of the first church built for Protestant worship, Torgau Castle, in 1544. Luther says of Christian worship "that nothing else be done in it than that our dear Lord Himself talk (*rede*) to us through His holy word and that we, in turn, talk (*reden*) to him in prayer and song of praise."[4] A similar approach appears in the *Large Catechism* where Luther says that in worship the people "assemble to hear and discuss God's Word and then praise God with song and prayer."[5] Thus worship has a duality, revelation and response—both of them empowered by the Holy Spirit.

Calvin

John Calvin had many negative things to say about idolatry and superstition in worship. But "God has given us a few ceremonies, not at all irksome, to show Christ present."[6] The ultimate purpose of

Christian worship is union with God: "We are lifted up even to God by the exercises of religion. What is the design of the preaching of the Word, the sacraments, the holy assemblies, and the whole external government of the church, but that we may be united (*conjungant*) to God."[7]

Anglican Archbishop Thomas Cranmer found the end of the ceremonies of worship to be the "setting forth of God's honor or glory, and to the reducing of the people to a most perfect and godly living."[8] Worship, then, is directed to God's glory and to human rectitude. Cranmer is echoed in modern theologies that link worship to social justice.

The duality of revelation and response is echoed by Russian Orthodox theologian George Florovsky: "Christian worship is the response of men to the Divine call, to the 'mighty deeds' of God, culminating in the redemptive act of Christ."[9] Florovsky is at pains to stress the corporate nature of this response to God's call: "Christian existence is essentially corporate; to be Christian means to be in the community, in the Church." It is in this community that God is active in worship as much as the worshipers themselves. As a response to God's work both in the past and in our midst, "Christian worship is primarily and essentially an act of praise and adoration, which also implies a thankful acknowledgement of God's embracing Love and redemptive loving-kindness."[10]

These ideas are reinforced by another Orthodox theologian Nikos A. Nissiotis, who stresses the presence and the actions of the Trinity in worship. He states: "Worship is not primarily man's initiative but God's redeeming act in Christ through his Spirit."[11] Nissiotis stresses the "absolute priority of God and his act," which humans can only acknowledge. By the power of the Holy Spirit, the church as the body of Christ can offer worship that is pleasing as an act both from and directed to the Trinity.

In Roman Catholic circles, it has been common to describe worship as "the glorification of God and the sanctification of humanity." This phrase comes from a landmark 1903 *moto proprio* on church music by Pope Pius X in which he spoke of worship as being for "the glory of God and the sanctification and edification of the faithful."[12] Pope Pius XII repeated this expression in his 1947 encyclical on worship, *Mediator Dei*. The same definition appears frequently in the 1963 Vatican II *Constitution on the Sacred Liturgy* which "in more than twenty places corrects the former definition of the liturgy and speaks first of the sanctification of man and then of the glorification of God."[13] That reversal of order presents this question: Which takes precedence, glorifying God or making people holy? Many of the debates about worship have revolved around that question, a question particularly pertinent for church musicians.

Should worship be the offering of our best talents and arts to God—even in forms unfamiliar or incomprehensible to people? Or should it be in familiar language and styles so that the meaning is grasped by all even though the result is less impressive artistically? Fortunately, these are false alternatives. Glorification and sanctification belong together. Irenaeus tells us the glory of God is a human *Both /* fully alive. Nothing glorifies God more than a human being made *And* holy; nothing is more likely to make a person holy than the desire to glorify God. Both the glorification of God and the sanctification of humans characterize Christian worship. Apparent tensions between them are superficial. Humans must be addressed in terms they can comprehend and must express their worship in forms that have integrity. Addressability and authenticity are both part of worship. Furthermore, artistically naive people have often created high art through their genuineness of expression.

In many churches it has also become normal to describe Christian worship as the "paschal mystery." Much of the popularity of this term is due to the writings of Dom Odo Casel, O.S.B., a German Benedictine monk who died in 1948. The roots of the term are as old as the church. The paschal mystery is the risen Christ present and active in our worship. "Mystery" in this sense is God's self-disclosure of that which surpasses human understanding, of the revelation that was hitherto hidden. The "paschal" element is the central redemptive act of Christ in his life, ministry, suffering, death, resurrection, and ascension. We can speak of the paschal mystery as the Christian community sharing in Christ's redemptive acts as it worships.

Casel discusses the way that Christians live, "our own sacred history," through worship. As the church commemorates the events of salvation history "Christ himself is present and acts through the church, his *ecclesia*, while she acts with him."[14] Thus these very acts of Christ again become present with all their power to save. What Christ has done in the past is again given to the worshiper to experience and appropriate in the present. It is a way of living with the Lord. The church presents what Christ has done through the worshiping congregation's reenactment of these events. The worshiper can thus reexperience them for his or her own salvation.

Each of these definitions is only a way station on the reader's own journey toward a personal understanding of Christian worship. One must remain open to discovering other definitions and coming to deeper understandings while continuing to experience and reflect upon what defines Christian worship.

Key Words in Christian Worship

Another useful way to clarify what we mean by Christian worship is to look at some of the key words that the Christian community has chosen to use when speaking about its worship. Often these words were originally secular but were chosen as the least inadequate means of expressing what the assembled community experienced in worship.

There is a rich variety of such words in past and current use. Each word and each language adds shades of meaning that complement the others. A quick survey of the most widely used words in several Western languages related to worship can show the realities being expressed.

The English language could well be envious of the German word *Gottesdienst*. Seven English words are needed to duplicate it: "God's service and our service to God." *God* is discernible, but less familiar is *Dienst,* which has no English cognate. Travelers will recognize it as the word identifying service stations in Germanic lands. *Service* is the nearest English equivalent and it is interesting that we, too, use this word for services of worship just as commonly as we use it for gas stations. *Service* means something done for others, whether we speak of a secretarial service, the Forest Service, or a catering service. It reflects work offered to the public even though usually for private profit. Ultimately it comes from the Latin word *servus,* a slave who was bound to serve others. The word *office* from the Latin *officium,* meaning "service" or "duty," is also used to mean a service of worship. *Gottesdienst* reflects a God who "emptied himself, taking the form of a slave" (Phil. 2:7) and our service to such a God.

There is only a slight difference between this concept and the one conveyed by our modern English word *liturgy*. Too often confused with smells and bells (ceremonial), *liturgy,* like *service,* has a secular origin. It comes from the Greek *leitourgía,* composed from words for *work* (*érgon*) and *people* (*laós*). In ancient Greece, a liturgy was a public work performed for the benefit of the city or state. Its principle was the same as the one for paying taxes, but it could involve donated service as well as taxes. Paul speaks of the Roman authorities literally as "liturgists [*leitourgoí*] of God" (Rom. 13:6) and of himself as "a liturgist [*leitourgón*] of Christ Jesus to the Gentiles" (Rom. 15:16 literal trans.).

Liturgy, then, is a work performed by the people for the benefit of others. In other words, it is the quintessence of the priesthood of believers that the whole priestly community of Christians shares. To call a service "liturgical" is to indicate that it was conceived so that all worshipers take an active part in offering their worship together. This could apply equally to a Quaker service and to a Roman Catholic mass as long as the congregation participated fully in either one. But it could not describe a worship in which the congregation was merely a passive audience. In Eastern Orthodox churches, the word *liturgy* is used in the specific sense of the Eucharist, but Western Christians use *liturgical* to apply to all forms of public worship of a participatory nature.

The concept of service, then, is fundamental in understanding worship. A different concept appears behind the word *common* in Latin and the Romance languages, a term reflected in our English word *cult.* In English, *cult* tends to suggest the bizarre or faddish, but it has an esteemed function in languages such as French and Italian. Its origin is the Latin *colere*, an agriculture term meaning "to cultivate." Both the French *le culte*, and the Italian *il culto*, preserve this Latin word as the usual term for worship. It is a rich term, even richer than the English word *worship*, for it catches the mutuality of responsibility between the farmer and the land or animals. If I do not feed and water my chickens, I know there will be no eggs; unless I weed my garden, there will be no vegetables. It is a relationship of mutual dependence, a lifelong engagement of caring for and looking after land or animals, a relationship that becomes almost part of the bone marrow of farmers, especially those whose families have farmed for generations on the same land. It is a relationship of giving and receiving, certainly not in equal measure, but the two are bound to each other. Unfortunately, the English language does not readily make the connection between cultivate and worship that is found in the Romance languages. Sometimes we find richer contents in the words of other languages such as the Italian *domenica* (Lord's Day-Sunday), *Pasqua* (Passover-Easter), or *crisma* (Christ-anoint) than in their English equivalents.

Our English word *worship* also has secular roots. It comes from the Old English word *weorthscipe*—literally *weorth* (*worthy*) and *-scipe* (*-ship*)—and signifies attributing worth, or respect, to someone. It was and still is used to address various lord mayors in England. The Church of England wedding service, since 1549, has contained the wonderful pledge: "with my body I thee worship." The intention in this last case is to respect or esteem another being with one's body. Unfortunately such frankness disturbs us and the term has vanished in American wedding services. Other English words such as *revere*, *venerate*, and *adore* derive ultimately from Latin words for fear, love, and pray.

The New Testament uses a variety of terms for worship; most of them words that also bear other meanings. One of the more common is *latreía*, often translated "service" or "worship." In Romans 9:4 and Hebrews 9:1 and 9:6, it implies the Jewish worship in the temple, or it can mean any religious duty, as in John 16:2. In Romans 12:1, it is usually translated simply "worship"; it has a similar meaning in Philippians 3:3.

An important insight appears in the word *proskyneîn* which carries the explicit physical connotation of falling down to show obeisance or prostration. In the temptation narrative (Matt. 4:10; Luke 4:8), Jesus tells Satan: "it is written, 'worship [*proskynéseis*] the Lord your God, and serve [*latreúseis*] only him.'" In another famous passage (John 4:23), Jesus tells the Samaritan woman that the time has come "when the true worshipers will worship the Father in spirit and truth." *Proskuneîn* in various forms is used repeatedly throughout this passage. In a less familiar passage (Rev. 5:14), the twenty-four elders "fell down and worshiped [*prosekýnesan*]." The physical reality of worship is underscored by this verb.

Two interesting words, *thysía* and *prosphorá*, are both translated as "sacrifice" or "offering." *Thysía* is an important term in the New Testament and to the early fathers even though it was used in both pagan worship ("to demons," 1 Cor. 10:20) and Christian ("a living sacrifice," Rom. 12:1; "sacrifice of praise," Heb. 13:15). *Prosphorá* is literally the act of offering or bearing before. It is a favorite term in 1 Clement—whether referring to Abraham's offering of Isaac or to those of the clergy or of Christ, "the high priest of our offerings" (3:1). Hebrews 10:10 speaks of "the offering of the body of Jesus Christ once for all." Both words play a significant, if controversial, role in the development of Christian eucharistic theology.

A much less prominent word in the New Testament literature is *threskeía*, which means "religious service" or "cult" (as in Acts 26:5; Col. 2:18; and James 1:26). *Sébein* signifies "to worship" (in Matt. 15:9; Mark 7:7; and Acts 18:3 and 19:27). In Acts, another use of the verb designates God-fearers, Gentiles who attend synagogue worship (13:50; 16:14; 17:4, 17; and 18:7). One other term from the New Testament has important uses to describe worship. *Homologeîn* has a variety of meanings: to confess sins (1 John 1:9), "if we confess our sins"; to declare or profess publicly (Rom. 10:9), "if you confess with your lips that Jesus is Lord"; or for the praise of God (Heb. 13:15), "the fruit of lips that confess his name."

These terms from other languages can expand the one-dimensional image of the English term *worship*. All are worth pondering for insights into what others have experienced at various times and places. A few English words related to worship need some clarification.

We need to make a clear distinction between two kinds of worship: common worship and personal devotions. The clearest aspect of common worship is that it is the worship offered by the gathered congregation, the Christian assembly. The importance of meeting or coming together can hardly be overstated. At times, the Jewish term *synagogue* ("coming together") was also used for the Christian assembly (James

2:2), but the chief term for the Christian assembly is the _church_, the _ekklesía_—those who are called out from the world. This word for the assemblage, congregating, meeting, convening, or gathering is used repeatedly throughout the New Testament for the local or universal church. One of the most easily overlooked aspects of common worship is that it begins with the gathering, in one place, of scattered Christians to be the church at worship. We usually treat the act of assembling as merely a mechanical necessity, but coming together in Christ's name is itself an important part of common worship. We assemble to meet God _and_ to encounter our neighbors.

In contrast, personal devotions usually, but not always, occur apart from the physical presence of the rest of the body of Christ. This is not to say they are not linked to the worship of other Christians. Indeed, personal devotions and common worship are both fully corporate since they share in the worship of the universal community of the body of Christ. But the individual engaging in personal devotions can determine his or her own pace and contents, even while following a widely used structure. On the other hand, for common worship to be possible, there must be consensus on structure, words, and actions or chaos would ensue. These ground rules are not necessary in devotions where the individual sets the discipline. (_Devotion_ comes from a Latin word for _vow._)

The relationship between common worship and personal devotions is important. Although the subject of this book is common worship and little will be said about personal devotions, it should be clear that common worship and personal devotions depend on each other. The Anglican theologian Evelyn Underhill tells us:

> [Common] and personal worship, though in practice one commonly tends to take precedence of the other, should complete, reinforce, and check each other. Only where this happens, indeed, do we find in its perfection the normal and balanced life of full Christian devotion. . . . No one soul—not even the greatest saint—can fully apprehend all that this has to reveal and demand of us, or perfectly achieve this balanced richness of response. That response must be the work of the whole Church; within which souls in their infinite variety each play a part, and give that part to the total life of the Body.[15]

Common worship needs to be supplemented by the individuality of personal devotions; personal devotions need the balance of common worship.

A widely used term in recent years is the word _celebration_. It is frequently used in secular contexts and seems to have developed a vagueness that makes it rather meaningless unless used with a specific object so that one knows what is being celebrated. If one speaks of celebration of the Eucharist or celebration of Christmas, the content may be clear. Since the whole community celebrates worship, the leader should be referred to as presider not as celebrant.

Ritual is a tricky term since it means different things to different people. To many people, it often implies emptiness (hence "empty ritual"), a rut of meaningless repetitions. Liturgists use the term to mean a book of rites. For Roman Catholics, the word *ritual* refers to the manual of pastoral offices for baptisms, weddings, funerals, and so on. In the Methodist tradition, *ritual* has been used since 1848 for all the official services of the church, including the Eucharist, the pastoral offices, and the ordinal. *Rites* are the actual words spoken or sung in a service of worship, though sometimes used for all aspects of a service. The term can also refer to those bodies, such as Eastern-rite Catholics, whose worship follows a distinctive pattern. Rites differ from actions or *ceremonial*, the actions done in worship. Ceremonial is usually indicated in service books by *rubrics*, or directions for carrying out the service. Rubrics are frequently printed in red as the name, derived from the Latin for red, indicates. Another essential element is the pattern for each service, one meaning of *ordo* or *order* (of worship). Order, rite, and rubrics—that is, pattern, words, and directions—are the basic components of most service books.

Diversity in Expression

Thus far, we have spoken of the common factors enabling us to speak of Christian worship in general terms. There is certainly enough basic unity that we can make many general statements and expect them to apply to most, if not all, of the forms of worship by Christian people. We need, however, to balance these general statements of *constancy* by considering the cultural and historical *diversity* that is also an important part of Christian worship. The constancy, as we have already seen, is enormous; the diversity is equally impressive. Christian worship is a fascinating mixture of constancy and diversity. We have practiced basically the same structures and services for two thousand years; people on the other side of town also practice them but in their own distinctive ways.

In recent years, we have become much more attuned to how important cultural and ethnic factors are in understanding Christian worship. A strong concern with the link between Christian *worship* and *justice* has emerged out of this. In a sense, this is nothing new for some Christians. Since the Quaker movement in the seventeenth century there has been a strong awareness among the Friends that worship must not marginalize anyone because of sex, color, or even servitude. Indeed, the Quaker insistence on human equality derives directly from their understanding of what happens in the worshiping community. That means, of course, that women and slaves were expected to speak in worship—hitherto an exclusively white male prerogative.

The nineteenth-century Anglican theologian Frederick Denison Mautice advanced our thinking about worship and justice as did Percy Dearmer, William Temple, Walter Rauschenbusch, and Virgil Michel in the twentieth century. But it is only in recent years that large numbers of Christians have become sensitive to the injustice of worship forms that marginalize large segments of worshipers because of gender, age, race, or other human distinctions. The result has been efforts to change the language of liturgical texts and hymns where they have tended to make women invisible, to redo buildings that have excluded the handicapped, and to open new roles for those who were previously not welcome to serve in them.

Closely allied with the move to include all people in worship has been the effort to take seriously the cultural and ethnic diversity within the world church. This involves encouraging respect for the variety in and the gifts of differing peoples as legitimate expressions of Christian worship. The technical name for such a process is *inculturation;* the reality is the acceptance of diversity as one of God's gifts to humanity and a willingness to incorporate such variety in the forms of worship. Music is often one of the best indicators of diversity of cultural expression. How limited have we been in emphasizing European expressions of Christian praise when a whole world sings God's glory? New hymnals have tended more and more to reflect cultural diversity, but most of them still have a long way to go before they mirror the variety of people in even a single nation.

The concern for the embodiment of justice in worship has taken many forms, but all of these efforts share a common goal of stressing the individual worth of every worshiper. Where some are neglected or relegated to inferior status because of age, gender, handicap, race, or linguistic background, these injustices are being recognized and alleviated. But it is a slow process to become aware of discriminatory practices then try to find the most equitable ways of redressing them. The result is that Christian worship becomes more complex and more diverse as it tries to reflect a worldwide community Thus, although what we have said about constancy remains valid, the cultural expressions of that constancy are becoming ever more diverse in the present. . . .

2

Worship as Adoration and Action

Reflections on a Christian Way of Being-in-the-World

Miroslav Volf

In this chapter Miroslav Volf discounts the false divide between contemplation and action, suggesting instead that Christian worship is built upon the rhythm of adoration and action.

I

One of the most significant accomplishments of the Protestant Reformation was overcoming the monastic understanding of the relation between the life of contemplation (*vita contemplativa*) and life of action (*vita activa*). Almost five centuries later, some important segments

Reprinted from *Worship: Adoration and Action*, ed. D. A. Carson (Carlisle: Paternoster, 1993), 203–11, 251–52. © 1993 by Paternoster. Used by permission of the publisher.

of Protestant Christianity (especially of the evangelical brand) are still caught in the false dichotomy between the sacred and the secular and are operating with a pre-Reformation understanding of the relation between (what they term) spiritual worship and secular work. In the context of the reflection on the Christian understanding of worship, it is important therefore to recall Martin Luther's rediscovery of the Christian calling to active service of God in the world and to reflect on its biblical roots.

The monastic understanding of the relationship between contemplation and action is rooted in the Greek philosophical tradition. Contemplation of the unchangeable order of things and of its divine origin was the highest possible human activity; it was considered the activity of the divine in human beings. Practical involvement in the world, though important, was inferior to contemplation.[1] The influences of Greek reflection on this issue on Christian spirituality and theology were strong and are easily observable, for instance, in Thomas Aquinas (though he was not the Christian theologian who adhered most slavishly to the Greek tradition on this point). For him, practical involvement in the world had no intrinsic value.[2] The ultimate reason for secular work lies in making the contemplation of God possible. Work keeps people alive by providing "for the necessities of the present life" so that they are able to contemplate God and it "quiets" and "directs" the internal passions of the soul thus making human beings more "apt for contemplation."[3] Like Mary, those who can devote themselves to a life of contemplation of God (monks and nuns) have chosen "the good portion"; like Martha, the rest who work for the maintenance of earthly existence must settle for the second best. Martha's work is not bad because it is a means to a good end. But Mary's contemplation is much better, because it is good in and of itself.

Together with the discovery of the merciful God who justifies sinners through faith alone, Luther overcame the medieval bias in favor of the contemplative life. This can be best seen in his views on Christian vocation. He came to believe that all Christians (and not only monks as was thought before him) have a vocation and that this vocation is twofold. The one vocation he called *spiritual*. It consists of the call of God through the proclamation of the gospel to enter the kingdom of God. The other vocation he called *external*. It consists in the call of God to serve God and fellow human beings in the world. For Luther, work in every profession—growing potatoes, proclaiming the gospel, governing a state—rests on a divine call. And if God calls to every type of work, there can be no hierarchy of human activities. Contemplation and action are fundamentally of equal value, because God calls to both.[4] Once Luther dismantled the hierarchy of activities, the way was open for the belief that one can equally honor God in all dimensions of one's life, provided that one obediently does the will of God.

Luther's understanding of Christians' active life in the world is no less biblical than his teaching on justification by faith.[5] He acquired both beliefs in the school of the apostle Paul. On the basis of his message of justification by faith, Paul wrote in Romans 12:1f: "Therefore I urge you, brothers, in view of God's mercy, to offer your bodies as living sacrifices, holy and pleasing to God—this is your spiritual act of worship. Do not conform any longer to the pattern of this world, but be transformed by the renewing of your mind. Then you will be able to test and approve what God's will is—his good, pleasing and perfect will" (NIV). As J. D. G. Dunn points out, Paul here transports the notion of worship "across a double line—from cultic ritual to everyday life, from previous epoch characterized by daily offering of animals to one characterized by a whole-person commitment lived out in daily existence."[6] There is no space in which worship should not take place, no time when it should not occur, and no activity through which it should not happen. All dimensions of human life are the "temples" in which Christians should honor their God—the God who created the whole reality, and the God who desires to redeem it.[7] In his essay in this book David Peterson has rightly emphasized that the understanding of worship as "daily obedience or service to God in every sphere of life" is not peculiar to Paul but permeates the whole New Testament.[8]

The liberation of worship from the cultic constraints of sacred space and time was, of course, not an accomplishment of the New Testament writers. They inherited and radicalized the Old Testament perspectives on worship in the light of the salvific work of Jesus Christ. As is well known, Hebrew has a single word to denote activities we have come to designate as work, service, and worship.[9] In the first chapters of Genesis we read that God created human beings in order for them to serve God, not simply in the realm of the cult, but explicitly in the realm of the *culture*. Human beings serve God by doing "worldly" things, like tilling and keeping the Garden of Eden (see Gen. 2:15).[10] Correspondingly in the proclamation of the prophets we encounter the stress on worship in the sphere of ethical responsibility. They stressed that the true worship consists not simply in the participation in cultic activities but in *doing justice:* "Is not this the kind of fasting I have chosen: to loose the chains of injustice and untie the cords of the yoke, to set the oppressed free and to break every yoke? Is it not to share your food with the hungry and to provide the poor wanderer with shelter—when you see the naked, to clothe him, and not to turn away from your own flesh and blood?" (Isa. 58:6–7 NIV; see Amos 5:21–24; James 1:27).

II

Luther's rejection of the monastic hierarchy of contemplative and active life was a result of a profound spiritual and theological insight. The new perspectives on involvement in the world were, however, not acquired in a social vacuum but were closely tied to a larger cultural movement of his time. It will suffice for my purposes here to enumerate some of the striking features of this transitional period in European history (without analyzing in detail each of them separately and their interrelations). In economic life, feudalism was in a state of collapse and a new, much more dynamic social order was being formed in which craftsmen and merchants would play the dominant role. In the political arena, the givenness of social structures was being called into question and the insight was emerging that these structures had been made by human beings and could therefore be altered by them. In relation to general culture, the Renaissance humanists were closing the gap between the sacred and the profane. In the sphere of intellectual pursuits, philosophers had boldly proclaimed the new experimental philosophy in which the researcher, who actively forced nature to reveal its truths, replaced the speculative scholar, who was satisfied to contemplate the truth.[11] Together with the affirmations of *sola scriptura* and of the priesthood of all believers, Luther's critique of monastic contemplative life and the rediscovery that God's calling pertains also to secular forms of activity is part and parcel of the one cultural movement infecting economics, politics, science, and theology alike. The movement marked the birth of modernity.

There is much talk today about the economically developed societies entering into a phase of postmodernity. The future will decide whether an epoch-making cultural shift is in fact taking place. In any case, activistic modernity still has a firm grip on our social and private lives. Despite a chorus of voices critical of Western culture the dominant goal of this culture still remains "to know everything in order to predict everything in order to control everything."[12] And although we are increasingly aware that technological rationality is incapable of steering the powers unleashed by technological advances, our technological successes ensure that the altar flame in honor of the god of technology is kept burning.

In this situation, it is increasingly difficult for Christians to hold seriously to the belief that God governs history and that the salvation of the world can, let alone must, come from God. And the more God is pushed out of our world—out of the spheres of nature, of society, and of individual human beings—the more difficult it will be to address this loving God in prayer and thanksgiving, and to stand before this holy God in awe and reverence. "When the modernizing reason has harnessed all the facts, figures and forces . . . prayer, worship and reliance on the Holy Spirit, along with humility and the sanctity of things, are out of place. Technique is all."[13] Technological culture does not deny God (it is not atheistic), but it makes God superfluous (it is a-theistic) and thus cuts off the worship of God at its roots. For adoration of a superfluous God is a religious impossibility. Where technique reigns, talking to God gives way to talking about God (or even to talking about talking about God!), reverence is replaced by manipulation, and joyous celebration of God's acts and God's character degenerates either into self-congratulatory praises of human vainglory or into oppressive demands for better and greater deeds.

Some modern theologians seem to think that it is their task to make a virtue out of our cultural predicaments. It is to be expected that the modern suppression of the contemplative life would be given a theological version, too. Summarizing the argument developed in *Marx and the Bible*,[14] J. P. Miranda—who is in this respect *not* typical of liberation theologians—claims that "God can *only* be known and approached through moral conscience."[15] This is the case, claims Miranda, because "God is God solely *in* the nonobjectifiable interpellation through which God's commandment is enjoined."[16] To claim to know or to be able to approach God directly would mean reducing God to an object. From this it seems to follow that every supplication and every thanksgiving turns God into an idol, that every liturgy is idolatry. Miranda absolutizes the prophetic critique of the cult, and proclaims the ethically responsible (social) action as the only true worship of God.[17] The monastic hierarchy in the relation between contemplation and action has been inverted: the subordination of the active life to the contemplative life has given way to a total suppression of the contemplative life by the active life.

There is an important truth in Miranda's position. A person cannot worship God and oppress his/her neighbor at the same time. Cult without justice is no worship of the true God but detestable idolatry (see Isa. 1:11–17); true worship is impossible without doing justice, indeed it consists partly in doing justice. But can worship be reduced to action—whether that action is ethical, evangelistic, or both? The biblical tradition affirms clearly the independent significance of adoration of God as a form of worship. I am not thinking here so much of the fact that the prophets do not call into question the cult as such but its misuse as justification of social oppression. For Christian theology this is of limited significance, because the New Testament clearly states that the ministry of Christ is the fulfillment of the priesthood and cult associated with the old covenant. But the songs of exuberant praise to God in the Psalter are certainly a model for Christian worship. The hymnal of the old covenant people of God remained the hymnal of the

Christian church. As Hattori states, the grand symphony of praise to God in Psalm 150 is a very appropriate finale for all the praises of God in the whole Psalter.[18] The Psalm is the call to the whole creation—to everything that has breath—to give praise to God for God's mighty deeds and exceeding greatness.

In the New Testament we find the new people of God adoring God with psalms, hymns, and spiritual songs (see Eph. 5:18f). The early Christians worshiped God not only through their obedient service in the church and the world, but by their celebration in response to God's mighty deeds of salvation as well. Luke portrays the earliest Christian community as full of joy, with lips full of praises to God (see Luke 24:52–53; Acts 2:26–47). Throughout the Revelation the heavenly beings and the heavenly church are portrayed as worshiping God and the Lamb (Rev. 4:8ff.; 5:9–10; 7:10; 15:3ff.; 16:5–7; 19:1–9). The different aspects of worship mentioned in Revelation—"rejoicing in God, giving him the glory and praising him"[19]—are clearly meant to be paradigmatic for the churches on the earth as they are facing godless economic and political powers desiring to crush them.

III

Christian worship consists both in obedient service to God and in the joyful praise of God. Both of these elements are brought together in Hebrews 13:15–16, a passage that comes close to giving a definition of Christian worship: "Through Jesus, therefore, let us continually offer to God a sacrifice of praise—the fruit of lips that confess his name. And do not forget to do good and to share with others, for with such sacrifices God is pleased" (NIV). The sacrifice of praise and the sacrifice of good works are two fundamental aspects of the Christian way of being-in-the-world. They are at the same time the two constitutive elements of Christian worship: *authentic Christian worship takes place in a rhythm of adoration and action.*

Why does Christian worship need to branch out into action and adoration? What is the reason for this biformity of worship? In what follows I will try to answer these questions.

First, why cannot worship consist simply in active life in the world? Why does adoration need to take place as a distinct activity beside action? Because God did not create human beings to be merely God's servants but above all to be God's children and friends. As much as they need to do God's will in the world, they also need to enjoy God's presence. The center of Christian life consists in personal *fellowship* of human beings with the Son of God through faith. Adoration is a time when this personal fellowship, which determines the whole life of Christians—their relation to themselves, to their neighbors, and nature—is nurtured, either privately or corporately.[20] This is the reason why human beings "need periodic moments of time in which God's commands concerning their work will disappear from the forefront of their consciousness as they adore the God of loving holiness and to thank and pray to the God of holy love."[21]

Second, why can we not make the adoration of God our supreme goal, and be satisfied to consider action in the world simply a necessary consequence of adoration? Because the world is God's creation and the object of God's redemptive purposes. Christian hope is not for the liberation of souls from the evil world, but for the redemption of human beings together *with* the world with which they comprise the good creation of God. The material creation is not a scaffolding that will be discarded once it has helped in the construction of the pure spiritual community of souls with one another and with their God; material creation represents the building materials from which, after they are transfigured, the glorified world will be made. This is why worship can never be an event taking place simply between the naked soul and its God. It must always include active striving to bring the eschatological new creation to bear on this world through proclamation of the good news, nurture of the community of faith, and socio-economic action. Fellowship with God is not possible without cooperation with God in the world; indeed cooperation with God is a dimension of fellowship with God.

As Christians worship God in adoration and action they anticipate the conditions of this world as God's new creation. Through action they seek to anticipate a world in which Satan will no longer "deceive the nations," a world in which God will "wipe away every tear" from the eyes of God's people, a world in which peace will reign between human beings and nature. Through their adoration they anticipate the enjoyment of God in the new creation where they will communally dwell in the triune God and the triune God will dwell among them (see Rev. 21–22). The eschatological bliss of God's people in the presence of their God and the eschatological *shalom* of God's world are two inseparable dimensions of Christian eschatological hope. It is this two-dimensional hope that makes Christian worship into a two-dimensional reality.

Adoration and action are two distinct aspects of Christian worship, each of which is valuable in its own right. The purpose of action is not merely to provide material support for the life of adoration. The purpose of adoration is not simply to provide spiritual strength for the life of action. When we adore God, we worship God by enjoying God's presence and by celebrating God's mighty deeds of liberation. When we are involved in the world, we worship God by announcing God's liberation, and we cooperate with God by the power of the Spirit through loving action.

Christian worship is bivalent. But do its two components stand merely side by side or are they also positively related to one another? I will return to this question after I consider the relation between adoration of God and seclusion from the world.

IV

I have argued that adoration is an activity distinct from involvement in the world. It would seem that as a distinct activity adoration requires distinct space and distinct time. If that is the case, are we not then back at the notions of sacred space and sacred time, which I have discarded earlier?

Does adoration need to take place in seclusion from the world? The answer to this question depends on where God is to be found. It is a consistent teaching of the Bible that God's presence is not limited to a particular locale. God is present in the whole created reality. No segment of it is secular in the sense that the transcendent God is absent from it. All dimensions of life in the world have what one might call a sacramental dimension: they can be places of meeting God in gratitude and adoration.[22] This is why the New Testament can ascribe redemptive significance to such an ordinary event as the table fellowship amongst Jesus' disciples: a meal can be an occasion for an encounter with the risen Lord.[23] Furthermore, if God is present in all of the created reality, then the soul ceases to be the privileged place for meeting God. We do not need to turn away from the world and search into the depths of our soul to find God there. Adoration does not require seclusion; indeed it is provoked by the apprehension of God's presence and activity in the world.

Still the New Testament does speak of taking time to go to a "secret" place (Matt. 6:6). The "secret" place should not be confused with "sacred space," however. It stands for the cessation of active involvement in the world, not for the exclusion of the profane reality. Every place can be a "secret space," and every moment a time reserved for God. But if we want to escape the tendency to dissolve the holy into the secular, which seems to be the danger of affirmation that the holy is not restricted to particular places,[24] then we need to reserve special time for the adoration of God, whether it means going to the "secret place" (as Jesus advised), spending a night in the mountains (as Jesus practiced), or gathering together in Jesus' name as a community of believers. The point of the talk about the *rhythm* of adoration and action is to *preserve profane reality as a meeting place with the holy God,* not to reintroduce the division between the sacred and the profane.

But does not the very act of adoring God, wherever it takes place, involve turning away from the world toward God? Even if we affirm the possibility of meeting God in the profane reality, do we not reduce this reality to a mere vehicle for encountering God? I will start answering these questions by noting the distinction between adoration and contemplation. As distinct from the modern way of knowing by which we manipulate things in order to grasp them, contemplation is a passive way of knowing by which we behold things as they present themselves to us (*theoria*). Its passivity notwithstanding, contemplation is a way of knowing *things* and *truths,* not persons. You can contemplate the works of a person, but you do not contemplate persons themselves; you know them by talking to them and letting them talk to you, by doing things with them. Seeing the persons (and touching them) is important, but only as a part of this conversation and cooperation which constitute our common history.

Since God is neither an a-personal truth nor anesthetic shape, contemplation is not appropriate as a way of relating to God. Adoration is. To adore God is not simply to behold the truth, goodness, and beauty of God in a disinterested way, but to affirm one's allegiance to God by praising God for his deeds in creation and redemption. The contemplation of God's works (like beholding the grandeur of creation or meditating on the passion of Christ) is a presupposition of adoration. But to adore is not to look at God, but to talk about God and to God, inspired by God's works in the world. This, however, means that *turning to God in adoration does not entail turning away from the world; it entails perceiving God in relation to the world and the world in relation to God*. The songs of praise to God are at the same time the songs about the world as God's creation and a place which God will transform into a new creation. And the songs about creation and redemption can be nothing else but songs about God the Creator and Redeemer.

Authentic Christian adoration cannot take place in isolation from the world. Because the God Christians adore is engaged in the world, adoration of God leads to action in the world and action in the world leads to adoration of God. Adoration and action are distinct, but nevertheless *interdependent* activities. So we need to investigate further the positive relationship they have to each other.

V

What is the significance of adoration of God for action in the world? We can answer this question best if we reflect on the nature of doxological language. At one level, in adoration a person is stating what is the case;

he or she is describing God's action (e.g., "he has condemned the great prostitute [economic and political power of Babylon] who corrupted the earth by her adulteries") and God's character (e.g., "true and just are his judgments" [Rev. 19:2 NIV]). There is no adoration without such description. But the actual point of adoration lies deeper than description. In thanking, blessing, or praising God, a person expresses his/her own relation toward the God he or she is adoring: joyous *gratitude* for what God has done and reverent *alignment* with God's character from which God's actions spring forth.

It is here that the significance of adoration for action becomes visible. First, by aligning with God's character and purposes in adoration one aligns oneself also with God's projects in the world. By praising God who renews the face of the earth and redeems the peoples one affirms at the same time one's desire to be a cooperator with God in the world. Adoration is the well-spring of action. Second, in adoration a person names and celebrates the context of meaning that gives significance to his or her action in the world and indicates the highest value that gives that action binding direction. In the pantheon of the modern world, adoration identifies the God in whose name one engages in action. Without adoration action is blind and easily degenerates into a hit-or-miss activism.

The dependence of action in the world on the adoration of God shows that the frequent disjunction found in cerebral and activistic Protestant circles between adoration and edification is inadmissible. As Psalm 119 shows, instruction in Torah could take place in doxological language. For Paul too, psalms, hymns, and spiritual songs were simultaneously expressions of adoration and a means of instruction and admonition.[25] Every authentic adoration is instruction, because it celebrates God's deeds and God's character, and expresses at the same time commitment to the God it celebrates. The inverse is also true. Every authentic Christian instruction is adoration. Instruction in faith which does not include (at least implicitly) adoration is deficient: it communicates knowledge without transmitting corresponding allegiance. Protestant theology (evangelical theology included!) on this point needs to learn from Eastern Orthodoxy which, in addition to maintaining that there is "no mysticism without theology," has stressed "above all" that there is "no theology without mysticism."[26]

What is the significance of action for adoration? In order to answer this question we need to look briefly at the nature and the purpose of Christian involvement in the world. Christian action is nothing less than cooperation with God. As Genesis 2 vividly portrays, there is a partnership between the creating God and working human beings.[27] Just as in Genesis a farmer is a cooperator of God, so Paul thinks of missionaries as fellow workers of God in God's field (1 Cor. 3:9).[28] Whether it consists in evangelism or mundane work, human activity is a means by which God accomplishes God's purposes in the world. If God's deeds in the world open the hearts and mouths of people to praise God, then human action, which God uses to accomplish God's purposes, must do the same: the purpose of evangelism and good works is the well-being of the people and of God's whole creation. And the integral well-being of God's world is the occasion for praise (see 2 Cor. 4:15; Matt. 5:16; 1 Peter 2:11). Christian action in the world leads to adoration of God. Action establishes conditions in which adoration of God surges out of the human heart.

But there is also another sense in which action is a precondition to adoration. There is something profoundly hypocritical about praising God for God's mighty deeds of salvation and cooperating at the same time with the demons of destruction, whether by neglecting to do good or by actively doing evil. Only those who help the Jews may sing the Gregorian chant, Dietrich Bonhoeffer rightly said, in the context of Nazi Germany. Only those who are actively concerned with the victims of economic, political, racial, or sexual oppression—who are doing "the significant something"—can genuinely worship God. Without action in the world, the adoration of God is empty and hypocritical, and degenerates into irresponsible and godless quietism.

VI

The distinction between action and adoration (just like the old distinction between action and contemplation[29]) is not a distinction between activity and passivity, but a distinction between two forms of human activity. Action designates deeds that are directed toward the world, adoration designates words and symbolic actions that are directed toward God. This is why the writer of Hebrews can describe both the action and the adoration as "sacrifices": the one is a sacrifice of good works, the other a sacrifice of praise (see Heb. 13:15–16). As sacrifices, action and adoration are something human beings give God. This is why both can properly be called "worship." For worship is something human beings owe God: in worship they are the givers, and God is the receiver.

But our arms are lifeless and our mouths dumb if God does not give them strength and facility of speech. We can give God only what we have first received from God. Reception is, therefore, a third dimension of Christian life that is even more fundamental than action and adoration. In distinction to the traditional two-dimensional understanding of Christian existence (*vita activa* and *vita contemplativa*), Luther rightly stressed that *vita passiva* is an additional dimension of Christian life, which underlies both Christian theory and practice.[30] At the foundation of Christian life lies passivity. Christians are receivers at the point when the beginning of the rebirth of the whole cosmos takes place in their new birth by the Holy Spirit (see John 3:3; Matt. 19:28; 2 Cor. 5:17). And the new life is sustained and flourishes only if they continue to be receivers throughout their Christian life. The rhythm of adoration and action must be embedded in the larger rhythmic phrase consisting of Christian passivity and activity.

The passivity of Christian existence can be described as receiving the Spirit by faith (which marks the beginning of Christian life: see Gal. 3:2) and being continually filled by the Spirit (which marks its continuation: see Eph. 5:18ff.). The secret of the whole Christian life is passivity in relation to the Spirit of God. For the Spirit is the source both of adoration (5:18–20) and of action (5:21–6:20).

3

Liturgical Assembly
as Locus of Mission

Thomas H. Schattauer

*Thomas Schattauer offers in this chapter another way of
understanding contemporary worship in terms of the relationship between the church in worship and mission, calling for a faith that is eucharistic, communal, prospective,
and symbolic.*

Over thirty years ago, J. G. Davies wrote a little book entitled
Worship and Mission. At the outset, he noted the lack of contemporary reflection on the relationship between the church's worship
and its mission:

Reprinted by permission from *Inside Out: Worship in an Age of Mission,* ed. Thomas H.
Schattauer (Minneapolis: Fortress Press, 1999), 1–21. © 1999 by Augsburg Fortress
(www.fortresspress.com). The bulk of this essay was initially prepared for the author's
inaugural lecture at Wartburg Seminary, Dubuque, Iowa, on May 5, 1999.

Those who make worship the object of their specialized study scarcely ever mention mission—not even in a footnote; while those who are concerned to develop the theology of mission seem in general to have little time for cultic acts. So worship and mission are treated as two totally distinct objects of theological investigation; they are placed in isolated compartments without the possibility of cross-fertilization and without the question of their unity being raised at all.[1]

Indeed, an examination of the work of liturgiologists and missiologists, according to Davies, might raise questions about the "complete dichotomy and even incompatibility" of worship and mission.[2]

It would not take too long to demonstrate that this disinterest in or aversion to considering the relationship between worship and mission no longer characterizes the work of those concerned primarily with either the church's mission or its worship. Much recent reflection about liturgy and mission has been motivated by questions about inculturation or contextualization in those parts of the world that have received patterns of worship from European and North American missionaries.[3] The advent of a post-Christian era in the West has encouraged significant reflection about the forms of worship appropriate to this new missional situation.[4]

The question remains whether we have reached any clarity about the relationship between liturgy and mission. There are, it seems to me, at least three approaches to the relationship: "inside and out" (conventional), "outside in" (contemporary), and "inside out" (radically traditional).

In the first approach, liturgy is understood and practiced as the quintessential activity for those inside the church community. Mission is what takes place on the outside when the gospel is proclaimed to those who have not heard or received it or, to broaden the notion of mission, when the neighbor is served in acts of love and justice. The relationship between the inside activity of worship and the outside activity of mission is portrayed thus: worship nurtures the individual and sustains the community in its life before God and in its life together and from where Christians go out to serve the church's mission as proclaimers and doers of the gospel. They return to worship, perhaps with a few more folk gathered by this witness, and the cycle begins again. In this model, worship spiritually empowers those inside the church who take up the church's mission in the outside world. Note that this process describes an indirectly instrumental relationship between worship and mission. Worship serves the purpose of mission, not because it directly accomplishes the tasks of evangelical proclamation and diaconal service but because it offers access to the means of grace that propel the individual and the community as a whole into such activity. Worship and mission, however, remain distinct activities within clearly demarcated spheres of the church's life—inside and out.

Although this conventional approach to the relationship between worship and mission upholds the autonomy of the church's liturgical life, the strict demarcation between the church's internal activity (worship) on behalf of its members and the church's external activity (mission) for the sake of the world bifurcates our understanding of Christian life and finally fails to grasp adequately their unity. A contemporary response to the conventional model has been to bring the "outside" activities of mission directly into the context of worship. The sacred precinct of the liturgy becomes one of two things—either a stage from which to present the gospel and reach out to the unchurched and irreligious, or a platform from which to issue the call to serve the neighbor and rally commitment for social and political action. The first represents the outside-in strategies of the church growth movement, which promotes what is called contemporary worship, most noticeably in the suburban megachurches but also in the many congregations seeking to imitate them. The second represents the outside-in strategies of both liberal and conservative Christians who seek to orient worship to specific social and political goals. Note that in either strategy, the relationship between worship and mission is understood instrumentally but more directly than in the conventional inside-and-out approach. The church's worship is reshaped to take up the tasks of the church's mission, construed as evangelical outreach, social transformation, or both. The tasks of mission become the principal purpose of the church's worship—outside in.

There is a third way—inside out. This approach locates the liturgical assembly itself within the arena of the *missio Dei*. The focus is on God's mission toward the world, to which the church witnesses and into which it is drawn, rather than on specific activities of the church undertaken in response to the divine saving initiative. The missio Dei is God's own movement outward in relation to the world—in creation and the covenant with Israel, and culminating in Jesus Christ and the community gathered in him. This community is created by the Spirit to witness to the ultimate purposes of God, to reconcile the world to God's own self (2 Cor. 5:18–19). The gathering of a people to witness to and participate in this reconciling movement of God toward the world is an integral part of God's mission. The visible act of assembly (in Christ by the power of the Spirit) and the forms of this assembly—what we call liturgy—enact and signify this mission. From this perspective, there is no separation between liturgy and mission. The liturgical assembly of God's people in the midst of the world enacts and signifies the outward movement of God for the life of the world. Note that in this approach, the relationship between worship and mission is not instrumental, either directly or indirectly, but rather the assembly for worship *is* mission. The liturgical assembly is the visible locus of God's reconciling mission toward the world. The seemingly most internal of activities, the church's worship, is ultimately directed outward to the world. The judgment and mercy of God enacted within the liturgical assembly signify God's ultimate judgment and mercy for the world. Like a reversible jacket, the liturgy can be turned and worn inside out, and by so doing we see the relationship between worship and mission—inside out.[5]

Inside Out

It is this third approach—inside out—to the relationship between worship and mission that I want to explore further. It is both thoroughly contemporary and radically traditional, and it moves us beyond the conventionally traditional inside-and-out as well as the radically contemporary outside-in approaches. This is the approach Davies himself adopted in his explication of worship and mission:

> In the past the theological understanding of worship has been developed mainly in one direction, i.e., *inwardly:* for example, it has been interpreted as that which builds up the Body of Christ. . . . I think the time has come when we must adopt another approach, which is complementary rather than an alternative; we must seek to understand worship *outwardly* in terms of mission.[6]

In some recent attempts to articulate the shape of the church's mission in the North American context, we can discern a similar inside-out approach to the church's worship. In *Missional Church*, the product of a team of North American Protestant (Reformed, Methodist, Baptist, and Mennonite) theologians, worship is described as central to a "missional ecclesiology for North America":[7]

> Our postmodern society has come to regard worship as the private, internal, and often arcane activity of religionists who retreat from the world to practice their mystical rites. By definition, however, the *ekklesia* is a public assembly, and its worship is its first form of mission. . . . The reality of God that is proclaimed in worship is to be announced to and for the entire world.[8]

In his reflections on the church as a distinctive culture within post-Christian society, Rodney Clapp, an Episcopalian with strong ties to American evangelicals, writes:

I reject the terms of those who think the church at its worship is necessarily inward focused and removed from the "public" world. I want Christians to stop thinking in the essentially modern and liberal categories that cut up our lives as "private" and "public," "inward" and "outward." . . . Liturgy is the public work par excellence of the church—something that, if omitted, would mean the church was no longer the church. Far from being a retreat from the real world, worship enables Christians to see what the real world is and equips them to live in it.

Liturgy also implies and enacts mission. . . .

All liturgy is related to mission. . . . The church exists for the sake of the world . . . . Worship teaches and forms us to live by the Jesus story so that others—the entire world, the church prays—will learn to live according to reality and wholeness. The people, the culture, that is now the church is joyful that God has already drawn it together, but it lives in hope of a greater joy, a joy that achieves fullness only in the kingdom's fullness.[9]

Some Lutherans have also taken up the inside-out approach. Bruce Marshall, for example, has argued for the central significance of the church's eucharistic worship for the way that God is encountered in the midst of the world, within as well as outside the church:

On the one hand, . . . the church's unifying participation in God's own life happens, not primarily in the minds and hearts of individuals (though it does, of course, happen there), but in the public eucharistic celebration by which Christ joins individuals to himself and so makes them his own community. On the other hand, the eucharistic fellowship of the church, in which human beings are joined to Christ, and so to the Father, by the Spirit, is the particular way in which the triune God visibly exhibits to and in the world his own single and eternal life.[10]

Frank Senn's book *The Witness of the Worshiping Community* is an extended explication of the claim that "worship is itself an aspect of the mission of God."[11] Or listen to Gordon Lathrop:

The local assembly . . . is itself the full presence, in this place, of all that Christians have to say about the ordering of place, time, and society. Christian liturgy means to invite people to discover the wide applicability—we may call it, poetically and religiously, the universal meaning—of what is done in the assembly. . . .

The world that is thereby suggested is not the status quo, but an alternative vision that waits for God, hopes for a wider order than has yet been achieved or than any ritual can embody, but still embraces the present environment of our experience.[12]

Certain statements in the Evangelical Lutheran Church in America's statement on liturgical practice, *The Use of the Means of Grace,* also evidence the inside-out approach to understanding the relationship between worship and mission:

> In every celebration of the means of grace, God acts to show forth both the need of the world and the truth of the Gospel. . . . Jesus Christ, who is God's living bread come down from heaven, has given his flesh to be the life of the world. This very flesh, given for all, is encountered in the Word and sacraments.
> . . . In the teaching and practice of congregations, the missional intention for the means of grace needs to be recalled. By God's gift, the Word and the sacraments are set in the midst of the world, for the life of the world.[13]

Statements like these, however, stand next to statements that continue to reflect the inside-and-out approach with its instrumental view of worship:

> In every gathering of Christians around the proclaimed Word and the holy sacraments, God acts to empower the Church for mission.[14]

The conventional distinction between worship on the inside and mission on the outside has not fully given way to a more radical understanding of their deep unity. Nonetheless, the inside-out impulse has gained a foothold.

Eucharistic Piety

The inside-out approach to the relationship between worship and mission bears with it concrete implications for the shape and content of the church's liturgical life and the piety of Christian people. Allow me to illustrate this with some reflection on my own liturgical genealogy.

Sunday services in the church of my youth invariably began with the confession of sins. I remember vividly the words from the *Service Book and Hymnal* (1958) that the pastor (who was also my father—liturgical genealogy is inevitably intertwined with family genealogy) spoke before the prayer of general confession:

> Almighty God, our Maker and Redeemer, we poor sinners confess unto thee, that we are by nature sinful and unclean, and that we have sinned against thee by thought, word, and deed. Wherefore we flee for refuge to

thine infinite mercy, seeking and imploring thy grace, for the sake of our
Lord Jesus Christ.[15]

I know that those beautiful and gracious words about fleeing for refuge
to God's infinite mercy sunk deeply into my being. I also know that I
spent a great deal of my spiritual energy reflecting about how I was
"by nature sinful and unclean" and precisely how I had sinned against
God "by thought, word, and deed," so that I could flee to God's mercy.
Paul's contorted speech in Romans 7 about the good that I would but
cannot do because of the "sin that dwells within me," including its note
of thanksgiving to God through Christ for deliverance from "this body of
death," provided a touchstone in my devotional life between Sundays.

Holy communion was celebrated monthly, and receiving Christ's body
and blood was for me an even more intense and personal confrontation
with my own sinfulness and the promise of forgiveness. I remember the
impression of the proper prefaces that wonderfully linked our thanksgiving to Christ in the unfolding feasts and seasons of the church year.
The words of institution, however, made the deepest impact: "my body,
which is given for you . . . , my blood, which is shed for you, and for
many, for the remission of sins; this do . . . in remembrance of me."[16]
My first communion took place on Maundy Thursday following confirmation on Palm Sunday of my ninth-grade year. This conjunction
of first communion with the Holy Week commemoration of our Lord's
last supper with his disciples provides an emblem for a significant piece
of my Lord's Supper piety. The mental picture that I brought to the reception of communion transported me back to the upper room on the
night of our Lord's betrayal, and there I took my place at table among
the Lord's disciples.

These recollections of the practice of confession and communion and
how they shaped my own piety are by no means the whole picture of my
early liturgical formation. That larger view would have to take account
of many things: the impact of the preaching that shaped every service;
the joy I always found hearing my voice joined with others in the song
of liturgy and hymns and choir anthems; the impression of a spatial
environment that visually gathered us around table, pulpit, and font;[17]
and much more. It would also have to take account of the turmoil I was
experiencing outside the church and my own struggle to understand it
in relation to what I did inside on Sunday morning: black Americans
marching, suffering, dying for fundamental civil rights; the specter of
environmental degradation and nuclear war; protests against the Vietnam War and the draft; apocalyptic predictions about overpopulation
and hunger; the voices of women raised for equal rights; and the youth

culture itself, with its hair and jeans and music and sex and drugs; and again much more.

This liturgical genealogy is my own, and at certain points it may even be idiosyncratic. Let me suggest, however, that the two reflections about confession and communion point to a pervasive liturgical piety characterized by the following abstractions. It was penitential, individual, retrospective, and institutional. It was about sin and forgiveness; it was about a personal relationship to God and to other people; it was focused on past events, especially Jesus' life, death, and resurrection; and it was about the administration of grace in the church through the means of word and sacrament. It corresponded to the conventional inside-and-out approach to worship and mission.

It would be difficult to identify the point where my own liturgical piety began to shift. As I have indicated, traces of something else were already present in my early liturgical formation. The Contemporary Worship series,[18] the trial materials that prepared the way for the publication of *Lutheran Book of Worship* (*LBW*)[19] in 1978, in conjunction with my own seminary studies in Bible, theology, liturgy, and Christian art and architecture were especially formative. In the new liturgical rites, I noted and welcomed the absence of the words "by nature sinful and unclean" in the order of confession and forgiveness that preceded the service of Holy Communion. Instead, we confessed that "we are in bondage to sin and cannot free ourselves."[20] And it was even possible to begin a Sunday service without the preparatory confession. *LBW* also promoted attention to the eucharistic center of Christian worship and exposed me to eucharistic praying that set the celebration of the Lord's Supper (and my Last Supper piety) within the sweep of God's activity from the creation of the world to the consummation of all things in the Lord's "coming in power to share with us the great and promised feast" (Eucharistic prayer I).[21]

There was a moment, however, when I began to articulate the movement that was taking place in my liturgical piety. In February 1977, Wolfhart Pannenberg gave some lectures at Yale Divinity School entitled "Theological Issues in Christian Spirituality," since published in the volume *Christian Spirituality*.[22] The first two lectures traced the shift from the penitential piety that has dominated Western Christianity since the Middle Ages to a eucharistic piety emerging in our own time.

Pannenberg described the development of a Protestant pietism that focused "on the awareness of sin and guilt as a condition for genuine faith. One could be certain of salvation precisely to the extent that one identified oneself as a sinner completely dependent on the grace of God."[23] And further, he said:

The strength of penitential pietism consisted in its support of those who felt themselves planted in the unshakable ground of the divine promise in Jesus Christ. But the price of this strength was self-aggression. . . . Another limitation has been its virtual individualism. . . . [A]n authentic conception of the Christian church was hard to develop on this basis, . . . for the body of Christ is more than an association of independent individuals.[24]

According to Pannenberg, there were signs that this penitential piety was giving way to a new type of piety, which he called eucharistic. Whereas the old piety had its origin in the medieval practice of penance, this new piety had its source in a renewed practice of the Eucharist. "The rediscovery of the Eucharist may prove to be the most important event in Christian spirituality of our time, of more revolutionary importance than even the liturgical renewal may realize."[25] In Pannenberg's view, the symbolism of the Eucharist in its communal, sacrificial, and eschatological dimensions represented a reorientation of Christian piety away from a narrow focus on the individual entangled in sin and toward the church as a communion of those united to Christ, toward the world as the object of God's reconciling mission in the death of Jesus, and toward the kingdom of God as the ultimate "social destiny of all human life."[26] For Pannenberg, worship is at the center of the church's mission in relation to God's own ultimate purposes for the world:

There is no reason for the existence of the church except to symbolize the future of the divine kingdom that Jesus came to proclaim. This explains in what specific sense worship is in the center of life of the church: The worship of the Christian community anticipates and symbolically celebrates the praise of God's glory that will be consummated in the eschatological renewal of all creation in the new Jerusalem.[27]

I listened attentively to all of this twenty-some years ago and realized that Pannenberg's description of an epochal shift in Christian piety summed up the reorientation of my own liturgical piety. His provocative reflections in those two essays have been a touchstone for my thinking about worship ever since. The focus of worship shifted from matters of personal salvation and devotion to matters of the liturgical assembly's significance "for the life of the world," to use the Johannine phrase (John 6:51—ὑπὲρ τῆς τοῦ κόσμου ζωῆς) found in the Byzantine anaphora of St. Basil[28] and popularized by the Russian Orthodox theologian Alexander Schmemann.[29] The liturgy, most especially the Eucharist, enacted God's world-redeeming and world-reconciling purpose in Christ, and it constituted a people to witness to that eschatological reality in every dimension of its life. The community of the church and its liturgical assembly was from this perspective the visible locus of the missio Dei, the symbolic enactment of God's eschatological purposes for the world in the midst of the world. Whereas my former liturgical piety was penitential, individual, retrospective, and institutional, the newly emerging piety was eucharistic, communal, prospective, and symbolic. It corresponded to the radically traditional inside-out approach to worship and mission.

For each of these adjectival abstractions about the contemporary liturgical assembly—eucharistic, communal, prospective, and symbolic—we can point to particular liturgical patterns and practices that constitute what it means to celebrate the liturgy of the church in its local assembly (inside) as a liturgy for a church in mission (out)—inside out. The "missional intention for the means of grace," "the Word and the sacraments . . . set in the midst of the world, for the life of the world" (*The Use of the Means of Grace*) are much more than newfangled ideas about worship meant to uphold the relevance of liturgy for a missional church. On the contrary, they represent the deepest movements of historic liturgical practice. What follows sketches some concrete examples of the inside-out approach to the liturgical practice of a missional church.

Liturgical Assembly as Eucharistic

The principal form of Christian prayer is *eucharistia* or "thanksgiving." The central prayer of the liturgy is a great thanksgiving, restored to its fullness in Lutheran liturgical books first in the American Lutheran *Service Book and Hymnal* (1958) and now in *Lutheran Book of Worship* (1978). Its deepest roots are to be found in forms of Jewish prayer called *berakoth* (blessings) and Jewish sacrifice, especially the *zebach todah* or sacrifice of thanksgiving, as well as in the pattern of Jesus' own meal fellowship, especially on the night in which he was given up to death on a cross for the sake of this world's life. Christian *eucharistia* gives thanks over the bread and wine of that same meal fellowship but now with the risen Lord. In its thanksgiving, the Christian assembly remembers its crucified and risen Lord. It also acknowledges the work of a gracious God in creating the world, calling out a people Israel, and gathering a new people as witness to the gospel of Jesus' death and resurrection. Moreover, the assembly that prays this prayer anticipates the fulfillment of God's promises and supplicates the Holy One for its own unity in the Spirit, which signifies already the promised unity of all tribes and nations in the kingdom of God.

Between its thankful remembrance and its hope-filled supplication, the church in its liturgical assembly carries out its eucharistic mission to witness to God's liberating judgment of the world and the world-encompassing mercy of God in the cross of Jesus Christ. The horizon of this great prayer of thanksgiving is always the world and the world's future in the unfolding of God's plan of salvation. Such a prayer celebrates *koinonia*, the reconciled communion with God that is already possible through Christ in the community of the church and yet remains a hope for the world and all its people, indeed, for the whole created order. In this way, the liturgical assembly in its *eucharistia* witnesses to and participates in the missio Dei. The liturgical assembly centered on such fervent praying in thanks for what God has done and in confident supplication for the world is far removed from one oriented around the prayer of the penitent and the Lord's Supper celebrated only as a promise of forgiveness, both of which focus on the self and its deliverance from sin.[30]

Liturgical Assembly as Communal

In liturgical formularies, the assembly itself is often designated by the term people (in Greek, λαός, in Latin, *populus*), and this usage is preserved, for example, in the English translation of the *Roman Sacramentary* and the American *Book of Common Prayer*. The reference of the term, it seems to me, is multiple—"this people" here gathered, that is, the local assembly; "a people," that is, the church as the visible people of God in the world; and even "the people," that is, the totality of all people. In the liturgy, all three of these meanings stand in relationship to one another. This local assembly is the church catholic in a particular place; it is also in communion with other local assemblies and as such represents the whole people of God; and this people finally also stands for all people, for in the liturgy, this people "does the world" as God would have it.[31]

All these meanings suggest the deeply communal character of Christianity. According to the Russian Orthodox theologian Georges Florovsky,

> Christianity entered history as a new social order, or rather a new social dimension. From the very beginning Christianity is not primarily a "doctrine," but exactly a "community." There was not only a "Message" to be proclaimed and delivered, and "Good News" to be declared. There was precisely a New Community, distinct and peculiar, in the process of growth and formation, to which members were called and recruited. Indeed, "fellowship" (*koinonia*) was the basic category of Christian existence.[32]

At the center of the gospel stand two things together, the message of salvation for the ungodly—for all—in Jesus Christ, embodied in an assembly for all, an assembly defined not by the markers of difference—age, race, gender, wealth, or status—but by baptism into Christ. In this way, the *koinonia* of the church, constituted and manifest in its liturgical assembly, is the missio Dei, as it happens now and in anticipation of the fullness of this communion in the kingdom of God. More than a collection of individuals with concern for personal salvation, the liturgical assembly enacts the communion that is the church, in the hope of that wider communion that is God's ultimate purpose.

Liturgical Assembly as Prospective

Much of Christian liturgical celebration appears to be about past events. At Christmas, we remember the birth of Jesus; at Epiphany, the visit of the magi; on Good Friday, Jesus' death on the cross, and at Easter, his resurrection; on Ascension Day, Jesus' going to the Father; and at Pentecost, the outpouring of the Spirit on the disciples. Whenever the Lord's Supper is celebrated, it is Jesus' last supper with his disciples or the crucifixion with Jesus' body given and blood poured out. The liturgy, from this perspective, becomes a ritual "bridging of the gap" between these events and our present, a ritual mechanism either to make the past somehow present to us or to make us somehow present to the past. This focus on the liturgical representation of the past, however, seems to miss the point that the liturgy is about a relationship with the risen Lord, who lives and reigns with the Father and the Holy Spirit, and to whom this past belongs. Moreover—and this is the critical point—the Risen One is himself the first fruits of the kingdom that lies before us, and consequently the remembrance of him always orients us to that future. Liturgical *anamnesis* is as much about the present and the future as it is about the past. Let us say it this way: Through the *memory* of Jesus Christ—his coming in the flesh, his life, death, and resurrection—our lives are directed in *hope* to the kingdom of God that Jesus proclaimed and to God's ultimate purposes for us and our world, just as we enjoy even now Christ's life-giving *presence* in the assembly of the faithful through word and sacrament by the power of the Holy Spirit.

As a community with prospective vision, the church in every present moment lives toward the reign of God inaugurated in Jesus Christ. The eschatological perspective permeates the liturgical assembly, because in Christ this community enacts the hope of the world for its ultimate reconciliation to God in a fellowship of love, peace, and justice. The missio Dei is nothing other than what the church as an eschatological community enacts in its liturgical assembly and in which it participates precisely by this enactment. Such an assembly is anything but focused on the past but lives in the present toward the future God has promised in Jesus Christ.

Liturgical Assembly as Symbolic

At the Vigil of Easter, there is an ancient and lengthy prayer, the Easter proclamation, that sings the meaning of that night in the light of the paschal candle. The proclamation begins with an extended invitation summoning the whole created order into the praise of God for the deliverance and restoration the Almighty One has wrought in Christ:

> Rejoice, now,
>   all heavenly choirs of angels. . . .
> Exult, also, O earth,
>   enlightened with such radiance . . . .
> Be glad also, O mother Church, . . .
>   and let this house resound
>   with the triumphant voices
>   of the peoples.
> Wherefore, dearly beloved,
>   who stand in the clarity
>   of this bright and holy light . . .[33]

This arena is a highly symbolic one in which the gathering of a local company of the faithful around a flickering flame in the middle of the night is set in relation to choirs of angels, the earth, and the whole church encompassing the peoples, all joined in a joyful eruption of cosmic praise. The liturgical assembly is never just what it appears to be. It always points to the eschatological reality beyond itself, to the purpose of God in Christ for the world and its peoples, for the whole created order. This is what it means to call the liturgical assembly symbolic.

The liturgical assembly is suffused with symbolic language and symbolic acts precisely because the church itself is a symbolic community.[34] The purpose of the church is essentially symbolic: in its very existence as a community in Christ, the church points to the kingdom of God as the ultimate shape of reality. The gathering of people into this symbolic representation of God's purposes for the world is the church's part in the missio Dei, all of which underscores the fundamental connection between the symbolic character of the liturgical assembly and the church's mission. More than a place for individuals to encounter word and sacrament as institutions of grace, the church in its assembly around word and sacrament enacts a ritual symbol of God's gracious purpose for the world and so participates in God's world-encompassing mission.

Engaging the Culture

The next step is to show how this inside-out approach to the relationship between the church's worship and its mission resonates in response to the greatest aspirations and the deepest needs at work in the contemporary cultural context. How do the eucharistic, communal, prospective, and symbolic dimensions of the liturgical assembly engage the vitality and delights, the lacks and longing of the contemporary moment in North American culture? How does the eucharistic gathering of God's people in a particular place as a sign of God's purposes for the world—as a visible enactment of the missio Dei—engage us as people shaped by the forces of life in the modern or postmodern world? These are large questions that ask us to ponder the intersection of the liturgical assembly and contemporary life and to articulate how the contours of this gathering are precisely about God's mission among us and in our world today. What follows is the beginning of such a reflection.

God at the Center

If the liturgical assembly is indeed pervasively eucharistic—consummately enacted in the great thanksgiving and the reception of communion—what does such thanksgiving to God mean for people today? How might such thanksgiving shape the experience of contemporary life in North America? First, it orients us to the source of all things, to the almighty and everlasting God, who has created and continually sustains the world and everything in it. Such a recognition is diminished, if not altogether eliminated, in the scientific rationality that permeates the daily existence of most people. The modern worldview gives place to God, if at all, at the margins of life and confines the divine to what is private and personal. The God of Christian *eucharistia*, however, stands at the center of all things and is not limited to any sphere of life. The practice of thanksgiving at the heart of Christian worship embodies the doxological foundation of human existence. As Nathan Mitchell writes,

> To be is to worship; human existence is inescapably liturgical, doxological. Doxology . . . is "ontologically constitutive"; it is what makes our existence as human subjects possible . . . Quite simply, we become ourselves only in the act of praising God.[35]

Furthermore, the *eucharistia* of the liturgical assembly offers a distinct alternative to the way of life shaped by modern consumer culture. The market economy is a dynamic, creative, and dominant force in contemporary life. It offers the promise of prosperity, freedom, and choice to large segments of North American society. At the same time, substantial numbers of people do not participate in this promise and struggle with poverty in the midst of affluence. Such an economy depends on consumption—on consumers who acquire things and enjoy them. Acquisition and enjoyment give shape to life in a consumer culture. The eucharistic gathering of Christians, however, "proclaim[s] the Lord's death until he comes" (1 Cor. 11:26; also eucharistic prayer I in *LBW*[36]) and seeks to shape our lives in relation to the cross of Christ. Instead of defining human existence in terms of the acquisition and enjoyment of things, the thanksgiving to God for Jesus' passion, death, and resurrection at the center of Christian worship defines the fullness of life in terms of the gift of communion with God and its corollary, the possibility of freedom to live for others according to God's purposes for the world.

Christian *eucharistia* in the contemporary North American liturgical assembly is about the mission of God in a time and place where there is forgetfulness about God and a compulsion to satisfy ourselves through the accumulation of many possessions. It redirects us to the living God, to our communion with this God through Christ, and to a life for others. Finally, this *eucharistia* is deeply connected to the fervent supplication that these blessings from God will extend beyond the assembly itself and encompass all who know this same forgetfulness and compulsion.

A Distinctive Community

The communal dimension of the liturgical assembly also meets the present moment in a very particular way. Many commentators have noted the radical individualism that characterizes the contemporary American way of life, including its religious life. If, however, the liturgical assembly is about "the people" in every sense of that word—the locally gathered people, the people of God throughout the world, and all people everywhere—then the matter of Christian worship is about something other than confirming us in our individual ways. It shapes a common life, a life decidedly with others. "Behold the church!" declared the nineteenth-century German Lutheran pastor and theologian Wilhelm Loehe. "It is the very opposite of loneliness—blessed fellowship!"[37] The fellowship of the church satisfies "the desire for fellowship . . . born in us," just as it directs us to the "real fellowship desired by God, a fellowship created by God for eternity."[38] The act of assembly for worship at the center of Christian life and practice enacts this fellowship, establishing the place of the individual in community. "There is no solitary earth and no solitary heaven,"[39] to again use Loehe's words. Because it enacts the essentially communal nature of human existence and human destiny, the liturgical assembly counters the distortions of contemporary individualism.

The communal vision at the heart of the church and its worship, however, also counters the distortions of communal claims and arrangements that destroy the dignity of the individual. Along side the impetus to individualism, the modern period is replete with nationalistic impulses, ideological movements, and utopian programs that seek to shape human communities and command the allegiance of individuals. In their extreme forms, such movements are coercive and exclusionary, and they often operate out of an understanding of human nature that fails to grasp fully the human capacity for evil. The inevitable result is a disregard for the individual and a lack of concern for the well-being of each person. It is important to acknowledge that such disregard can also infect the church as a community. Nonetheless, the kind of community to which the church is committed—especially in its worship—is not determined by territory, ideology, or fantasy. It is a place where each individual stands equally before God's judgment and mercy and where the well-being of the least cannot be ignored.

The communal character of the liturgical assembly is a critical aspect of the mission of God in contemporary circumstances. On the one hand, it critiques every notion of the autonomous individual and affirms the fundamentally social nature of human existence. On the other hand, it critiques every form of human community that disregards the dignity and well-being of the individual, including the structures and practices of churchly life itself. This critique takes place because the church, constituted in its liturgical assembly, is a distinctive community amid the plurality of human communities, the one community that refers us ultimately to the fellowship that God establishes and promises to be the destiny of human existence.

God's Future

Because the community of the church refers beyond itself to the fellowship of all people in the kingdom of God, its assembly for worship has a prospective character as we have seen. This theological orientation to the future provides a connection to the contemporary focus on the future. One characteristic of the modern sensibility is to cast off the weight of the past and to look forward with confidence in human progress. The meaning of things is in what lies ahead of us, and this is where our cultural energy is directed. The Christian eschatology that shapes the prospective dimension of the liturgical assembly is similar to this outlook but with two important qualifications. First, the past is understood more positively, it is not just a limit to be surpassed. Rather, through the activity of God in human history, the past bears relation to the future—especially in the life, death, and resurrection of Jesus, which contain the meaning of the future. Second, the future that concerns the liturgical assembly is a particular future. It is God's future, a future beyond all human projection and imagining. So the prospective orientation is finally trust in God, to whom the future belongs, not a misplaced confidence in human progress.

Indeed, there are many who do not share the modern confidence about the future. Nurtured by postmodern disillusionment about human progress, they are skeptical, even despairing, about the future. What remains is the present, a present dissociated from the past and the future. Robert Jenson has addressed the difficulty of having no future orientation:

> It is the whole vision of an Eschaton that is now missing outside the church. The assembly of believers must therefore itself be the event in which we may behold what is to come. . . . If, in the *post*-modern world, a congregation or whatever wants to be "relevant," its assemblies must be unabashedly events of shared apocalyptic vision. "Going to church" must be a journey to the place where we will behold our destiny, where we will see what is to come of us.[40]

The prospective vision of the Christian liturgical assembly shapes a context in which people isolated in the present moment are broken open to the testimony of God's activity in human history and to the hope for a future determined by God's purposes for the world. Such a response to contemporary cynicism offers a framework for living that upholds connections to the past and the future while acknowledging the complexities and limitations of human existence.

Once again the church in its assembly for worship is about the mission of God in the present as that assembly engages contemporary perspectives on the world's future (and its past). Where there is unlimited confidence about the human ability to understand and shape the future, the prospective dimension of the liturgical assembly directs that confidence instead to the future that God promises. Where there is doubt about the future, it constructs a framework of hope in God's purposes for the world.

Engaging the Culture's Images

We come finally to the symbolic dimension of the liturgical assembly and its intersection with contemporary life. One clear point of intersection is the role that visual images play both in the symbolic environment of the liturgy and in the electronic media. Present-day North Americans are awash in a sea of images emanating from the television and increasingly from the computer. Whereas words—spoken, written, and printed—have been the dominant form of human communication, the visual image has emerged as a powerful force in contemporary mass communication. The visual image is also critical to the liturgy's ritual and symbolic communication, and indeed the importance of the visual image in contemporary culture has helped to heighten sensitivity to the visual experience of worship and to what is imaged in the ritual activity of worshiping assemblies.

Attending to the visual image in Christian worship becomes all the more important when we look further into the messages communicated by the electronic media. In her study of television images, Gregor Goethals has labeled television "the electronic golden calf," suggesting a correspondence between America's worship at this video altar and Israel's idolatrous worship of the golden calf at the foot of Mount Sinai (Exodus 32).[41] She convincingly interprets the constant flow of images from the television, which saturates our experience, as an "expression of an encompassing faith in the American way of life."[42] These electronic images construct a "symbolic canopy" that shapes a way of life, particularly in relation to the values of individualism and consumerism:

> "Choice" is . . . the most magical word in American culture. . . . The steady hum over radio and television about the choices we have is a litany to liberty, to the freedom to choose one product over another, and above all to define one's individuality through one's choices.[43]

She concludes that "unless we recognize the power of the media to construct symbolic worlds, we will not even grasp the range of mediated values or recognize the real choices to be made. Nor will we understand the need for a daring iconoclasm."[44]

The images at work within the church's own symbolic life, especially its liturgical assembly, are potentially the Christian community's most powerful force for engaging and critiquing the electronic images of contemporary life and breaking the idolatrous images that contend for our worship. The ritual images of worship—derived from Scripture and enacted in the reading of the Word and its proclamation, in the gathering at the font, and in the eating and drinking at the table of thanksgiving—all relate to the saving death of Jesus and to the hope found there for the whole world. This symbolic canopy mediates God's judgment and God's generosity. It is not so much about choice as it is about being chosen "in Christ before the foundation of the world" (Eph. 1:4); it is not so much about individuality as it is about being part of "a chosen race, a royal priesthood, a holy nation, God's own people" (1 Peter 2:9). Those who participate in the liturgical assembly are encompassed by its images and in that symbolic canopy themselves become the image of God's purposes for the world. The liturgical assembly is about the missio Dei in the midst of the symbolic world of contemporary popular culture.

Liturgy for a Church in Mission

These embryonic reflections are intended to show that the liturgical assembly is where God's mission takes place—a locus of mission—not merely in the abstraction of theological ideas but in the concrete reality of North American cultural circumstances. In its eucharistic, communal, prospective, and symbolic dimensions, that local gathering of God's people does engage the vitality and delights, the lacks and longing of this time and place. The words of Wilhelm Loehe, whose own pastoral work over a century ago demonstrated the deep connections of liturgy and mission, offer us a fitting conclusion: "The church has put together according to holy orders . . . services of various kinds and esteems them to be understood by all the faithful as the highest harmony of earthly life and not only to be sung and spoken but to be lived."[45] The liturgy sung, spoken, *and lived* is liturgy for a church in mission—inside out.

4

On Starting with People

James F. White

*In this chapter James White draws relevant conclusions for
contemporary worship by examining the cultural revolution of the fifteenth and sixteenth centuries.*

I

The shape of present-day Protestant worship is largely a consequence of
the communications revolution of the fifteenth and sixteenth centuries.
The Reformation coincided with one of the greatest communications
revolutions of all time—the invention of the cheap book. The combination of this revolution and the theological revolution of the Reformation
shaped Protestant worship for four hundred years.

Christian worship had known the use of written formularies from at
least the third century. Hippolytus' liturgy, which dates from the early-
third century, presents a written form of prayer, though he testifies to

Reprinted from James F. White, *New Forms of Worship* (Nashville, Abingdon Press, 1971),
21–37. © 1971 by Abingdon Press. Used by permission.

elasticity in his provision that bishops may improvise. Serapion's prayer-book from the fourth century is further evidence of the use of written texts, and from that time onward the use of written rites is clear. Even so, it was only the clergy who had a missal, a ritual, or whatever service book was needed. The very terms "cleric" or "clerk" often referred to someone who could read and write, since the average layman was illiterate or "lewd," that is, nonclerical.

In the Middle Ages, books were used by the clergy, but what they had to say in the mass, apart from the sermon, was usually hard to hear and even harder to understand for those who did not know Latin. The priest was the man with the book, and he was the only one who could "say" mass. For most people, both the culture and worship were pre-literate. People participated at mass largely by watching the actions of the priest at the altar. The laity had few, if any, words to offer in their worship. Stephen Gardiner, Catholic bishop of Winchester, England, wrote in 1547:

> It was never meant that the people should indeed hear the Matins or hear the Mass, but be present there and pray themselves in silence; with common credit to the priests and clerks, that although they hear not a distinct sound to know what they say, yet to judge that they for their part were and be well occupied, and in prayer; and so should they be.[1]

The laity were to keep quiet and occupy themselves with their own private devotions.

Johannes Gutenberg changed all that though not in the most obvious way. His invention, of course, was a means of mass-producing books. Books, formerly possessions only of clergy and men of wealth, could be mass produced after the 1450s with each printed page being identical with all others from the same type.[2] At last books could be sold cheaply. William Tyndale's hope that his biblical translations could be read by "a boy that driveth the plough" was possible only in a print culture. The 1549 *Book of Common Prayer* was limited in price by royal authority to no more than two shillings two pence unbound.[3]

But the most important result of the invention of printing was not that in the course of more than a century books became available to most people. What matters most is what reading did to people. Learning to read does things to people as can be observed by watching any first-grade school child. Reading is an individual act. You need no one to do it for you. The child stops demanding, "tell me a story," and goes into a corner to read by himself. What he learns does not come through a person but through little splotches of black ink pressed into a white page. Reading is a solitary act; we put up quiet signs in libraries. It is also depersonalized, since things communicate to us rather than people. And consequently reading is more likely to stimulate the intellect than the emotions. It is hard to get quite as excited about what ink and paper say to us compared to what flesh and blood say when we are confronted by a living human. Only one medium communicates to us in print, rather than the multiplicity of voice, facial expressions, and gestures of a human being. In reading we are accustomed to reality being mediated to us through a single and impersonal medium, the printed page.

There is another important consequence which Marshall McLuhan called "the linear structuring of rational life of phonetic literacy."[4] The printed page metes out information in a neat orderly sequence, word after word, line after line. One thing comes at a time. Instead of the instantaneous impact of meeting a person and seeing and hearing him at the same time, we read about these one item at a time. So the reader becomes doubly detached from the reality the book describes. Reality is mediated through cold print and in a sequential and linear pattern rather than instantaneously.

The invention of printing drastically changed people and the ways they perceived reality. Reading heightened their individualistic self-reliance. It also pushed them to approach reality in terms of sequential analysis, taking things in an orderly fashion. At the same time, the senses of taste, touch, and smell, instantaneous in impact and completely absent from printing, were eclipsed. The importance of printing for Protestant worship lies much more in what it did to people than in the mechanical possibilities that it opened up for the conduct of services. People had changed and the Reformers could make a new start in worship because they were dealing with a new kind of person, literate man.

All this had tremendous consequences for the shaping of Protestant worship. Indeed, in some areas it may have overcome the theological preferences of the Reformers themselves. One of the great accomplishments of the Reformers with regard to worship was that they seemed to grasp what was happening to people in northern Europe and the opportunities these changes presented for renewing the forms of worship. In part it was a chain reaction just as the introduction of the vernacular has been in Roman Catholic worship in our own time. The Reformers differed in how far they followed out the consequences of the print revolution, the churches of the Reformed tradition being the most consistent in shaping their worship around the new emphasis on the word.

The first and most obvious consequence of a literate laity was that they could participate verbally in services of worship in a much fuller way. No longer were they restricted to litanies and those few phrases that memory could recover. Hymns, prayers, lections, psalms now became accessible to them. The clerical monopoly was broken, for now all could be clerics, that is, readers. Gutenberg made possible in worship what Martin Luther proclaimed about the priesthood of all believers. The result was a raising of the status of the laity rather than a lowering of the clergy.

But there were other effects. The laity, for the most part, read their native tongues, not Latin. Luther began by preparing a Latin liturgy. But for most people a book in Latin was no better than none. Others preceded Luther in enabling a literate laity to participate in worship through vernacular translations. Soon all important Protestant leaders recognized this necessity though themselves fluent in Latin. The language of the laity was adopted in every land of the Reformation. Since any translation expresses ideas in new forms and thus subtly changes those same concepts, translation was the crucial act in shaping each Protestant tradition of worship. Even the most careful translation is couched in the new language into which the ideas are rendered, and thus the various liturgies adopted the thought patterns of sixteenth-century German, French, Dutch, English, and other languages.

It was also evident that drastic simplification would be necessary for the laity to participate verbally in the service. Thomas Cranmer's complaint in 1549 with regard to the old service books: "That many times, there was more business to fynd out what should be read, then to read it when it was founde out"[5] led to considerable pruning and simplification. His prayer book distilled into one volume the contents of the missal, breviary, ritual, and pontifical and put it all into the hands of the laity. A Bible was the only other book necessary for the conduct of the services of the Church of England. Simplification, then, was a keynote of Protestant worship, achieved largely by subtraction rather than new additions.

Worship for Protestants came to be expressed primarily through two mediums, the word spoken and the word read. It is no accident that the biblical image of the "Word of God" came to be so important. Whether identified with Christ himself, Scripture, preaching, or inward perception, the "Word of God" remains the most conspicuous image of the Reformation. The Puritans treated the Bible itself as a book of canons as to what was suitable for worship, reformed according to God's Word.

The preaching of the Word of God came to occupy the longest time of any part of public worship. Luther felt that the congregation "should never gather together without the preaching of God's Word and prayer."[6] In much of Protestantism even the prayers eventually took on the nature of brief homilies, and the whole service seemed to be a frame for the sermon. Hourglasses were placed in many English churches to measure the length of the sermon. God's Word was not just expounded; it was expounded fully and frequently.

A good indication of what was happening is provided in the fate of the church year. Many of the Reformers were convinced that all Scripture was written for man's instruction (Rom. 15:4), hence lectionaries based on the calendar were scrapped for a *lectio continua* in which one plodded through whole books of the Bible instead of reading the appropriate selections for special days and seasons of the calendar. None of God's Word was neglected, but the peaks and valleys of the church year were leveled to a flat plain of continuous reading.

A linear mentality had come to dominate man. It often worked contrary to the desires of the Reformers. Martin Luther, John Calvin, and Thomas Cranmer desired that the main Sunday service be the Lord's Supper as it had been since New Testament times. But in each case their wishes were frustrated. Instead, the service of the Word from the Lord's Supper or the pattern of the divine office (based on the Scriptures, psalms, and prayer) ousted the full Lord's Supper from dominance. In effect, the synagogue triumphed over the upper room.

The causes of this great change in the main diet of congregational worship (undoubtedly the greatest transformation in Reformation worship though neither desired nor anticipated by many of the Reformers) was largely due to what had happened to man. The communications impact of the Lord's Supper is instantaneous. In one service is represented the very heart of the gospel: Christ's passion, death, and resurrection. The impact of the divine office and the service of the Word, on the other hand, is cumulative. Bits of salvation history are commemorated week after week in lessons, psalms, hymns, and sermons. In the course of time these add up to the whole gospel, but the approach is basically one item at a time in a steady progression, week after week. Nothing could be better suited to the mentality of literate man, for he looks at reality in a linear and sequential fashion. Thus the pattern of the divine office or service of the Word became his most natural form of worship. The Lord's Supper became an occasional ceremony, eventually celebrated only three times a year in the Church of England or quarterly in the Church of Scotland. The triumph of the linear mentality was complete.

For Protestants, worship came to be equated with the reading, singing, and speaking of words. "Reading prayers," or "going to the sermon" came to be Protestant ways of speaking of worship. In short, the ethos of Protestant worship came to be bookish just as did the culture of Protestant regions. Unfortunately, the great stress on the word read, sung, and spoken led to corresponding losses in other areas. The whole vocabulary of gestures that had been so important in medieval worship was sloughed off. The Puritans denounced many bits of ceremonial as "popish abuses" and "badges of Antichrist" unless "gathered out of the word of God." But it may be equally significant that the Protestant emphasis on verbalization made them superfluous. The visual arts withered away, and Protestant worship became, for all purposes, color-blind. Color was as absent from churches as from the printed page. Vestments disappeared except in Sweden to be replaced by conservative black street dress or professors' gowns. Sir Christopher Wren designed his churches by calculating the optimum distance that a preacher's voice could be heard and referred to Protestant church buildings as "to be fitted for Auditories." To be sure, his buildings did employ bits of baroque carving as adornment, and the New England meetinghouses were often painted colors until the Greek revival of the nineteenth century whitened them all. But none of this adornment could properly be called liturgical art, nor did it bear any intrinsic relationship to the building's function in worship.

Sixteenth-century Protestant worship, then, was shaped by the same forces that were shaping men at the time, especially by the new development of widespread literacy. The forms of worship became those most natural to the people of the time. Catholicism, on the other hand, made little acknowledgment of what was happening to men except to seize the possibility of standardizing liturgical texts. A variety of local uses still survived, but these were abolished (with few exceptions) at the advent of printing. The Roman breviary of 1568, the missal of 1570, and subsequent books led the way to a standardization of texts no matter in what part of the world the divine office or mass was said. Mass-produced books led to identical rites. Protestantism succumbed to the same temptation, and various acts of uniformity provided for one identical prayer book in England and Wales so that "all the whole realme shall haue but one use." Catholicism managed to ignore the consequences of Gutenberg's revolution except for accomplishing the standardization of texts.

Protestantism allowed people to worship in the forms most natural to them. This has been the strength of Protestant worship for more than four hundred years. There were, of course, occasional variations. On the American frontier, where literacy could not be taken for granted, some quite divergent forms of worship developed. They made more use of the emotions and stressed various gestures through use of the sawdust trail, the mourner's bench, and the altar call. Similar features tended to be characteristic in the black churches.

A further development considerably affected Protestant worship though not mentioned in any liturgical textbooks. In 1884 a Chicago businessman, A. B. Dick, solved a business need for rapid duplication by inventing a process for stencil duplication. It proved so efficient that he marketed it under the name of "Mimeograph." Gutenberg made it possible to put prayer books in the hands of people; Dick made prayer books obsolete. Prayer books are mostly propers which are hard to locate and confusing to most people. Dick gave each minister his own printing press and a new possibility of printing only what was needed on any specific occasion. Xerox and other processes promise to do the same for hymnals. These developments have simply completed what Gutenberg began, and in worship as elsewhere we are now flooded with printed paper.

II

Protestant worship, then, was shaped by the communications and theological revolutions of the sixteenth century and made creative use of what had happened to man. Basically these premises remained valid until very recently when we find ourselves in the midst of an equally tremendous new communications revolution, a similar theological one having already occurred in the accommodation of religion to scientific discoveries. The new communications revolution is much more impatient than its predecessor. It has not required a hundred years or more to affect whole populations. Technology has provided a variety of new media and, even more significant, has made them available cheaply. Television, the most conspicuous of the new media, has not turned out to be a luxury of the privileged few (like medieval books) but a necessity of the masses. Its importance, like printed books, lies in the fact that it knows no elite.

This new communications revolution has happened to us so fast that we are hardly aware of its effects on us. We still judge it in terms of our past, putting movies on television just as we made movies out of books. Yet the great importance of what television (along with the telephone, speed in travel, and other new possibilities) has done for us is often ignored when it is seen just as an alternate way of presenting the same information. That is to miss the point altogether. Marshall McLuhan has argued that the medium itself is the message and we must perceive what the new media do to us, not just the message that they present.[7] Our thesis here is that the new media, especially television, have caused a drastic change in our means of perceiving reality, just as the advent of mass literacy did in the sixteenth century. This is particularly true of those who have grown up on television. Since half of the American population has been born since World War II, that includes vast numbers of people. In 1954, for the first time, television surpassed radio in the amount of broadcast revenues it produced.

Television plugs each of us into the events of the whole world. McLuhan has popularized the phrase, "the global village."[8] It is as if we all once again were squatted around a tribal campfire, taking part in whatever was happening to the tribe. But that tribe is now worldwide. Instead of the perimeter of the village campfire being our widest horizon, we now find ourselves elbow to elbow with the whole human race. When man first stepped on the moon, it is estimated that one fifth of the human race saw him do so. In a very real sense we were all there.

It is this quality of being a direct participant in the event which makes television so different from reading. One reads about an event, seeing it through the eyes of the writer. In television he sees it happen directly with his own eyes. The old phrase "seeing is believing" describes the television event. But television excites more than just eyesight since the sense of touch is so closely related to seeing. Affected is the sense of touch as well as hearing and seeing. Television involves the emotions, too. One reacts directly to what he sees and hears, not to something described by a writer. So our emotions and our senses of touch, hearing, and seeing are all sucked into the television event.

Television demands a much greater degree of participation than reading or radio since several senses work simultaneously. We become part of the event. No one could have watched the riots at the 1968 Democratic Convention in Chicago and remained neutral. One had to take sides, either with the youth or the police. The same event, printed in the newspapers the next day, could be analyzed without passion or commitment. The detached act of reading about such an event was a completely different experience of its reality from that of being there via television. A medium such as television demands our full involvement for we become a part of the action. We do not remain passive, analytical, noninvolved.

Television's impact on us is instantaneous. Partly because the value of broadcast seconds is measured in thousands of dollars, television works on compression, leaving us much to fill in ourselves. A television program compresses into half an hour or an hour a story that the more leisurely medium of the movies loiters over for double that time. We do not have to rely on an author to set the setting. It's there; we see it immediately. A whole variety of circumstances can be grasped from a few short glimpses, or they can even be superimposed on one another.

Part of the problem with television is that it is still a new medium for those of us over thirty. Our children never knew a world without television. They start watching it long before they learn to read. They see, it has been calculated, about 15,000 hours of television before they reach eighteen. During the same years they have been in the classroom about 10,800 hours.[9] The child who once had to wait till he was six to learn to read and thus to expand his horizon beyond those near him now accomplishes the same by the flick of a switch. Furthermore, it is often just as much entertainment as it is education. Parents rarely have to force their children to watch television. The same can hardly be said with regard to reading!

Those under twenty-five have grown up with different modes of perceiving reality than their parents. We older people expect information to be supplied us in the sequential forms of print. We read about Guadalcanal the day after. Our children see war in Vietnam as it happens. We grew up on media where everything was spelled out for us. Our children see for themselves. There is no need to reduce events to words when they are participants via television. And so their methods of perceiving reality are quite different from those of their parents who grew up under quite different circumstances.

In some ways our children are like men before the invention of printing when information had to be communicated to the illiterate through other persons or at least through visual representations on the walls of churches and in the market. They are sensitive to many forms of sensory input, and their basic orientation is to the immediate and instantaneous rather than to the linear and sequential. McLuhan calls the "now" generation "post-literate." It has come to perceive reality through the immediacy of direct experience.

Small wonder then that we have problems with our forms of worship. The forms most natural for perceiving reality on the part of the youth do not coincide with those of the older adult. Several national magazines failed to attract younger readers and their eventual demise should be a word of warning to the church. Worship in the mainline white churches still consists almost entirely of a diet of words spooned out to us by the minister. We adults prefer to be nourished this way, but the youth feel underfed. We adults are largely oriented to verbal forms of perception, since we have been watching television for fewer years than we have been reading. The question we still ask when we miss church is, "What did he say?"—meaning, "What was the sermon about?" The younger generation is more likely to ask, "What happened?" For them the problem is that nothing happened, or at least very little and much of that was insignificant. The congregation stood, sang a few hymns, and went home.

By and large, Protestant worship is still in the realm of the communications revolution of the sixteenth century. After 450 years the times have changed, most of all within the last twenty years. We must realize that people have changed. They are accustomed to much more immediate forms of communication than words read from a book. And consequently the forms by which worship is expressed must change, too.

III

To say that there is an imperative for changes in the forms of worship, at least for some people, does not indicate what those changes should be. We can approach this problem on a theoretical level by establishing norms by which forms of worship can be evaluated. Then, in chapters four through nine, we shall discuss specific parts of worship.

Three norms seem to be crucial in evaluating any form of worship, old or new. The first of these we have been considering in this chapter—the forms of worship must be natural to the perceptual and expressive character of the worshipers. This we may call the *pastoral norm:* the forms of worship should reflect the people who worship. In the next chapter we shall discuss a *theological norm*: the forms must express Christian faith. Then we shall expound a *historical norm*: we must learn from those forms which have functioned well in expressing Christian worship in the past.

In essence, we have been discussing the present crisis in terms of the pastoral norm throughout this chapter, but a few specific comments at this point may prove helpful. The chief brunt of the pastoral norm is the need for a minister to know his people. It is no accident that the cutting edge in liturgical studies today seems to be in sociology, anthropology, and communications theory. What we do not know in these areas will hurt us.

The day of universal liturgical reform is past. *The Constitution on the Sacred Liturgy* acknowledged the need to respect and foster "the spiritual adornments and gifts of various races and peoples."[10] The "in" word is "indigenization." The issues of *Notitiae*, the organ of the Consilium for the Implementation of the Constitution on the Sacred Liturgy, are replete in requests from different parts of the world for variations in the mass and other rites. The *agnus dei* proved offensive when translated in parts of India, the baptismal ceremonies were misconstrued in Africa, liturgical colors produced different responses in parts of the world where white might be associated with mourning or red with weddings.

Even more so do we need to become sensitive to the various subcultures within any given culture. The type of worship emanating from a youth culture and described in *Multi-Media Worship*[11] proved to be most offensive to many outside that age group when telecast nationally. It was natural in one situation, it was outrageous in others. The experience is familiar. Anyone who is asked to "come and do an experimental service" soon realizes how impossible this is without a knowledge of the people who will be worshiping. Only a pastor who knows his people can effectively introduce and nurture new forms of worship that are authentic expressions of his people.

The splintering of society means that to be true and relevant to people as they now are, we will need to be all things to all people. In the past we have offered what businessmen call a manufacturing mentality. We produced a product and then looked for someone to take it. Now, instead, we need a marketing mentality. Businesses operating on a manufacturing mentality are not apt to survive since their competitors can produce something that people really want. Yet such has been the mentality of the church. A marketing mentality searches for what people want and need and then resolves to satisfy that need. Our pastoral norm emphasizes the need to recognize the great variety of persons in the church today and their varying conditions of life. This almost automatically demands a greater number of choices of types of worship. Henry Ford is reputed to have promised the customer any color as long as it was black, but Ford Motor Company would not be in business today if it had kept that policy.

One of the obvious consequences of acceptance of the generation gap as inevitable and healthy is the divisiveness it produces within the family. It has become increasingly difficult for members of the same family to find things that they enjoy doing in common. We take it for granted that the family will receive its education with peer groups. We have become accustomed to each age group in the family finding its own form of recreation. When children become teenagers they practically have to be coerced to take their recreation with their parents. The appeal of the peer group in establishing fashions, makeup, taste in music, favorite television programs, and almost everything else is extremely hard to resist. It even becomes a struggle to force the family to eat together at the same time despite the advantage (to the parents) of this opportunity for passing laws!

It then seems a bit romantic and quaint to argue that at least the family ought to worship together. If they do little else together, is it not a bit unnatural to make worship the exception? We may not like what is happening to the family, but we can ill afford to ignore these effects. Why should we demand that little children "sit still during church" when everyone knows that nowhere else do little children sit still? We long ago gave up using the same educational methods and subjects with every age group. Why should we expect the same forms of worship to be normative for each age within the family?

Our worship must be constructed around a healthy respect for the varieties of people who will be worshiping either in homogeneous or heterogeneous groups. What is appropriate worship for children may not be so for teenagers or for their parents. No longer can we afford to offer a menu with only one dinner on it. For years we have, in effect, said: "This is it and you can take it or leave it."

We ministers are often hardly aware of how arrogant our presuppositions with regard to worship have been. We knew what was good for people, and that we gave them. Nowhere is this more evident than with regard to church music. We wanted "good" music, so schools of sacred music flourished to train musicians who would see that the church got the best. It might not be the music that the congregation would sing. It might not be the music that was represented in their record collections at home. But at least it fitted our standards of classical good taste.

Rarely did we stop to consider how arbitrary our actions were. Can we any longer defend such aesthetic snobbery? I personally may prefer not to listen to church music past Mozart and Haydn. But what right do I have to enforce such preferences on a congregation? Unfortunately, we often thought we were doing the congregation a favor by imposing standards of quality on them. Too often this concern for "quality" as determined by past artistic forms has been more "symbolic of a snob church for an elite than a part of the culture of the masses."[12] Few present-day clergy realize just how classical the presuppositions of their education have been or how rigid and inflexible their mentality is. And this applies to far more than church music. Perhaps this is philistinism, but maybe the alternative has too long been an aesthetic snobbery that is no more defensible. Our knowing what is best for congregations needs to be based on more than those standards of good taste that we learned years ago in seminary. Perhaps the people know what is best for them and we ought to take them into our confidence. The Roman Catholic Consilium on the Liturgy had two laymen (both church musicians) and one lay woman and a couple of hundred clerical consultors. Yet the Catholic Church is more than ninety-nine percent laity. Most other denominations do not do much better, and the imbalance is often found even on commissions on worship in the local church.

We need, then, to accept people and the forms of perception and expression most natural to them, not to prescribe them. It should be pointed out that the forms of communication are theologically ambiguous. A verbal form of expression is neither more nor less Christian than a visual one. Indeed all forms are inherently secular since they have been taken from normal forms of human intercourse. Only long association has given religious connotations. Organ music is considered churchly in the West, associated with taverns in the East. The mass is just as Christian in English and Swahili as in Latin. But it may mean a great deal more to the worshiper if it is in his native tongue.

On the other hand, there are people who have changed little. It would be the worst of mistakes to force them to change simply because others have. We have no right to yank the rug out from under those who are quite satisfied with the normal eleven o'clock Protestant service. The almost exclusively verbal forms of expression may be just right for those over thirty since these are the forms of expression and perception most congenial for them. If these forms are valid for those people, then the use of such forms must be continued. We have no right to force people to accept anything less valid for them. They have no need of new forms of worship. The usual eleven o'clock style of service ought to be continued as long as there are people who find it a satisfactory way of offering their worship to God.

But the converse is also true. These people need to be tolerant of those who find such forms of worship dull and meaningless. It is no longer realistic to say that everyone ought to worship in the way that seems natural to a forty-year-old, middle-class white person. To meet the needs of others, the church must provide alternate forms before those who are not middle-aged and middle-class vacate the church altogether. For many it is already too late. It is to help minister to these people for whom purely verbal forms are insufficient that this book is written. We do not mean for an instant that anything goes as long as it is relevant and currently modish. That is why we join to our pastoral norm theological and historical ones. But we do want to emphasize the need to start with people.

It is easier, after all, to change forms than people, so long as we abide within sound theological and historical norms. It should not surprise us that the possibilities before us are infinitely more varied than ever before in history since never before has human life been so complex and so rich.

Our pastoral norm, then, demands that we not only know people but that we accept them. Obviously we cannot as individuals accept and share with enthusiasm in all the forms of worship that a diverse society will need. But we do need to recognize the varieties of needs and to accept their legitimacy. Of course this means that the minister's work as leader of worship is likely to expand considerably in the future. Just as we have turned much of the educational work of the ministry on the large church staff over to a specialist—the director of religious education—so we may one day look for another specialist on such staffs—the liturgical director. He may not lead services himself (some have been laymen), but he will coordinate the numerous services of worship offered each week by differing groups within the congregation. And in some of these he may very well have a function not dissimilar to that of a producer in the theater.

In this aspect of ministry we are called upon to know people, to accept them, and to serve them. The pastoral norm for developing new forms of worship will test our adequacy at each of these steps—knowing, accepting, and serving.

5

The Triumph of the Praise Songs
How Guitars Beat Out the Organ in the Worship Wars

Michael S. Hamilton

By studying the recent history of the traditional/ contemporary worship debate, Michael Hamilton suggests we celebrate the healthy diversity and creative growth of the one living Church.

It's Sunday morning at the 5,000-member Vestavia Hills United Methodist Church near Birmingham, Alabama. Early risers, mostly middle-aged and older, gather at 8:30 A.M. for a traditional worship service in the 700-seat sanctuary. The organ and one of the church's three smaller choirs are the musical heart of the service. Music director Mark Ridings (who moonlights as the director of the Alabama Symphony Chorus) usually

Reprinted from *Christianity Today* 43, no. 8 (July 12, 1999): 29–35. © 1999 by Michael S. Hamilton. All rights reserved. Used by permission.

selects standard hymns from the new United Methodist hymnal—something from Isaac Watts, Charles Wesley, or Fanny Crosby.

An hour later the sanctuary empties and is immediately reoccupied with a younger, more casually dressed crowd. The organ sits silent in favor of a piano and sometimes a guitar. These accompany a somewhat introspective version of a praise and worship service, where the people sing Southern gospel standards ("I'll Fly Away") and traditional hymns ("Great Is Thy Faithfulness"), done in a contemporary style with projected lyrics.

At eleven o'clock the sanctuary again empties and refills, this time with a mixed-age group for another traditional service with organ, hymns, and the large Sanctuary Choir. At the same time, in another part of the building, the 300-seat fellowship hall fills with young adults and young children. This is the "Son Shine" service, also known as "Rock & Roll Church." A worship team of singers and instrumentalists—piano, amplified guitar, drums, and tambourine—leads a lively, hand-clapping congregation in a potpourri of crowd pleasers. These range from Southern gospel, to old rock and roll songs like the Doobie Brothers' "Jesus Is Just Alright With Me," to repackaged hymns ("Amazing Grace" sung to the tune of the Eagles' "I Got a Peaceful Easy Feeling"), to contemporary praise and worship standards (Michael O'Shields' "I Will Call Upon the Lord").

At noon most everyone goes home, and the building is relatively quiet until the five o'clock Vespers in the chapel. There fifty to sixty retirement-age folks gather to sing favorite hymns and simple gospel songs ("In the Garden") from the old Methodist *Cokesbury Hymnal*, accompanied by the piano. They finish up at six o'clock, leaving a one-hour buffer before Youth Worship begins. This is a monthly service where the teenagers are the musicians, singing both contemporary praise choruses and songs from the radio with rewritten lyrics. The music is amplified, raucous, and very loud; in the words of church member Lee Benson, "not for the faint of heart."

With five musical styles for six services, Vestavia Hills embodies the new reality of congregational singing in America. All over the country, churches are customizing worship-music styles for particular demographic groups. Vestavia Hills is living evidence that American churchgoers no longer sort themselves out by denomination so much as by musical preference.

Since the 1950s, denominational divisions have steadily become less important in American church life. We have the baby boom generation (of which I am a part) to thank for much of this. But at bottom we are all still sectarians; we still prefer to congregate with the like-minded. Our new sectarianism is a sectarianism of worship style. The new sectarian creeds are dogmas of music. Worship seminars are the seminaries of the new sectarianism; their directors are its theologians. The ministers of the new sectarianism are our church worship leaders.

Some large churches, like Vestavia Hills, are able to hold the new sects together under one roof. Churches that are too small to sustain separate congregations with separate worship styles are either trying to mix musical styles ("blended worship"), or they are fighting and dividing over which music to use.

For this, too, we have the baby boomers to thank, for they set into motion two movements that have profoundly reshaped what congregations sing. Reformers working from within the church music tradition—animated by baby-boom concerns—began writing new hymns with contemporary themes and experimental styles. Revolutionaries starting from outside the church tradition—baby boomers themselves—began adapting popular secular music for religious purposes.

The turbulence produced by these crosscurrents has put traditionalists everywhere on the defensive. Liturgical churches are borrowing pietistic practices, while pietistic churches are introducing liturgical elements. Conflicts over worship in general and music in particular have erupted in churches of every denomination. Forty years ago, this heightened sensitivity to the details of worship and music would have been unheard of, but now it is the norm. All over North America, worship has become contested ground.

The contemporary proliferation of different worship and music styles may well be the next century's test of our commitment to Christian unity. We seem to have learned charity in regard to differences over mode of baptism, church polity, and a number of doctrines like eternal security or the second blessing—differences that have already produced their schisms. It is not as clear, however, that we have developed the Christian maturity to deal with the deepening differences over music and worship that are now producing our new sectarianism.

The Baby Boom

The recent avalanche of change in worship life generally, and in congregational singing particularly, is not unique to church life. All of the changes that have precipitated our worship wars are in fact part of a long trail of cultural dislocations left behind by that abnormally large generation of Americans we call the baby boomers. The baby boom generation was like a supertanker, tied to its cultural wharf by too-small mooring lines. When the storms kicked up in the 1960s—unprecedented mobility, the communications revolution, the hot and cold wars against communism, civil rights—the mooring lines of cultural continuity sheared, setting this generation free to create its own youth culture.

Unwilling to follow their parents' lead, they grew up distrusting established institutions like government, schools, and churches. They have since turned this distrust into a social norm. Never has an American generation been so convinced that other cultures—almost all other cultures—are wiser and better organized than its own.

As a consequence, baby boomers have reoriented our society toward peers and away from family. They have moved the psychic center of the family away from obligations to others and toward self-fulfillment. They have raised to new ideological heights the ideal of individual autonomy fused with democratic egalitarianism. And they have transformed music from a carrier of cultural tradition into the symbolic fencing that marks off a noisy multitude of peer-oriented subcultures.

Once this oversized generation decided that music would be the primary carrier of its symbols and values, music quickly became, in the words of George Steiner, the new literacy of Western culture. When one chooses a musical style today, one is making a statement about whom one identifies with, what one's values are, and ultimately, who one is. As a result, music has become a divisive and fractionalizing force, Balkanizing Western culture into an ever-expanding array of subcultures—each with its own stylistic national anthem.

A generation so at odds with the traditions it has inherited is going to change the way it does church; a generation this large is going to change lots and lots of churches. Baby boomers have abandoned the denominational loyalties of their parents. The generation that was crowded into maternity wards and grade schools and rock concerts now crowds into megachurches. (Only a generation that loved Woodstock could love Willow Creek.) The generation that reorganized family around the ideal of self-fulfillment has done the same with religion. Surveys consistently show that baby boomers—whether evangelical or liberal, Protestant or Catholic—attend church not out of loyalty, duty, obligation, or gratitude, but only if it meets their needs.

Not surprisingly, a generation that sought its youthful identity in music searches for its religious identity in music as well. For better or worse, the kind of music a church offers increasingly defines the kind of person who will attend, because for this generation music is at the very center of self-understanding. Music for baby boomers is the mediator of emotions, the carrier of dreams, and the marker of social location. It is therefore bound to be an integral part of baby boomers' connection to the eternal truth of life in God. Therefore, in worship and music, the received tradition could not be allowed to stand unaltered.

This left only two possibilities—reform of the tradition or revolution against the tradition.

The Reformers

The English-language church music scene of the 1950s was ripe for reform. Classically trained musicians on both sides of the Atlantic grumbled that so-called sacred music had reached a creative dead end, characterized by what American Robert Mitchell remembers as a "dreary seeking after reverence and solemnity."

What finally shook things loose was the surprising new popularity of folk music around 1960. Rock 'n' roll from the 1950s had failed to influence church musicians partly because its main lyrical theme—teenage romance—showed little promise for any connection to Christian concerns. However, folk music—most famously represented by Bob Dylan's fusion of white-folk working-class ballads, African-American blues, and Celtic laments—brought its long tradition of sympathy for the poor and outrage at injustice to the popular music scene. This shocked some church musicians into awareness that their hymnic tradition was not only artistically stunted; worse yet, it had lost touch with the pressing moral issues of the day.

The reform of American hymnody unexpectedly began in Dunblane, Scotland. In 1962, a group of dissatisfied British church musicians gathered to try to revitalize church singing. The group was led and inspired by Eric Routley, a Congregationalist minister and one of the leading organists in Britain. (Routley had earlier tried to enlist C. S. Lewis, whom he greatly admired, in efforts to improve British hymnody. Lewis declined, cheerfully confessing that he disliked hymns altogether.) Under Routley's prodding, the Dunblane group searched for a new, simple music without traditional ecclesiastical accent "that would catch the ear of our time." They experimented with new poetic structures for the hymn lyrics and new instrumentation to accompany hymns. But most of all they tried to connect church singing to the contemporary social issues that preoccupied the baby boomers. The reformers listened to Bob Dylan records, and they studied the work of British folk songwriter Sydney Carter (best known for "Lord of the Dance," in which he used the American Shaker tune "Simple Gifts" as a setting for new lyrics about Jesus).

The work of Routley and those he inspired was spread to the U.S. by George Shorney, Jr., of the independent Hope Publishing Company, a long-time mainstay of evangelical music publishing. This gave the British reformers the backing and encouragement of a large American audience. In the process, American church musicians were inspired to revise nearly all of their denominational hymnals and to produce a flood of new independent hymn collections.

The main result of the reformers' labors was a phenomenal outpouring of new English-language hymnody that dovetailed perfectly with baby-boom concerns. Catering to a generation that looks for wisdom outside its own culture, the hymn reformers have gathered for their revised hymnals Christian songs from all over the globe. They have also written new hymns emphasizing global awareness (Carl P. Daw, "We Marvel at Your Mighty Deeds"), and making confession for the social sins of Western culture (Herman Steumpfle, "O God, the Wounded Earth Cries Out"). The baby boom's visceral uncertainty about all inherited tradition reveals itself both in recent hymn writers' wariness about doctrinal matters and in their eagerness to ruminate on God's incomprehensibility (Dorothy R. Fulton, "Elusive God").

If the baby boom harbors uncertainties about Christian tradition, it entertains none about the evils of war, and this has generated a bevy of antiwar hymns (Thomas H. Troeger, "Fierce the Force that Curled Cain's Fist"). The baby-boom commitment to the equality of all persons has likewise inspired recent hymn writers (Fred Kaan, "Help Us Accept Each Other"). The reformers have, however, abstained from writing hymns that cater to the baby boom's legendary self-preoccupation (this they left to the revolutionaries).

The reformers were not satisfied merely to produce a new body of hymns that embodied baby-boom ideals. They also insisted on cleaning up the old hymns. This urge to sanitize the language of hymns is, of course, a part of a larger social phenomenon that has produced campus speech codes, business seminars on avoiding offensive language, and laws against hate speech. (Parenthetically, we Americans have tried this before. In the Victorian era, the guardians of culture attempted to purge public language of all profanity, vulgarity, and references to sex and to the body. Legs became "limbs," women's underwear became "lingerie.") Critics of this movement have labeled it "political correctness," a polemically effective but not particularly accurate term. This is not so much a controversy about politics as it is a controversy about morality.

Today's correctitude originates in moral values and is driven by a supercharged sense of propriety. This leads our contemporary moral guardians—most of them baby boomers—to take offense, and to worry about giving offense, when the boundaries of the new propriety are breached. As regarding hymn language, the new sensibilities have occasionally led editors beyond inclusiveness to outright bowdlerization. The example that always comes to my mind is one denomination's new version of

William Cowper's "O for a closer walk with God." In this new version, the editors worried that the noun *walk* excluded the disabled, so the hymn was changed to "O for a closer *bond* with God." My seven-year-old son, who cannot walk, much prefers the original version. He likes the word *walk* better because it speaks directly to his most cherished hope, which is that after his body is resurrected and made whole, he will walk—literally walk—closely alongside his Lord.

The main point here, however, is not to take sides in this matter, but simply to note that this is a particularly baby-boom form of moral fussiness. The eagerness to change language is yet another manifestation of the baby boom's readiness to reshape its inheritance; yet another manifestation of its self-sure conviction that its own values are superior to those of the past. The impulse to address modern concerns originates in the baby boomers' quest for relevance. The impulse toward inclusiveness originates in the baby boomers' democratic commitment to equality of all persons. The squeamishness about royal and military imagery comes from this generation's antiwar sensibilities.

The hymn reformers are, nonetheless, reformers, not revolutionaries. They start their work from within the church music tradition, and, at bottom, they are still trying to save elements of that tradition by reforming it. Despite their acquired taste for carefully limited doses of non-Western folk music, they have never been able to develop any real affection for the musical tastes of the ordinary people who are their next-door neighbors. Despite their professed egalitarianism, they assume that the people in the pews need instruction through didactic hymn texts. Despite their commitment to change, the reformers still largely remain comfortably inside the taste culture of formal church music.

The Revolutionaries

Baby boom ideas gave the hymn reform movement its distinctive flavor, but baby boomers themselves were more apt to become revolutionaries. They are revolutionaries precisely because their starting place is outside the church music tradition. The reformers began with church music forms and sought to incorporate baby-boom values; the revolutionaries began with baby-boom music forms and baby-boom values, and sought to adapt these to the Christian faith.

For all their openness to new creative currents, Routley and the English hymn reformers failed to make any connection with the indigenous music of the baby boom generation—rock 'n' roll. The same was true of the evangelical "pop" musicians in America, like Ralph Carmichael, John W. Peterson, and Bill and Gloria Gaither.

Rock 'n' roll was simple. It engaged deep emotions, and it portrayed itself as free of hypocrisy. But above all else, it focused the baby boomers' longings and anxieties, their values and ideals. This music became their primary marker of social location and their medium for articulating identity. Music was so important to baby boomers, it was inevitable that if they came to church at all, they would be bringing their music with them.

But because neither the hymn reformers in England nor the creators of evangelical pop in America would engage teenage music, "Jesus rock" was slow to get rolling. It started with longhaired Christian teenagers themselves who loved the Beatles, the Rolling Stones, and Bob Dylan. In the mid-1960s they began forming garage bands that married Jesus lyrics to the electric thump of rock 'n' roll, but this music was most unwelcome in sanctuaries. So an underground circuit of Jesus rock musicians began to form, playing in parks, coffeehouses, and in a few more daring churches.

It is no accident that Chuck Smith's Calvary Chapel, one of the first congregations to welcome the counterculture, was one of the first to welcome its music. And it is no accident that in 1973 Calvary Chapel started Maranatha! Music to spread the new music to other churches. As baby boomers moved into the churches, this music came along, too. It soon acquired a new name—"praise and worship"—but it began as baptized rock 'n' roll. In the quarter-century since Maranatha! was founded, the enterprise of praise and worship music has precipitated a blizzard of creative activity. There are dozens of nonprofit and for-profit companies producing this music, with hundreds of musicians involved. They cover a surprisingly wide landscape of popular music genres, produce a bewildering variety of high-tech products to aid church worship leaders, and sponsor workshops all over the world.

Despite complaints about commercialization, this music continues to bubble up from the wellsprings of local churches. All three of the largest praise-and-worship companies (Maranatha!, Integrity, and Vineyard) began in local churches, and musicians in local churches all over the country are today writing, recording, and marketing new music to other churches. Over 100,000 churches in the United States (nearly one-third of all churches) participate in the reporting program of Christian Copyright Licensing Inc., which distributes royalties to publishers based on how many overhead projector transparencies churches make of each song. Most of their songs are in the praise and worship genre, the most popular of all being Rick Founds's "Lord, I Lift Your Name on High."

Because praise and worship music is a baby-boom creation, it is impregnated with many of the same values that characterize the new hymnody—though sometimes the same values work themselves out in different ways. The old denominational concerns, missing in the reformers' hymns, are also absent from the praise and worship songs. Likewise, both schools draw some of their inspiration from international sources.

The reformers have been influenced by international church music and the revolutionaries by international popular music. Both, curiously enough, have been influenced by the interdenominational Taizé community in France, whose simple yet rich songs (the Taizé "Alleluias" are sung the world over) are rooted in both traditional church music and in the baby boom's guitar-and-folk-chorus style of the 1960s.

The same democratic sensibilities that prodded the reformers to revise hymn language have prompted the revolutionaries to do away with hymnals. The overhead projector means that no one needs to be able to read music, everyone is singing in unison, and everyone is—literally—reading off the same page. The quest for relevance in the new hymnody finds expression in contemporary social concerns, while in praise and worship music it focuses on intensifying the individual's experience of God.

Not coincidentally, the focus on individual experience aligns perfectly with the baby boom's luxuriant self-concern. Just as one cannot sing the reformers' new hymns for long without noticing their didactic character and preachy tone, one cannot sing praise songs without noticing how first person pronouns tend to eclipse every other subject.

There are, of course, differences between the new hymnody and praise and worship music that are not the outworking of common values. The starting place for the revolutionaries was secular rock 'n' roll, so they eagerly used guitars and drums, simple accessible lyrics, and the conventions of popular music—simple harmonies, steady rhythm, frequent repetition. The reformers, however, retained many of the conventions of formal church music, even while experimenting more cautiously with new themes and modes of presentation. The revolutionaries freely employed parachurch networks to disseminate their music, while the reformers remained more closely tied to the denominational church organizations. This, by the way, accounts for the not-quite-fair criticism that praise and worship music is too "commercialized." Parachurch groups, such as evangelistic organizations, missionary agencies, and publishing houses always behave more like businesses than do denominations.

Perhaps the most important difference is that the hymn reformers still cherish the pre-baby-boom hope that the ideal of Christian unity can be achieved in worship. Praise-and-worship musicians, by contrast, bring the baby-boom assumption that different groups will all need their own kind of music.

In this last argument, the baby boomers are, as usual, having their way. There are just too many of them. Increasingly, people choose their churches by the type of worship and music they feature. Increasingly, churches sponsor multiple services for multiple musical tastes. Increasingly, we are grouping ourselves with the musically like-minded. This is the root, stem, and branch of the new sectarianism that is flowering in American church life.

What Now?

There is nothing we can do to stop the new worship divisions, any more than we could stop the doctrinal divisions over who, when, and how to baptize. So the question is: How will we respond to the new tribalism of worship and music? How can we keep our sectarian worship from becoming a sectarianism of the soul?

First, we need to remember that differing expressions of Christianity are not necessarily a bad thing. For decades, theologians have wrung their hands over America's ecclesiastical fragmentation. "Denominationalism . . . represents the moral failure of Christianity," claimed H. Richard Niebuhr in *The Social Sources of Denominationalism*. Well, maybe. In fact, the United States, with the most denominationally divided Christianity of the Western world, also has the highest levels of Christian faith in the Western world. This empirical reality has led some people recently to wonder if the organizational splintering of the American church has not, in fact, been a strength as well as a weakness. The advantage of multiple expressions of Christianity—whether they are based in doctrine or based in worship—is that there is an expression for everyone. Anyone can find a home. And in this world of brokenness and homelessness, maybe having many different homes is a good thing.

Second, it is right and good to put different expressions of orthodox Christianity to a functional test rather than a theological test. Every complaint about worship music, no matter which style, claims to be rooted in theological principles. Yet in every critique, the theology aligns perfectly with the critic's own musical taste. What may be more helpful instead is a pragmatic test based on a bit of wisdom from the Gospels: "The tree is known by its fruit." If this is so, then worship music ought to be judged not by the songs themselves but by the people who sing them. Looking at the songs themselves is rather like looking at the bark of the tree and then pronouncing the tree good or bad. Better to look at the fruit itself—the lives of the people who are singing the songs. The job of the local church is to communicate the good news of Jesus Christ, to draw people into a living relationship with God, and to remold disciples of Jesus into a Sermon-on-the-Mount shape. Any worship music that aids a church in these tasks is almost certainly a conduit of the Holy Spirit. In light of this, maybe it is time to substitute charity for condescension.

Another path out of the wilderness of disdain is to begin to see others' music with new eyes. When the hymn reformers introduced music from other cultures into their canon, a handful of them noticed that the characteristics of praise and worship music that they most disliked are abundantly present in Christian folk songs from Africa, Latin America, and Asia. Many of these international songs have simple music, driving beat, repetitive lyrics, light theology, and an emphasis on experience. Here is a South African folksong that appears in the current United Methodist hymnal:

> Send me, Jesus, send me, Jesus, send me, Jesus, send me, Lord.
> Lead me, Jesus, lead me, Jesus, lead me, Jesus, lead me, Lord.
> Fill me, Jesus, fill me, Jesus, fill me, Jesus, fill me, Lord.

An openness to simple, repetitive international songs like this opened some reformers to accepting contemporary praise music produced domestically.

Meanwhile, a parallel movement is taking place on the other side of today's church music divide. Several musicians working out of the praise and worship genre are beginning to explore and appreciate music from different cultures around the world—including the classic English hymnody. The revolutionaries are already starting to include such hymns in their catalogs. One hopes it will not be long before they begin to draw upon the best of contemporary hymnody as well.

Does an openness to the varied musical expressions of different Christian cultures and subcultures leave us stuck in relativism, the tar baby of contemporary secular thought? By no means. It is merely to remember that the God who created this world did so with exuberant extravagance, his unchanging purpose often hidden in a tumbling cascade of variety. The resulting multiplicity has, ever since, been the medium of an infinitely dexterous Holy Artist, furthering the work of redemption in whatever cultural forms human beings have been able to devise. The Bible has four different Gospels; no single one of them tells us the whole truth about the life of Jesus. Likewise, no single musical style brings to full flower more than a few of the many possibilities for communion with God. It is said that when King George II of England heard Handel's Hallelujah chorus for the first time, it was not the glory of the music that—to the astonishment of the audience—pulled him to his feet. It was, rather, the glory of the Lord, surging through the conduit of the music. It was much the same when my elderly neighbor Elsie Hudson lay for several days in a coma. She responded to no one, not even her closest family members, until her pastor sat beside her and softly sang the simple gospel songs that she had sung all her life. The power of God surged through that music also—to the astonishment of the hospice workers—waking her up one last time before she went home to her Lord.

It is fruitless to search for a single musical style, or even any blend of musical styles, that can assist all Christians with true worship. The followers of Jesus are a far too diverse group of people—which is exactly as it should be. We need, rather, to welcome any worship music that helps churches produce disciples of Jesus Christ. We need to welcome the experimental creativity that is always searching out new ways of singing the gospel, and banish the fear that grips us when familiar music passes away. For this kind of change is the mark of a living church—the church of a living God, who restlessly ranges back and forth across the face of the earth seeking out any who would respond to his voice.

6

The Crisis of Evangelical Worship

Authentic Worship in a Changing World

Robert E. Webber

Drawing from a broad base of experience and scholarship,
Robert Webber challenges evangelicals to add to the strong
characteristics of evangelicalism the historical content and
process of worship carefully contextualized into our post-
modern world.

Postmodern philosopher Hans Georg Gadamer effectively argued that we do our interpretive work out of our prejudice, dialogue, and historical consciousness. Following his advice I will begin this presentation with an appraisal of my own prejudices, dialogue, and historical consciousness. I will then clarify the audience to whom I am

Reprinted from *Ancient and Postmodern Christianity: Paleo-Orthodoxy in the 21st Century,* eds. Kenneth Tanner and Christopher A. Hall (Downers Grove, IL: InterVarsity Press, 2002), 140–54. © 2002 by Kenneth Tanner and Christopher A. Hall. Used by permission of InterVarsity Press, P.O. Box 1400, Downers Grove, IL 60151 (www.ivpress.com).

speaking, and after that I will explore the crisis of evangelical worship: authentic worship in a changing world.

Prejudice, Dialogue, Historical Consciousness

The word *prejudice* is not used by Gadamer in the negative and pejorative sense of unacceptable attitudes. Rather, prejudice refers to the subliminal influences that have shaped our mindset—those ways of thinking communicated to us through our family of origin, education, and general group consciousness. Gadamer calls us to a conscious awareness of these influences, to an intelligent and examined life. I am certainly not aware of all my prejudices, but I want to mention a few I have examined and consider important to the shaping of my mindset.

The first seven years of my life were spent in the heart of the African jungle where my parents were missionaries. My parents returned to the States where my father pastored a congregation associated with the American Baptist Church. I was educated at Bob Jones University (fundamentalist), Reformed Episcopal Seminary (Calvinist), Covenant Theological Seminary (Presbyterian), and Concordia Theological Seminary (Lutheran). I have taught at Covenant College (five years), Covenant Seminary (three years), Wheaton College (thirty-two years), and while still a member of the Episcopal Church, I am now Myers Professor of Ministry at Northern Baptist Theological Seminary. This history undeniably puts me in a camp of interdenominational evangelical influences and names my prejudices with a degree of clarity.

Second, I have also been shaped by what Gadamer calls dialogue. Dialogue, as I understand it, is genuine conversation with those who live a set of prejudices different from your own. I want to mention two such dialogues that have enriched and expanded my horizons. First, while doing graduate studies at Concordia Seminary I was a member of an ecumenical prayer and study group, 50 percent of whom were Catholic priests or seminarians. Here I was introduced to persons characterized by warm Christian piety and deep devotion to Christ and the church. My experience with Catholic clergy brought me to a new and appreciative reading of Catholic thought and to a continued personal friendship with my brothers and sisters in the Roman tradition. The next life-changing experience was the opportunity to teach missionaries Orthodox theology at a school established by the Slavic Gospel Mission. My exposure to the works of Georges Florovsky, Vladimir Lossky, Alexander Schmemman, Timothy Ware, and John Myendorff introduced me to the most important theological reading of my life.

And then there is the matter of historical consciousness. My graduate work was in the area of historical theology where I was exposed to the great fathers, doctors, and reformers of the church. While I have sought to appreciate all of these leaders within their own cultural paradigm, my interests have always been drawn to the thought of the common era, to the formulators of the classical Christian tradition, to the foundational thought of the Rule of Faith, the Apostles' Creed, the Nicene Creed, and the Chalcedon Creed.

Now where has prejudice, dialogue, and historical consciousness placed me? I am an evangelical with a love for the whole church, a distaste for modernity, and a commitment to the thought and practice of classical Christianity, which I think should be recovered and contextualized into a postmodern world. This is the set of glasses I wear when I think about authentic worship in a changing world.

To Whom Do I Write?

My second introductory concern is to address the audience to whom I speak. While I want to borrow from the whole church, I am keenly aware that I speak to a very small minority within it. I am not speaking to the Roman Church nor am I speaking to the Orthodox Church. My audience is Protestant, and within Protestantism my audience is primarily limited to those who identify themselves as evangelicals. This term needs to be defined.

As I see it, there are four ways in which the word *evangelical* is used. First, the linguistic use is drawn from the Greek word *euangelion* and refers simply to a commitment to the gospel. In this sense all Christians can be referred to as *evangelical* because all adhere to the gospel. Second, theologically the word *evangelical* is used of all who confess the historic creeds of the church—the Apostles' Creed, the Nicene Creed, and the Chalcedon Creed. These creeds define classical Christianity and tighten the boundaries of evangelicalism. The third use of *evangelical* refers to those movements of reform and renewal within the church. So far as I know, the word was first used by Desiderius Erasmus when he jeeringly referred to Martin Luther as "that evangelical." Since Luther, awakenings of the church have been called evangelical movements. For example, the evangelical movement attached to John Wesley in England and Jonathan Edwards in America. This more recent use of *evangelical* has given the word a decidedly Protestant flavor and has limited its use particularly to movements of reform and renewal that seek to get behind a tired experience of faith to a refreshing discovery of the simple yet powerful message of basic Christianity. The fourth use of *evangelical*, which is the most complicated and much more limiting than the three previous uses, is the sociological use.

In order to understand the sociological use of *evangelical*, it is first necessary to explain its sociological use as peculiar to the twentieth century. Let me begin with a crude but nevertheless quite accurate sociological use of the word. An evangelical is a "son of a fundamentalist." Current evangelical parentage goes back to the liberal-fundamentalist controversy in the beginning of the twentieth century. After 1925 the fundamentalists, defeated by liberalism, retreated from the mainline churches and began a new movement of churches, schools, mission agencies, and publishing houses. This first phase of fundamentalism was characterized by anti-intellectualism, anti-ecumenism, and anti–social action. A second phase of fundamentalism developed after World War II. Many children of fundamentalism wanted to distance themselves from their parentage. In the mid-1950s Harold Ockenga, then the young pastor of Park Street Church in Boston, coined the term *neo-evangelical* and called for new initiatives in scholarship, ecumenical dialogue, and social action. This "new" evangelicalism is identified with Billy Graham and the new schools, mission agencies, churches, and publishing houses spawned after World War II. The word *evangelical* stuck. The history of the word's evolution is beyond the scope of this presentation, but let it be sufficient to say that the word in its broadest sense is used by those who do not want to be identified as fundamentalists or liberal Protestants.

Regarding worship, these evangelicals of the last fifty years can be divided in two groups: traditional evangelicals and contemporary evangelicals. Traditional evangelicals are those who have not been directly affected by the worship renewal of the twentieth century. Their worship is quite the same as it was in the 1950s: primarily a sermon along with traditional forms of music such as hymns and choirs. Contemporary evangelicals, on the other hand, have been affected by the rise of the contemporary worship movement of the 1960s, 1970s, and 1980s. Their worship is either seeker-centered or seeker-sensitive. Like its traditional parentage, contemporary evangelical worship is still sermon-centered, but it has exchanged traditional hymns and choirs for contemporary instrumentation, singing of choruses, worship teams, and an atmosphere of intimacy. These two approaches to worship represent two cultures. Traditional worship represents the booster culture of people born before the end of World War II. Contemporary worship represents the boomer culture, people born after World War II but before 1981. Obviously not everybody fits neatly into these two categories. There are boosters who are attracted to contemporary worship and boomers who are drawn to the more traditional forms of worship. While these two groups represent two distinct histories, they also have become the center point for intense conflict in an increasing number of churches. Furthermore, the conflict has spread beyond the walls of the evangelical church into nearly every major denomination and fellowship of churches. While it is these groups to whom this presentation is directed, it has ramifications for all the churches torn by the conflict over traditional and contemporary forms of worship.

Now that I have explained my prejudices, dialogues, and historical consciousness that are part of my interpretive background and have identified the particular evangelical audience to whom I write, I am prepared to identify the crisis of evangelical worship.

The Crisis of Evangelical Worship

In terms of strengths, evangelicals bring a deep, heartfelt commitment to Christ, a loyalty to the authority of Scripture, and a desire to meet the needs of people. The most obvious weakness of the evangelical community is an antihistorical bias that shapes its inadequate theology of worship, its programlike nature, and its overemphasis on an accommodation to culture.

Inadequate theology of worship. The average evangelical does not have a theology of worship. For evangelicals, worship is not *leitourgia*, but *kerygma*. Evangelicalism by its very nature is an evangelizing community. The primary mandate that gives shape to the evangelical ethos and mission is the Great Commission. What is called worship in the evangelical community is outreach. What drives contemporary evangelicalism is the market. The questions generally asked by evangelicals are, Who is the audience? How can we target their needs? What is it that attracts the audience? How can we sell Jesus to our target market?

I recently attended an evangelical market-driven megachurch. The building and the grounds were beautiful and compelling. There was an enthusiastic buzz among the people gathered on the patio. (I overheard one person say, "Wow! This is just like Disneyland!") The service began with a light jazz piece that gathered the people. A few songs focusing on love were sung by a worship team. There were a few announcements and then the sermon. The theme of the sermon was "Love is time and time is love." If, the preacher urged, you want to have a good relationship with your spouse and children, you need to love them and loving them means giving quality time. The response to the sermon was to promise to give fifteen minutes of quality time to each member of your family this week. I liked the sermon and felt empowered by it. But nowhere in that sermon was the gospel. It was peppered with verses and frequent reference was made to God, but there was no mention made of Jesus or the Holy Spirit. I feel confident that that church believes and proclaims the gospel, but it was nowhere evident in its worship. Its worship was not about God or the *missio Dei*. It was all about how you can help yourself to have a better and more fulfilled relationship with your family. As good and helpful as that is, it isn't what worship is all about.

Worship as program. My second critique of this popular kind of evangelical worship is that the content lends itself to a program, to an entertainment form of worship. Worship is not the unfolding of God's mission but a variety of acts of worship offered as musical or dramatic events designed as entertainment to catch the attention of the "audience." This presentational form or program of worship is a natural outcome of its culturally conditioned, Enlightenment-oriented, self-focused style. The program is simple and almost always follows a threefold pattern: music that puts the crowd in the right mood, a sermon oriented toward an intended accomplishment, and a response focused toward the desired outcome. This pattern does not follow the biblical fourfold pattern of gathering, hearing the Word, celebrating at the Table, and going forth to love and serve the Lord.

I have been in communities where worship has been intentionally programmed. In one church the worship leader repeatedly announced each new act of the program by saying, "now the next part of our package is . . ." In another church the pastor had deliberately shaped the worship event according to a Phil Donahue TV program and proudly announced that they had achieved participatory worship.

Accommodation to culture. A third critique of evangelical worship is its overemphasis on relevance achieved through an accommodation to culture. Evangelicalism, following the Enlightenment culture, asks, What is in it for me? Its approach to worship is self-focused. It focuses on knowledge, experience, self-help, or empowerment. The person who focuses on knowledge asks, What did I learn? What new "aha" did I get? How does the discovery of the authorial intent of the passage speak to me? In this scenario authentic worship is verified by its pedagogical value. If the worshiper has been edified, educated, or informed by God's Word, then, according to this paradigm, true authentic worship has happened.

Next, those who focus on subjective experience ask, Did I experience the presence of God? Was my heart strangely warmed? Did the worship experience make me feel good? In this scenario worship is verified as authentic when the worshiper is made to feel good or has felt conviction or the comforting presence of God.

A third culturally bound self-focused approach regards worship as authentic when it accomplishes emotional or physical healing. When worship touches the worshiper's pain or results in the alleviation of the worshiper's anxieties, then it is authentic.

Another self-focused understanding of worship occurs when worship is authenticated by its empowerment value. If it empowers the worshiper to live a life that is holy, socially useful, or directed toward the accomplishment of this or that mission, then worship is regarded as authentic. In these scenarios, worship is authenticated by what it accomplishes. If it has edified the saint, saved the sinner, healed the brokenhearted, or empowered mission in the world, then it must be good, biblical, and authentic worship.

This instrumental or causation approach to worship can be illustrated in both traditional and contemporary worship. For example, traditional worship of the 1950s has been influenced by either the rationalism of the Enlightenment or the subjective emotionalism of the impulses of nineteenth-century romanticism. Worship influenced by rationalism is heady and intellectual; it is sermon-driven and aimed primarily toward growth in biblical knowledge and a life lived out of biblical principle. Worship influenced by emotion is primarily evangelistic and aimed at an emotional response culminating in the invitation to receive and to live in a warmhearted relationship with Jesus. These traditions, like the Enlightenment and romantic impulses with which they identify, are self-focused. The cultural identification is "what's in it for me?" Questions about an authentic biblical or historical understanding or practice of worship are seldom asked.

Next, contemporary worship that emerged among evangelicals after the revolution of the 1960s continues the same preoccupation with culture, but with a new twist. The emphasis falls on a pop-culture style of worship, characterized by a need-oriented, market-driven awareness. This approach to worship has resulted in the megachurch movement, which has attracted thousands of people to the faith. Despite its numerical accomplishments and the spiritual refreshment that these churches have brought to many, its approach to worship is still a cultural accommodation. This culturally conditioned worship has led many churches into an antihistorical rejection of all tradition, and a reductionism in worship that heralds popular chorus music as the new sacrament of God's presence; regards Scripture reading, intercessory prayer, and communion as offensive to the seeker; and makes the sermon a presentation of Christianity 101. Worship and evangelism are confused. Contemporary worship leaders still ask, What does our worship accomplish?

I realize that I have given the worst possible examples of the crisis in evangelical worship. There are numerous smaller and mid-sized evangelical worshiping communities that are appalled by this current evangelical scene. So why then did I use these examples? For the simple reason that the megachurch these examples largely represent is holding itself and is being held up by the church-growth movement as the bright light of the future church. Unfortunately, many evangelicals as well as mainline Protestant and some Catholic churches are looking to the megachurch market model for leadership.

The Future of Evangelical Worship

Since I have suggested that the crisis of evangelical worship is related to its lack of a theology of worship, its approach to worship as a program, and its accommodation to culture, my prescription for the future is that these trends be reversed. I suggest evangelicals first work toward a trinitarian view of worship; second, recover the historic process of worship; and third, develop a more appropriate relationship to culture.

Recover a Biblical Theology of Worship

Worship from the very beginning of the church has been in the name of the Father, the Son, and the Holy Spirit. This is not the time to try to develop a full view of trinitarian worship, so I will suggest a possible direction for an evangelical worship that is triune in nature.

Worship of the Father. The Arians, who were major opponents of the Trinity in the fourth century, were characterized by the saying "I know God as He is known to Himself." St. John Chrysostom, the fourth-century bishop of Constantinople, wrote it is an impertinence to say that He who is beyond the apprehension of even the higher powers can be comprehended by us earthworms or compassed and comprised by the weak forces of our understanding. In his five discourses on the incomprehensibility of God (*De Incomprehensible*), Chrysostom asserts, "he *insults* God who seeks to apprehend his essential being." When God, he argues, is even incomprehensible in his works, how much more is he incomprehensible in his essential nature. And, if God is unknown in his transcendent majesty, even to the cherubim and seraphim, how much more unknown is God to humanity!

The notion of God's incomprehensibility is certainly attested in Scripture. The visions of God like that of Isaiah (Isa. 6:1–6), Daniel (Dan. 10:5–8), and John (Revelation 4–5) speak in the language of poetry and metaphor, not in propositions that can be dissected and analyzed. Paul speaks of God as unapproachable light (1 Tim. 6:6), and in the great doxological cry to the Romans Paul cries, "O the depth of the riches both of the wisdom and knowledge of God! how unsearchable are his judgments, and his ways past finding out!" (Rom. 11:33 KJV).

Throughout history this sense of the incomprehensibility of God is clearly expressed in worship. We find it in the great words of the *Gloria in Excelsis Deo,* the *Te Deum,* the *Kyrie,* and the *Sanctus.* We find it in the attention given the great vaults of space, in the quiet sounds of contemplation and prayer, in the powerful use of light and shadow, and in the visions of heaven.

Father worship evokes the sense of God's mystery and our response of awe, wonder, and reverence. As Rudolf Otto said in *The Idea of the Holy,* "before God becomes for us a rationality, absolute reason, a personality, a moral will, he is the wholly nonrational and 'other', the being of sheer mystery and marvel."[1] This worship of God, the source of all being who is the mystery beyond being, is offered by us in our feeble, fumbling, and faulty language of praise. For it is only in the language of praise that we can approach what we cannot know.

Worship of the Son. While we confess we worship one God, we recognize God in three persons. For this reason we are able to distinguish the revelatory work of God most fully expressed in the incarnation, the Word made flesh (John 1:14). Unlike the mystery of God's otherness, the work of God in history is knowable. While we don't confess to know everything about God's revelatory presence in history, we do acknowledge that our worship of God in this instance lies in the realm of intelligibility. The Eastern church fathers summarized God's work in history with the three words—*creation, incarnation, recreation,* whereas the Western church has used the words *creation, fall, redemption.* While there are different emphases in these theologies, what is common to them is the biblical record of creation; the fall; the account of how God initiated a relationship with Abraham; called a people into being in Israel; became incarnate in Jesus; was crucified, buried, and resurrected to forgive sin and overcome death. He ascended into heaven and established the church by the gift of the Spirit to witness to the overcoming of the powers and principalities. He now sits at the right hand of God to intercede for us continually and will return to restore the created order where his shalom will rule forever and ever in the new heavens and the new earth.

This litany, the Christian metanarrative, is characterized by a particular story we confess to be not just *our* story; but even in the face of a pluralistic world it is *the* story for all people. This story forms us as a community, gives shape to our ethic, and makes us an eschatological people (not just a people who have an eschatology).

Common images of the narrative of God's activity in history, and the creation of God's special community of people who are to remember God's action, be shaped by it, and live in it, are found in New Testament descriptions of the worshiping communities such as Acts 2:42–47 and 1 Corinthians 12–14. We are admonished not to forsake worship but to gather to exhort each other to good works (Heb. 10:25). This worship is for the edification of the saints (Eph. 4:12). It has to do with God's revelation, which is not mere knowledge for the sake of knowledge but the record of God's truth for guidance, wisdom, and a life that pleases God and brings glory to God's name. This metanarrative in which we are immersed in public worship shapes our personal worship so that all of life is a "living sacrifice, holy and acceptable to God" (Rom. 12:1).

History attests to the significant role given to the worship of the Son in public worship. Sermons, hymns, choruses, prayers, litanies, Eucharistic prayers, anthems, and the like sing, proclaim, enact, and extol God's work of creating the world and redeeming it—all of it—to the glory of God. This is the *missio Dei* that worship signifies and represents to the glory of God and to the formation of a people who testify by their very existence to the glory of God and grace. Therefore, when we worship the Son, we do so in the language of a knowable narrative. We remember, proclaim, and enact the story that tells the truth about the mystery of life.

Spirit worship. While Father worship evokes mystery and Son worship recalls a knowable narrative, Spirit worship is apprehended primarily through the concept of presence. We encounter the very presence of God in the experience of the Spirit through the language of symbol.

We confess, of course, that God is present everywhere by virtue of creation. But we also acknowledge that the presence of God is made available in greater intensity through visible and tangible sign. In the Old Testament, God was present on the mountain, then in the tabernacle, especially in the holy of holies at the ark and between the cherubim. In the New Testament, God becomes present in the Word made flesh. Jesus is the image of God (Col. 1:15): what is invisible has been made flesh.

God has been earthed and concretized into our historical reality. The God who cannot be contained in all the universe is voluntarily confined in the womb of woman, was born of her, and participated in our earthly life constricted by time, space, and history. This incarnational theology affirms that the God who is immaterial actually communicates to us through materiality. Thus the enfleshed God continues to be present to us by the power of the Spirit in visible and tangible ways.

This God, we confess, dwells within the church. God's people are the temples of the Holy Spirit. Consequently, the primary locus of God's presence in worship is in the assembly. When we gather to worship we become the actualized church, the body of Christ mystically united with the head of the church, Christ. In this assembly, the priesthood of all believers, there are distinct visible signs of God's presence—tangible ways that Spirit worship happens.

Historically the church has acknowledged the work and worship of the Spirit in the visible signs of Word, ministry, and sacraments. The Spirit attends the reading and preaching of the Word; the Spirit empowers the pastor; the Spirit communicates through water, bread, wine, and oil (to name the chief visible signs). For this reason the act of gathering, the presence and work of the ordained pastor, the reading and preaching of the Word, the rite of baptism, the celebration of the Eucharist, the anointing of oil, and the hands raised in benediction are not empty symbols but performative symbols that participate in the reality they re-present.

A goal then for evangelical worship is to become triune: to worship the mystery of the Father in the language of praise, to thankfully remember and enact the work of the Son in the language of story, and to worshipfully receive the empowering presence of the Holy Spirit through visible and tangible sign. In this way the church and each believer personally are drawn into an experience of union with the triune God, a momentary existential experience of the eschatological kingdom yet to come in its fullness.

The Process of Worship

The next prescription for evangelical worship is to recover the historic fourfold pattern of worship as the unfolding story of gathering, hearing God's Word, thankfully celebrating God's redeeming work at the table, and going forth to serve God in every area of life. If evangelicals are to recover this fourfold pattern, they will have to break with their proclivity toward programs and performances. Fortunately, a recovery of the biblical understanding of worship in both content and process will already undermine the presentational nature of worship. But evangelicals will need to pay more attention to the internal process of each of these phases in the fourfold pattern. This task includes first the recovery of the gathering as the acts by which the community is formed as the body of Christ. In the gathering, greater attention needs to be paid to the reality of Christ, the head of the church who is made mystically present in the congregation's act of centering so that a prayerful lingering in God's presence occurs. Second, there is a need to recover the dialogic nature of the Word. In reading and preaching there is a real presence of Jesus through a speech communication. There is a need to probe how the congregation can become more interactive with the Word. There is a need to return psalm singing, talk-back sermons, and bidding prayer to the service of the Word. The third need is to recover the celebratory nature of the Eucharist. The current practice of the Lord's Supper is a funeral dirge. The sense of resurrection can be retained through prayerful singing and the simultaneous act of the laying on of hands with an anointing for healing. Finally, there is a need to recover the sense of God's presence in the going forth. More attention needs to be paid to the way the benediction is communicated and how people are sent forth.

Hopefully recovering the historic fourfold pattern of worship will result in a more clear distinction between worship and evangelism. The hallmark of evangelical Christianity is evangelism, not worship. The primacy given to evangelism turns what should be worship into an evangelistic event. This distorts the nature of worship from what it signifies to what it accomplishes. It then turns worship into a program or performance as opposed to the unfolding narrative of the mission of God. The recovery of the fourfold pattern as the distinct structure of *leitourgia* should help clarify the distinct nature of worship from the programmatic nature of evangelistic events.

Worship and Culture

There is one more question that we must deal with—evangelical worship in the changing world, a world shaped by postmodern culture. I have already suggested authentic worship is characterized by a triune content and a fourfold process. But worship is to be contextualized into the culture we are a part of. The questions are, What are the influences of a postmodern culture that are to be taken into account by evangelical worship, and what will an authentic biblical worship contextualized into this culture look like?

Postmodern cultural changes. The term postmodernism has been used in nearly all disciplines of thought, including postmodern philosophy, science, literature, politics, and economics. The various ways in which the word has been used speaks to the complexity of thought implied by the term. My usage of the term is limited to those revolutions that are currently creating a postmodern culture. I can do no more in this presentation than refer to the revolutions and hint at the changes that appear to be emerging for the evangelical worshiping community.

First, consider the sociological changes resulting from technological and digital forms of communication. The world which was once lands and cultures foreign to our experiences is now on our doorstep. The result is the rise of pluralism, knowledge of many competing metanarratives, and new questions about the uniqueness of Christian worship. At the very least, evangelicals will need to become more clear about the Christian metanarrative, how it is shared by the whole church, what this means for relations between Catholics, Orthodox, and Protestants, and how the Christian story relates to the metanarratives of world religions.

Second, the revolution in historical understanding has shifted society away from the nineteenth-century evolutionary theory of history. Evangelicals have been influenced by the evolutionary view of history that regards the past as irrelevant to the future. The boomer generation, a product of the 1960s revolution, turned its back on all tradition and introduced contemporary and seeker-oriented worship as a brand new start for Christianity. Generation X and Millennial young people, who constitute the next generation of leaders in the evangelical church, do not share their parents' convictions. They question the future and honor the past. They are characterized by a nostalgia for the past, a return to the liturgies of the ancient church, a longing for substance and depth.

Third, the scientific revolution, introduced by Einstein's theory of relativity and quantum physics, has created a new worldview. The Newtonian mechanistic worldview with its emphasis on an understandable world has been changed to a much more dynamic and interrelated view of the world characterized by complexity and mystery. This interconnected view has resulted in a new emphasis on community, a more humble posture regarding our ability to know, and a new interest in ecology and the survival of a natural order in which humans can thrive.

The fourth revolution affecting the emergence of a postmodern culture is the shift taking place in philosophy. The interconnected understanding of all things questions the previous notion of the absolute distinction made between object and subject, and the subsequent conviction that it is possible to arrive at objective propositional truth. Postmodern science collapses the subject and object into a philosophical theory of coherence. The new science should lead us into a more humble stance of mystery and ambiguity.

A fifth revolution, proceeding from the scientific and philosophical changes, is the religious revolution. Modern science and philosophy fostered religious skepticism and convinced atheism, but postmodern science and philosophy have the opposite effect. The new interest in transcendence, in a spiritual reality, and in getting in touch with one's own spirituality is an obvious response to the recovery of mystery.

Finally, the communication revolution is shifting us from a near exclusive emphasis on print to a greater use of the visual. We have become a world of graphics and symbols. This shift has sparked new interests in imagination and creativity.

These six revolutions—the sociological, historical, scientific, philosophical, religious, and communications—are only the most obvious changes taking place. How, we must ask, will evangelical worship be influenced by these changes?

The Impact of Postmodern Cultural Change on Evangelical Worship

In summary, postmodern trends are moving society toward a recovery of the supernatural, a desire to be connected to the past, a concern for intercultural affirmation, a longing for community, an openness to mystery, and an affirmation of a more visual and symbolic form of communication.

In order to determine the impact of these postmodern trends on the next generation of evangelical leaders, I conducted a survey in the fall of 1999 among 176 twenty-somethings from 38 states, 41 denominations, and 14 countries. The respondents were all committed evangelical Christians, active in the church and likely to have positions of clergy and lay leadership in the church by 2010. The goal of the survey was to discover the direction of the next generation of leaders.

The survey consisted of about forty characteristics of worship that were to be placed in columns designated "very important to me, important, neutral, unimportant," and "very unimportant." The results were very interesting, to say the least.

First, the survey showed that there seems to be a general reaction against the contemporary style of worship developed in the 1970s, 1980s, and 1990s. Eighty-seven percent of those surveyed listed "entertainment" worship as a style that least interested them. Forty-eight percent registered a negative attitude toward contemporary worship and the style of music generally associated with it such as band (63 percent), drums (59 percent), keyboard (56 percent), and guitar (38 percent).

On the other hand, the survey demonstrated that the twenty-something evangelical leaders of tomorrow are characterized by the following nine interests:

1. The strongest and deepest desire of the twenty-something worshiper is to have a genuine encounter with God (88 percent).
2. This longing for an encounter with God is not merely individualistic, but one that takes place within the context of genuine community (88 percent).
3. It follows that there is high concern to recover depth and substance in worship (87 percent).
4. There is a deep desire to return to a more frequent and meaningful experience of communion. Here is where a deep, substance-filled

encounter with God is most fully experienced on the personal level (86 percent).

5. Another significant way we are encountered by God shows up in the demand for challenging sermons (69 percent) and more use of Scripture (49 percent).

6. Worship in the future will be more participatory. Worship is not a lecture or a concert done *for* us. Authentic worship is done *by* us. We are the players, God is the audience (73 percent).

7. This generation wants a more creative use of the senses (51 percent). The current communication revolution has shifted us toward a participation that is more visual.

8. Worship will become more quiet, characterized by more contemplative music and time for quiet personal reflection and intimate relationship with God (58 percent).

9. Worship will focus more on the transcendence and otherness of God (45 percent) even as the demand for an encounter with the nearness of God remains high (88 percent).

Conclusion

This essay has dealt with evangelical worship, its lack of a theology of worship, its failure to have an adequate order of worship, and its attachment to culture. My concern has been to analyze the crisis of evangelical worship and to suggest an agenda for authentic evangelical worship in a postmodern world. I admit the difficulty of this endeavor, and I hesitate to offer an answer to a movement that despite its weakness in worship, is growing numerically and in influence throughout North America. So instead of an answer, I will summarize my thoughts as a suggested direction.

First and foremost, evangelicals need to recover an authentic biblical worship. This is worship that is not outreach but upreach. It is not driven by what it accomplishes but by what it signifies or represents. Its focus is on God and God's saving mission to the world accomplished in Jesus Christ by the power of the Spirit. Worship celebrates the *missio Dei*. It prays, sings, preaches, and enacts it.

Second, evangelicals need to discover the unfolding process of worship. Worship is not a program but an unfolding process of gathering under divine call; listening to the living, active, life-giving voice of God in the Word of God read and preached; enacting the Christian narrative at the Table in a response of praise and thanksgiving; and a going forth with the promise of God's presence in every area of life.

To these two directions—recovery of a biblical content and process of worship—I suggest a critical listening to the text of culture. The impulses arising from the revolution in our postmodern culture support the recovery of an ancient worship with a contemporary flair. The continual task of contextual adaptation asks how we can take the ancient classical paradigm of worship, the paradigm common to the whole church and to all worshiping communities, and faithfully re-present it into a postmodern culture. My prejudices, my dialogue with the church, and my historical consciousness suggest that this is the direction we evangelicals should consider taking in order to do authentic evangelical worship in a changing world.

What an evangelical brings to the table is the experience of transformation, a commitment of will, an enthusiastic discipleship, a desire for spiritual formation, and a dynamic, infectious sharing of the gospel story with others. I simply suggest we add to these strong characteristics of evangelicalism the historical content and process of worship carefully contextualized into our postmodern world. I think it would result in a dynamic worship rooted in the biblical story, shaped by the test of history, and spiritually expressive in a postmodern culture.

7

A New Reformation

Re-creating Worship for a Postmodern World

Leonard Sweet

*Noted postmodern theologian Leonard Sweet describes the
need for experiential, participatory, image-driven, and communal (EPIC) corporate worship.*

The journal *Philosophy and Literature*, published by the University
of Canterbury, in Christchurch, New Zealand, periodically gives
Gold Medal awards in the "Bad Writing Contest." One of the recent
award winners was the distinguished scholar Fredric Jameson, whose
opening sentence in *Signatures of the Visible* (1998) gives a portent of
what follows:

Reprinted from *Experience God in Worship: Perspectives on the Future of Worship in the
Church from Today's Most Prominent Leaders* (Loveland, CO: Group Publishing, 2000),
171–91. © 2000 by Group Publishing, Inc., P.O. Box 481, Loveland, CO 80539 (www.group
publishing.com). Used by permission.

The visual is *essentially* pornographic, which is to say that it has its end in rapt, mindless fascination; thinking about its attributes becomes an attribute to that, if it is unwilling to betray its object; while the most austere films necessarily draw their energy from the attempt to repress their own excess (rather than from the more thankless effort to discipline the viewer).

In close second was a professor of English, Rob Wilson. His "winning" paragraph went like this:

> If such a sublime cyborg would insinuate the future as post-Fordist sub-ject, his palpably masochistic locations as ecstatic agent of the sublime superstate need to be decoded as the 'now-all-but-unreadable DNA' of a fast deindustrializing Detroit, just as his Robocop-like strategy of carceral negotiation and street control remains the tirelessly American one of inflicting regeneration through violence upon the racially heteroglossic wilds and others of the inner city.[1]

Easy for him to say. But it is not just academics who are speaking and writing in "secret code" language that reflects their professional class or occupational superiority. From the perspective of "outsiders" in this post-Christian culture, much of mainline Protestantism has been speaking in a foreign language for decades.

In the midst of one of the greatest transitions in the history of Chris-tianity—from modern to postmodern—mainline churches remain stuck in a modern paradigm. They have clung to modern modes of thought and action, their ways of embodying and enacting the Christian tradi-tion frozen in patterns of modernity.

The decline of mainline Christianity is so well-documented it needs no rehearsing here. In fact, the mainline plight has passed into the realm of humor. At a recent board meeting of a community agency, someone used the phrase "mainline churches." Someone else asked, "What are mainline churches?" A third snapped back, "The ones with the fewest people."

For the first time in U.S. American history more people are attending non-denominational than denominationally affiliated churches. In one year alone (1997 to 1998), average church size plummeted over 10 per-cent, with a drop of 15 percent during the same twelve-month period in annual operating budgets.[2] The fact is that most of the mainline church is in serious deterioration or comatose.

My favorite example of how out of touch mainliners can be with the emerging postmodern world all around them is a throwaway line from Marc Driscoll, Gen-X pastor at Seattle's thriving Mars Hill Fellowship. Driscoll says his challenge in reaching postmoderns is not convincing them that Jesus rose from the dead or that there could be such a thing as a resurrection. His biggest challenge is in convincing postmoderns that there was only one resurrection.

The mainline church went to sleep in a modern world governed by the gods of reason and observation. It is awakening to a postmodern world open to revelation and hungry for experience. Indeed, one of the last places postmoderns expect to be "spiritual" is the church. In the midst of a spiritual heat wave in the host culture, the mainline church is in the midst of a deep freeze.

The mainline crisis is of "EPIC" proportions. It will take more than a Martha Stewart makeover or spiritual plastic surgery to make mainline worship vital to a postmodern culture. Unless mainline churches can transition their worship into more EPIC directions—Experiential, Participatory, Image-Based, and Communal—they stand the real risk of becoming museum churches, nostalgic testimonies to a culture that is no more.

From Rational to Experiential

A modernist dies and finds himself surrounded by dense, billowy clouds which only allow him to see a short distance ahead of him. He sees that he is walking down a road paved in gold. Ahead, there is a slight break in the clouds. He sees a signpost and a fork in the road. The signpost has inscriptions with golden arrows pointing to the left and right.

The modernist reads them. The right arrows says, "This way to heaven." The left arrow says, "This way to a discussion about heaven."

Guess which fork the modernist took?

The perpetual openness to experience of postmoderns is such that one can never underestimate the e-factor: experiential.

Welsh priest and poet R. S. Thomas, when out walking in the countryside of Wales, has a custom of putting his hand in the place where a hare has recently lain, hoping to find it still warm.[3]

Postmoderns are constantly putting their hands and the rest of themselves where God may have visited, hoping it's still warm. They are hungry for experiences, especially experiences of God.

The postmodern economy is an experience-based economy. In my lifetime we have transitioned from an industrial economy (which manufactured widgets) to an information economy (which generated information) to an experience economy (which traffics in experiences). The precise nature of this new economy has been summarized exquisitely by Marilyn Carlson Nelson, the new Chair, President, and CEO of Carlson Companies, one of the world's largest privately held companies:

Anyone who views a sale as a transaction is going to be toast down the line. Selling is not about peddling a product. It's about wrapping that product in a service—and about selling both the product and the service as an experience. That approach to selling helps create a vital element of the process: a relationship. In a world where things move at hyperspeed, what was relevant yesterday may not be relevant tomorrow. But one thing that endures is a dynamic relationship that is grounded in an experience that you've provided.[4]

Already U.S. American consumers spend more on entertainment than on health care or clothing.[5] Whatever happened to the fountain pen? Ask Mont Blanc how much high-tech postmoderns want high-touch experiences with their fingers.

REI's flagship store in Seattle looks more like a retail amusement park than a store. One of the country's largest wilderness-sports stores (100,000 square feet; 60,000 stock items), the consumer cooperative Recreational Equipment, Inc. (REI), boasts places for customers to interact with and experience some of the products it sells—a 7-story climbing wall; a 300-foot waterfall; a 475-foot-long biking trail and test track; a 100-seat cafe; a rain room for testing how waterproof Leak-Tex is; a lab where camp stoves can be tried out; and so on. The aisles between departments are even designed to resemble hiking trails.

Honda has based an entire sales strategy on an "experiential" foundation. Honda's success with its four hundred supplier companies throughout North America is based on what it calls The Three Joys. According to The Three Joys, each component in the "car experience" (customer, employee, supplier) should enjoy the "experience." Customers should have a positive experience of ownership. The dealer who connects the customer to the supplier should enjoy the experience of bringing pleasure to the customer—high customer satisfaction. Honda, who supplies the product, should enjoy the experience of pleasing both other parties with such a superb product.

Why is tourism one of if not the fastest growing industry in the world? It creates a new job every 2.5 seconds and generates investments of $3.2 billion a day. Almost two trillion dollars is spent annually on tourism worldwide, accounting for one-tenth of the global economic impact. More than 200 million people are employed worldwide by an industry that will grow to 350 million employees by 2005.[6]

Some scholars interpret the touristic phenomenon as a postmodern ritual that performs the same role as sacred rites did in pre-modern societies. Heritage tourism appeals to a culture's search for "authenticity," "otherness," "identity," and educational experiences while vacationing.

In 1994, 528 million people traveled for the pleasure of experiences of "otherness." By 2010 this figure is expected to rise to 937 million. Half the world's vacationers head to the sea each year—and half the world's people live within fifty miles or so of saltwater. But tourism has reached every region of the globe—from the mountains to the desert, from the polar icecaps to the tropical rain forests. It will soon reach the moon first and then Mars. What will get us there will not be government space agencies, but Hilton and Ritz-Carlton.

Why is travel and tourism the United States' largest export industry as well as our second largest employer (after health) and third largest retail industry (after automotive and food store sales)?

Because tourism is an experience industry. The fastest-growing segment of tourism is adventure travel, with over two hundred travel books appearing each month catered to this clientele. Adventure travel will likely become in our lifetime the largest commercial use of space once reusable launchers reduce costs sufficiently for space tours to orbiting space stations. It is not surprising that in an experience economy frequent mall shopping would plummet, down from 16 percent in 1987 to fewer than 10 percent in 1998. Yet at the same time the Mall of America (Bloomington, Minnesota) now hosts more visitors than Walt Disney World, Disneyland, and the Grand Canyon *combined*.[7] Why? It's not a mall, but an experience center.

Here's the point? *In postmodern culture, the experience is the message.* Postmoderns literally "feel" their way through life. If postmodern worship can't make people furiously *feel* and *think* (in the old "modern" world, we would have said only "think"), it can't show them how God's Word transforms the way we "feel."

Postmodern preachers don't "write sermons"—they create experiences. And these *Shekhinah* experiences (*Shekhinah* is the Hebrew term for the divine presence) bring together all the senses—sound, sight, touch, taste, and smell—into a radiant glowing of God's presence dwelling with God's people suffused in the ethereal light of beauty, truth, and goodness.

It will not be easy for mainline Protestantism to make this transition to worship that meets the "wow" standard. As much as the modern university, the mainline church is the intellectual outgrowth of the Enlightenment, which tried to make the critical use of reason, not experience, the touchstone of knowledge. Jane Miller recalls her experience at Cambridge in the mid-twentieth century: "I have to admit, I believed you should not include anything you actually thought or felt in an essay."[8]

The triumph of Enlightenment rationalism in worship is demonstrated in the statistics of a 1998 Barna Research Group study, which found that 32 percent of all types of regular churchgoers have never experienced God's presence in worship. Forty-four percent have not experienced God's presence in the past year. And the younger you are, the less likely you are to have a religious experience in worship.

As appalling as these figures are, the percentages would be even higher if mainline Protestants were isolated out for comparison.

At a gathering of seven hundred mainliners, I watched in amazement as the entire congregation obediently followed the instructions in the bulletin, turned to the page for the black spiritual "Amen, Amen" and read from their hymnals, with heads bowed and legs braced, the one-word song: "A-men, a-men, a-men, a-men, a-men." It's definitely time for a change.

From Representative to Participatory

Here's a conversation overheard in a restaurant:
"Give me a Coke."
"Would you like a Classic Coke, a New Coke, a Cherry Coke, or a Diet Coke?"
"I'd like a Diet Coke."
"Would you like a regular Diet Coke or a caffeine-free Diet Coke?"
"The heck with it. Give me a 7 UP."

A choice culture is by definition a participatory culture. Postmoderns don't give their undivided attention to much of anything without it being interactive. In fact, the more digital the culture becomes, the more participatory it gets. The notion that electronic culture produces "couch potatoes" has pockmarked the mind of the church for too long. The truth is just the opposite. The more you surf the Internet, the more you become "surf bored," as Jim L. Wilson puts it,[9] and want to surf the real thing.

This is one reason for the decreasing popularity of television in postmodern culture. The finale of *Seinfeld* attracted 76.3 million viewers in 1998. The finale of *Cheers* attracted 80.5 million viewers in 1993. The finale of *M*A*S*H* attracted 106 million viewers in 1983. That's a drop of 30 million viewers while during the same time the total number of television households grew by 16 million.[10]

Why? Television isn't nearly interactive enough. With a wired universe, each person can be a programmer; not just an observer. Television news has a stable audience only among those fifty or older. Everyone else is getting his or her information elsewhere. No wonder interactivity is the central focus of content providers, with an interactive *Sesame Street* now being prepared that will run on WebTV.

In economics there are fewer "professionals" as more people are becoming their own online stockbrokers and with an astonishing 41 percent of U.S. households having become stockholders.

In religion there are no more "professional clergy" and pew-sitting laity. There are only ministers who look to leaders to mobilize and release ministry through them.

Naturally this shift in culture also applies in worship. Postmoderns want interactive, immersive, in-your-face participation in the mystery of God. That's why they are attracted to the power and mystery of Pentecostalism—which is the fastest growing religious movement in the world.[11] That desire to explore the "mystery" of worship has also drawn postmoderns toward neo-traditional faiths. Sometimes, in fact, the Pentecostals and the neo-traditionalists have actually combined forces. For example, there is a 1,500-seat sanctuary Pentecostal church in Valdosta, Georgia, which converted en masse to the Book of Common Prayer, with a bishop of the Episcopal Church carrying out the confirmation of the entire congregation on Good Friday 1990.

Postmodern worship is body worship. Body piercings show postmodern desperation for rituals, including body rituals. People are narrating the story of their lives on their bodies through multiple piercings (a dozen piercings are not uncommon). The role of spectacle in worship is only beginning to be understood.

Ironically it is the screen that releases postmoderns to "put their whole being" into worship and frees them up from being chained in place by books. Sometimes the preaching will become more karaoke, other times more kinesthetic. But whatever form preaching takes, the interactive component is crucial. Unless postmoderns can complete the sentence for themselves, or at least have the opportunity to hold the mike themselves, worship will insufficiently help them create new realities for their lives.

Faced with a smorgasbord of choices, some people don't select one or the other. They select nothing at all. That's why the neo-traditional movement will become stronger than it is now. But while many couples want traditional weddings with all the trimmings, they want tradition "neo." "Neo" for them means tradition customized and personalized. Even neo-traditionalists make the tradition interactive. If they can't take tradition and run with it down their own path, they won't pick it up.

From Word-Based to Image-Driven

"If you want people to think differently," Buckminster Fuller used to say, "don't tell them how to think, give them a tool." The best tool worship leaders can give people to help them think and live differently is a metaphor or image. Nietzsche was right: "We do not think good metaphors are anything very important, but I think a good metaphor is something even the police should keep an eye on."[12]

To sculpt a metaphor is to transform the world. Metaphor (such as metaphor evangelism or metaphor preaching) is the medium through which postmodern spirituality is created for a variety of reasons.

First, humans think in images, not words. In a visualholic culture like postmodernity it is difficult not to believe that using metaphorical "pictures" would make worship more meaningful. But our "image-driven" lifestyle isn't distinctive to postmodern culture, but to the human mind itself. The human mind is made-up of metaphors. In defining realities, metaphors create realities. Metaphors consist of both thought and action. Metaphors are more than matters of language.

> Metaphor is a matter of conceptual structure. And conceptual structure is not merely a matter of the intellect—it involves all the natural dimensions of our experience, including aspects of our sense experiences: color, shape, texture, sound, and so on. These dimensions structure not only mundane experience but aesthetic experience as well.[13]

That's why the power of liturgy is so immense. The ultimate in power is the ability to order and ordain metaphors.

Postmodern spirituality is image-based for a second reason. Postmodern culture is a double-ring culture,[14] and metaphors are themselves a double ring. Philosopher Max Black calls them "two ideas in one phrase" (for example, "sweet smile" or "sharp tongue"). Part of this double-ring effect comes from the shaping influence of chaos theory and complexity science, which look at the whole—the system—rather than the parts. In searching for similarities, complexity thinking invites metaphorical thinking and linking.

Third, worship is not about style; it's about spirit. If the "spirit" isn't right, presentation means little—no matter how contemporary or high-tech. Ten times zero is still zero. And, if the Spirit is there, presentation also means little—no matter how traditional or bookish.

Linda S. McCoy is pastor of The Garden in Indianapolis, which meets in a Beef and Boards Dinner Theater facility. The musical group The Good Earth Band leads worshipers seated around tables through heavy helpings of video clips, drama, secular music, and contemporary Christian music—keeping the service to a thrifty forty minutes. A flowerpot container at the door is the only offering plate.

The importance of shifting worship from the exegesis of words to the exegesis of images in the postmodern world was hammered home from studies of companies in *Built to Last* (1996). Two Stanford Business School professors discovered to their surprise that the key to great companies is not "visionary leadership" by some entrepreneurial CEO, but the creation of a network of shared meaning and values around common metaphors that abide and guide the company into the future.[15]

From Individual to Communal

Why is Times Square the most popular place to greet the new millennium? Why are coffee bars the new dating places? Why is the Internet becoming less an information medium than a social medium, with more and more people logging on, not to gain information but to hear "You've Got Mail" and even to find love online?

Relationship issues stand at the heart of postmodern culture. In classic double-ring fashion, the more digitally enhanced the culture becomes, the more we are drawn to flesh-and-blood interaction.

At the heart of postmodernity lies a theological dyslexia: Call it "me/we," or the experience of individual-in-community. Think back on the flowers that were strewn on the sidewalks as part of Princess Diana's funeral. Something registered in your subconscious about those mounds of flowers, even if you didn't call it to rational or verbal consciousness. What was unique about those flowers?

In the medieval world, where everything was communal and nothing was individual, grieving villagers would have been content to simply pile flowers on top of other flowers. In the modern world, where everything was individual and little was communal, we arranged single bouquets of flowers in individual vases and put them on the altar or grave. In postmodern culture, we put our flowers back on the communal pile, but wrap them in cellophane or plastic to separate them from the crowd. A postmodern "me" needs "we" to "be."

Electronic culture necessitates longer pastoral tenures, not shorter. Building relationships of trust and intimacy in a post-Christian culture takes time. The transient nature of the culture requires that our community-building and hospitality be more aggressive, not less—more premeditated, not haphazard. Dietrich Bonhoeffer's conviction that an anti-Christian culture can actually work for the good of Christianity presupposes a vibrant communal life where people of faith can teach each other to live by faith—which is what God intended in the first place.

The future promises a second coming of communal customs and values. Postmoderns are disillusioned with the hyper-individualism of modern society. In the words of Gen Xer Tom Beaudoin, "My generation inherited not free love but AIDS, not peace but nuclear anxiety, not cheap communal lifestyles but crushing costs of living, not free teach-ins but colleges priced for aristocracy."[16]

Part of this quest for community and communal dimensions of life appear retro and neo-traditional: white wedding gowns, dance halls (swing dancing, ballroom dancing), even church fellowship halls. But the individual quest for communal rituals runs deep. To address this hunger for community, vital worship will need to upgrade four elements. First, three-quarters of all pastors see themselves as gifted either at teaching or preaching.[17] Yet Jesus' ministry had three components: preaching, teaching, and healing. If moral and spiritual transformation is to occur communally as well as individually, pastors will need to upgrade their healing role and hone their healing skills to at least the same levels as preaching and teaching.

Second, like everything else in postmodern culture, worship needs to be decentralized. Postmodern culture brings in its wake a double edge toward global hypercentralization and local decentralization. The one big refrigerator has been replaced by refrigerators you can find in places other than kitchens—bedrooms, family room bars, play-rooms, grill areas, custom installed in every cabinet or drawer. Already the California Legislature has considered two proposals to divide California into two new states. Already some twenty-five counties have voted to secede from California.

Worship must become a key component to every small, separate cell group that is free to worship in its own way while integrated into the larger church. Eighty-five percent of churches now offer cell group opportunities, each one of which should include a worship component.

Third, storytelling creates community. The narrative quality of experience is a deeply religious issue. We organize our experience through narrative. We inhabit a storied reality.[18] The modern world exalted abstract principles over "stories." In fact, the poet John Betjeman defined an intellectual as simply a nonvisual person.[19]

The very word "abstract" comes from the Greek *ab*, which means "to move away from," and *strahere*, which means "to stand." To have an abstract relationship with something, one has to stand away from it. To tell a story, one has to step into it and hold it tightly. In fact, according to New Testament scholar Tom Boomershine, "To say 'Let me tell you a story' is like saying, 'Let's go play.'"[20]

The gospel has lost its original character as a living storytelling tradition of messengers who told the good news of the victory of Jesus . . . telling stories is foreign to contemporary experience. We continue to read Bible stories to children. But the assumption is that once you grow up and learn to think you will stop telling stories and start telling the truth. Telling the truth means you will speak in conceptual abstractions.[21]

Telling stories in a digital culture may take any number of forms in worship: oral, audio, video, television, films, multimedia, and CD-ROM. Fourth, postmoderns need active worship that leads to service and social transformation. In the words of history of religions scholar Huston Smith, "The heart of religion is not altered states but altered traits of character. For me, then, the test of a substance's religious worth or validity is not what kind of far-out experience it can produce, but is the life improved by its use?"[22]

Forget an annual Mission Sunday. Make every day a mission day and every worship service a mission service. In fact, worship services need to be precisely what they say they are: worship service.

Worship and the "New" Way of Thinking

Modern worship has been trapped in foundationalist thinking where the divine is "out there" to be hauled in by objective methods. EPIC worship will need to evolve in concert with three forces of thought and culture, all of which are creating what is known as a "postmodern." These three forces are (1) postmodern hermeneutics, (2) the hard sciences themselves, and (3) cognition research.

Mainline Protestantism's predominant model of sit-and-soak worship cannot hold up under postmodern hermeneutics and philosophy. It's helpful to remember that just as the Protestant Reformation was a worship revolution wrought by changes in hermeneutics and epistemology, so the current Postmodern Reformation is witnessing revolutions in worship styles and functions wrought by similar forces.

Postmodern Hermeneutics. Why has "praise" music had such a hard time of it in mainline circles? Partly because the modern age was temperamentally allergic to praise. The scientific method was a "critical" method, and moderns were trained to critique, not to cheerlead—to assess, not to applaud.

The postmodern hermeneutics of learning through "interactive observation" are dethroning the old epistemological beliefs that pure learning comes via an under-glass analysis of cold logic, hard facts, and critical distance from the "object" of knowledge. Postmodern theorists are charting the course to a new "scientific method," one whose modes of knowledge are more relational, more experiential, more image-based, and more celebratory and communal.

Unlike their cerebral predecessors, postmodernists believe there are multiple ways of seeing the world. For example, there is more than a single way of "knowing" a flower. One way (more Western) of "knowing" a flower is to be full of oneself, one's wits and wisdom, and to throw oneself against the flower as an object. The other way (more Eastern) of "knowing" is really a way of "unknowing": to be "empty" of oneself and to let the flower reveal itself as it is. The first way of "knowing" a flower is to experiment with it as something separate, to stand at a distance from it, and pick it apart. The second way of knowing a flower is to experience it, to enter in rather than stand back; to stand under (there is no ultimate understanding without standing under) and participate in its beauty.

Knowledge by dissection analytically takes apart; knowledge by dance synthetically puts together. In one you are rich—full of yourself. In one you are poor—empty of yourself. In one you are a distant observer or critic. In one you are an intimate lover.

For the postmodern worshiper, objectivity can no longer be the sole objective of the pursuit of truth. Love can be as much a mode of knowledge as the old scientific method's detachment. Thus a worshiper is both active and reflective, participating and observing, both in and out of the experience.

Hard Sciences. The second influence turning the church toward an EPIC methodology is the "hard" sciences themselves. Chilean immunologist/biologist turned neuroscientist Francisco Varela once remarked that the "hard" sciences deal with the "soft" questions, and the "soft" sciences deal with the "hard" questions. But one of the hardest issues of life is the nature of truth, and here science itself is leading the way in pioneering a new "scientific method" and showing how the old "objective" pursuit of truth is not intellectually sound. The implications of this new "scientific method" for the worshiper are monumental.

Let me give a smattering of examples to explain what I mean. Particle physicist Edwin Schrödinger states the new paradigm eloquently: The world has not been given to us twice—once in spiritual or psychological terms and once in material terms. The world has been given once. The distinction between subjectivity and objectivity has been useful, but specious.

When Thomas Kuhn wrote his classic text on the *Structure of Scientific Revolutions,* he was only embellishing what Albert Einstein and Karl Popper, in their ruminations on the course of scientific discovery, had already taught us. Both stressed that science advances not through the logic of induction or deduction but through imaginative leaps of faith.[23] A "paradigm shift" is an act of faith which creates new facts and new realities.

In this new approach to science, value and faith commitments become rational parts of a scholar's search for truth. Lorraine Code puts it this way: "Subjectivity—however conflicted and multiple—becomes part of the conditions that make knowledge possible."[24]

Physicist Fred Alan Wolf also lent his support to this new view of reality when he boiled quantum physics down to this statement: "The universe does not exist independent of the thought of the observer" and "You will see it when you believe it."[25] Physicist John Wheeler has advised his colleagues to "cross out that old word 'observer' and replace it by the new word 'participator.'"[26]

Of course, the old scientific method still has its defenders. But one of the untold stories of our time is the movement of the scientific community beyond the modern scientific method. One can see it manifested in British science writer Bryan Appleyard's protestations about "the appalling spiritual damage that science has done" by ignoring questions of meaning and purpose.[27] Or scientist Donald A. Norman's laments over the spiritual and moral vacuum in which much of science is conducted.[28]

Cognition Theories. The third set of influences pushing the church in EPIC directions is the postmodern critique of the modern mindset and especially the emergence of "cognitive sciences." The field of cognition, which includes multiple academic disciplines of neuroscience, psychology, linguistics, genetics, computer science (especially artificial intelligence), anthropology, and philosophy, is generating new insights almost faster than they can be written down.

While some theologians whimper over the loss of modernity's fixed foundations and grounded reference points, scholars such as Humberto Maturana, Gregory Bateson, Heinz von Foerster, George Lakoff, Zenon W. Pylyshyn, Francisco Varela, Eleanor Rosch, and Michael Polanyi are showing how to live and move in an interdependent, relational mindset. Their work is shifting our perspectives from control to flow, from abstract and disembodied reason to embodied and imaginative reason, from representation to participation, from literalism to metaphor.[29]

Barbara McClintock, a geneticist who won the Nobel Prize in 1983 for her lifetime work on the genetics of corn, dissented from modern ways of knowing and suspended the boundaries between subject and object. She developed "a feeling for the organism," and told her biographer Evelyn Fox Keller that things are "much more marvelous than the scientific method allows us to conceive."[30]

The work in the biology of cognition done by Humberto R. Maturana and Francisco J. Varela has show that cognition is not a representation of the world out there but "an ongoing bringing forth of a world through the process of living itself."[31]

In many Mediterranean cultures, beauty is more than an intellectual aesthetic. It is an aesthetic of experience, participation, images, and communal celebration. The French scholar Pierre Babin tells of seeing a number of elders sitting motionless under a tree, staring at a picturesque mountain range. He commented to the elders, "Beautiful, isn't it?" They responded, "We feel good here." Babin, unsure whether they understood him properly, tried again. "Your village is so beautiful!" Once more they replied, "Do you feel good in our village?" For them beauty was not fullness of artistry or perfection of lines. It was fullness of being and perfection of presence.

EPIC worship does not give up critical methods of understanding, but rather places them within a larger context of personal reality and experience. And while a worship methodology that is more Experiential, Participative, Imaged-based, and Communal may be classified as "postmodern," it's really nothing new. For Jesus, truth was not a matter of distant observations or scientifically tested theories. Rather, truth was revealed through our participation and interaction with him, others, and the world around us. The same approach rings true for worshipers in a postmodern age.

8

Moshing for Jesus

Adolescence as a Cultural Context for Worship

Kenda Creasy Dean

The author of this chapter provides grounded suggestions for corporate worship by analyzing the socio-cultural characteristics of the mosh pit.

Worshiping God is fun and all. The only thing that makes people think it's boring is church.

Brendan Dean, age 11

The concert is hard rock all the way. "No rap music lovers here," notes journalist Patricia Hersch, observing the Reston, Virginia, Com-

Reprinted from *Making Room at the Table: An Invitation to Multicultural Worship,* eds. Brian K. Blount and Leonora Tubbs Tisdale (Louisville: Westminster John Knox Press, 2001), 131–44. © 2001 by Westminster John Knox Press. Used by permission of Westminster John Knox Press.

munity Center event. The youth pushing their way in—partially shaved heads, lots of Megadeth T-shirts and earrings (on boys and girls)—look like the least likely species on the planet to show up in worship. They have come to the "Jam the Man" concert for the roar of the music, the surging beat, the indistinguishable lyrics, the time with their friends. But most of all they have come together to mosh:

> Joan and her friends . . . stand happily at the perimeter of the dance floor grooving to the music. Joan is sizing up the scene, watching especially to see how the girls are faring. Her petite friend Carol is a monster on the floor, her arms like propellers, her footwork like a boxer's. Sweaty, dirty, bloody and bruised, she keeps "dancing." She is jerked out momentarily when a cut on her nose bleeds onto her shirt, then is back in the middle a few moments later, a Mickey Mouse Band-Aid on her wound. One boy leaves with what appears to be a broken nose. Boys and girls, faces frozen in furious grimaces, circle about, shoving, jabbing, hurling themselves against one another, their hair damp and matted. In this rolling sea of flesh, occasionally someone gets pushed to the floor and stomped on. Alert fellow dancers or one of the brave wide-eyed adult chaperones . . . will dart in and scoop up the victim. One very preppie honor student . . . looks like she wandered into the wrong dance. But looks are deceiving. She goes in and within moments her sleeve is torn as she whips around slamming into people until she disappears, having slipped and fallen. She emerges from underfoot tearfully, with the help of a chaperone. Her friends rush to comfort her, and a few minutes later she goes back into the fray. . . . When the music stops the vicious looks fade, the kids put happy faces back on, and everyone hugs.[1]

The Pit—the "mosh pit" to the uninitiated, the floor space bordering center stage at any rock concert—contains one of millennial adolescents' weirdest rituals. "Like the era it reflects," Hersch observes, "[moshing] has no synchronicity, no steps, just action, sensation, and physicality."[2] Rock diva Alanis Morissette recently stopped a concert midsong to advise overly enthusiastic fans in the pit: "Instead of hitting each other, jump up and down, like this."[3] Unspoken rules of touch don't apply here. Boundaries—psychological and physical—fade away. In the adrenaline rush, endorphins surge and stress dissolves.

Moshing fails to register even the slightest comprehension among those of us born on the far end of the 1960s. In the 1990s, however, teenagers turn to moshing for many of the same reasons adults attend worship: the chance "to be close to people"; for an intense if temporary bond to others who subscribe to the same practices; for the promise of being moved ("It's a rush, literally," one of my students explained); for the transporting experience of being part of something bigger than they are.[4] Youth who mosh do not deny that pain accompanies it—on the contrary, hard contact is intentional—but they insist that getting hurt is beside the point. One student told me, "The point is that you're not in control. Moshing gives you a safe place to get primal." Another noted: "Even if you get hurt, at least you feel like something *happened*."

Something *happened*. Compare that to the overwhelming adolescent critique of Sunday morning in American mainline congregations, namely, that *nothing* happens. Church, as it turns out, is about the last place we expect anything to "happen," including the presence of God. George Barna's research reveals that more than a third (34 percent) of church going adults say they have "never" experienced God's presence in worship.[5] In 1962, cognitive psychologists David and Sally Elkind asked young adolescents where they were most likely to experience God. The most common response was "in a church or synagogue."[6] By 1999, however, only one in seven adolescents believed that participating in a church, synagogue, or other religious group was necessary to being "religious."[7]

American adolescents (like many adults) go to church to feel moved, to feel changed, to feel God, to feel *something*. Theologically, of course this is a misguided instinct. Worship is for the benefit of God, not primarily for the benefit of teenagers. After all, hunger for visceral personal experience also causes adolescents to drive too fast, to have sex too early, to go to *Star Wars* movies. Faith gets confused with feeling all the time. As George Lucas told Bill Moyers in a recent *Time* interview, Luke Skywalker, the *Star Wars* protagonist, must learn "not to rely on pure logic, not to rely on the computers, but to rely on faith. That is what that 'Use the Force' is, a leap of faith. There are mysteries and powers larger than we are, and you have to trust your feelings in order to access them."[8]

If Christian worship is construed as "meaningful human action oriented toward the divine, celebrated communally and in public,"[9] then "feeling" has little to do with it. Modern Christians have tended to interpret "meaning" in terms of rational discourse. Despite the fact that humans also construct meaning intuitively and emotionally, and communicate this meaning through story, symbol, and ritual as well as by discursive means, for most of the twentieth century mainline Protestant worship has aimed for rational eloquence, punctuating it with a few well-placed, lyrically sensible hymns. As a result, by the late-twentieth century, mainline Protestant youth seeking self-transcendence, ecstatic release, and direct access to the sacred overwhelmingly—left. Viscerally, moshing just made more sense.

Affect Matters

When worship addresses the cultural context of adolescence, feelings matter. This is a generation in touch with its sensitive side. Churches can no longer acknowledge the affective needs of adolescents only on "Youth Sunday." According to one estimate, the U.S. teen population will rise in the next decade from 29 to 36 million. "In other words," observed *Rolling Stone* (no stranger to teen marketing), "resistance is futile. Teenagers are driving our culture—and they won't be giving the keys back anytime soon."[10]

Embracing affect in worship has little to do—very little—with naked emotionalism. Let me be clear: I am not making a case for turning worship into an emotional mosh pit of whirling sensation. Nor am I advocating tearful televangelism or even "celebration services," narrowly defined. Contemporary youth recognize emotional manipulation even when they play into it; this, after all, is the first generation raised on cable TV and omnipresent advertising, where emotional excess has made them wary consumers of advertising even while making them lavish consumers of everything else.[11] Affect simply acknowledges the subjective side of God's gift of faith, the "religious affections," variously named, important in the theology of Martin Luther, Jonathan Edwards, John and Charles Wesley, and others for whom religious experience (despite charges to the contrary) had less to do with outward "enthusiasm" than with an inward conviction of love toward God and neighbor.[12]

Postmodern adolescents raised in a global culture want to experience their religion. To them, worship is a verb. "To worship" is to invoke God's immediacy—God's awesome "nowness" in which divine presence is subjectively apprehended. Although worship's primary purpose is doxological, worshiping also marks us objectively as people to whom something subjective has *happened:* the inward conviction of faith, the subjective knowledge that Christ loves us enough to die for us. In the practices of worship, Jesus reveals his mystery as often as his message, and invites us—by playful, ecstatic, and sacramental means—into the passionate love of God.

By emphasizing God's immediacy, contemporary adolescents call the mainline church to reclaim subjective aspects of faith undervalued by modernity. Practices of play, ecstasy, and sacrament acknowledge the subjective experience of God alongside more discursive forms of prayer, praise, and proclamation. Adolescent worship cannot be reduced to the "Jesus is my buddy" theology often ascribed to youth ministry (which ignores the fact that God's immediacy comes in majesty and mystery as often as in interpersonal identification). For youth, traditional elements of worship—the order of service, the presence of Scripture, prayer, proclamation, musical intercession, and so on—serve as scaffolding for existential experience, sacred "dots" to be connected by leaps of faith invited by God's playfulness, affection, and grace.

The God Who "Happens": Adolescents' Hunger for Immediacy

For three centuries American youth have tried to rescue mainstream Christianity from intellectual aridity through the divine immediacy available in nondiscursive practices of worship. The First and Second Great Awakenings, the Pentecostal turn of the twentieth century, the charismatic renewal of the 1960s—all of these began as youth movements, primarily guided by and aimed at young people whose futures seemed uncertain in light of swift cultural change.[13] Some historians claim that religious renewal is the predictable companion of cultural upheaval, as religious institutions become vehicles through which culture reinvents its master-narratives. Not surprisingly, then, the seismic cultural shifts accompanying global postmodernity have yielded intense interest in adolescent "spirituality."[14]

Contemporary youth worship movements can be viewed as direct descendants of these renewal movements. The Christian rock concert, the Christian "Woodstock" experience (e.g., "Creation," "TomFest," "Agape," and "Ichthus" festivals), and the "youth worship" movement (teen services that either evolve into separate intergenerational congregations or function as generationally specific congregations within a large body) have been linked to the eighteenth-century camp meetings as well as to the revivals of the Second Great Awakening.[15] Contemporary forms of adolescent worship, like their forebears, tend to be dismissed by parent congregations, only to be embraced a generation later as "mainstream" expressions of faith. Choruses banished from traditional worship as "camp songs" in 1970, for instance, have gained legitimacy as "worship music," as "contemporary" services in the 1990s became willing to baptize rock and roll in the sanctuary.[16] A case in point: A few weeks ago our congregation's contemporary praise band planned to teach a chorus of Micah 6:8, a song I learned at a youth conference years ago. When it was omitted from the service, I asked why. "It wasn't appropriate," our pastor told me. "That's really a camp song." My husband and I found it hilarious to open the bulletin for the traditional service that same morning and see "Pass It On" (now in the *United Methodist Hymnal*) listed as the closing "hymn."

Like all worship, worship in an adolescent context must operate within the culture's primary idioms. The idiom of adolescents shaped by global postmodernity is immediacy. Today, fifty years after "the adolescent society" was first observed by sociologists, youth culture and popular culture in the United States have become virtually synonymous. Postmodernity increasingly views adolescence as a life*style* rather than a life *stage*, a choice available to adults as well as to youth. In a universalized youth culture, everyone, from toddlers to middle-aged adults, wants to be a teenager, forcing youth to turn to "alternative" cultures for self-definition.

Compounding the problem of self-definition for teenagers is global consumerism, which calls every imaginable boundary into question with worldwide commercial, communication, and transportation systems eradicating a need for "place," issues of location become insignificant. Teenagers wear jeans made abroad, eat dim sum with Diet Coke, chat online with friends whom they have never met, drive to noncustodial parents' homes on weekends. For adolescents raised in a global culture, mobility and placelessness are ways of life, with jarring effects on religion. Adolescents shun the symbolic territoriality of denominations and institutional religion in favor of "portable" spiritual practices.[17] Contemporary youth, whom sociologist Wade Clark Roof describes as a generation of "questers," view life as a spiritual journey that may or may not lead somewhere. Locale is unimportant, but the journey matters enormously.[18]

Without physical geography to mark their pilgrimages, adolescents use emotional terrain as a source of spiritual landmarks. Adolescents employ distance as a primary metaphor for understanding God, but translate it to an emotion (I "feel" *close* to God). Claiming a near and intimate God—a God you can feel *close* to—risks conflating the Other with the self ("God is me": meaning, "We are *really* close"). This, of course, is the appeal of many New Age movements: becoming God ourselves suggests our ultimate emotional identification with God.

Immediacy, as it turns out, is not just an issue of popular culture. The word *now* appears in Scripture 190 times, and it is usually ascribed to God. The word *wait* appears in Scripture 74 times, and it is usually ascribed to a man or a woman. God acts now; human beings wait—but not very well. The lack of immediacy in much mainline worship has alienated countless young people, for whom emotional terrain is primary. For youth raised in global postmodernity, God does not merely exist; God "happens." Truth is an event.[19] Even more than the personalized gospel common to much evangelical spirituality, the acid test of meaningful worship for adolescents is objective evidence of inward "contact" between human and divine. Whether invoked through ancient liturgies (recast, for instance, in contemplative prayer or Taizé chants), through Christian youth "raves" that address youth's appetite for electronic stimulation, or through a traditional Eucharist, worship praises the God who "happens," and who chooses to be "God with us" in perceptible but subjective ways.

How to Worship like a Teenager

Worship in the cultural context of adolescence calls for alternative metaphors besides time and distance to describe the religious affections. The God of Jesus Christ cannot be reduced to the categories of global postmodernity. Christians worship a God of paradoxes: in Jesus Christ, God is at once near and far, now and forever, immanent and transcendent, revealed and hidden, active and still, dead and resurrected. The rituals of adolescence—like Christian worship throughout the centuries—dramatize paradox rather than give in to reductionist interpretations. Adolescence is at once exhilarating and painful; hence, rituals like moshing. To omit either the thrill or the anguish would make the ritual untrue. Dramatization is immediate; by practicing the paradoxical love of God, we not only communicate the meaning of the Christ-event more faithfully, we somehow gain access to it. Practices of worship invite God to "happen" to us again and again. They bring every divine paradox into full view by reenacting the life, death, and resurrection of Jesus Christ in imperfect, partial, but authentic ways.

Practicing Transcendence: Worshiping the Playful God

Liturgy means "the work of the people." Unfortunately, we have interpreted this work as the opposite of play. Most of us learned early on that playing in worship is off-limits (as is playing on Sundays generally, in some strict Christian sects). Besides distracting the folks in the pew behind us, playing risks trivializing what we have come to celebrate in worship in the first place: the life, death, and resurrection of Jesus Christ, undertaken on our behalf. Church nurseries—a telling development in twentieth-century liturgical life—were conceived so playing children could be extracted from worship until they reached the age of reason. Once they could apprehend the significance of the Christ event, they became "old enough" to know *not* to play in church, and were permitted to "worship."

The irony, of course, is that worship constitutes one of the oldest forms of play known to human society. Human beings have always engaged in "sacred games" that dramatize the values of their cultic communities.[20] Play points to a larger reality, a "true order" of things intuited but not fully grasped intellectually.[21] Children practice relationships and enact their culture's role expectations by playing house, school, doctor. Americans love football in part because it dramatizes basic (if flawed) assumptions about competitive American culture: success belongs, not to stature or birthright, but to practice, strategy, a willingness to tackle your opponents, and, above all, the ability to get up and keep going after they have tackled you.

The act of playing has a "back and forth" quality to it; it is always relational, always involves an "other"—an imaginative object, a playmate, a conversation partner, a community. Play's reward comes from the deep satisfaction of losing ourselves in the play, the moment of self-abandonment in which the reality we glimpse but cannot grasp somehow grasps us. In this surrender, "something happens" indeed: the self is re-created, infused with intrinsic worth and meaning as we give ourselves over to an Other—an Other that has already given itself over to us.

When youth call us to worship playfully, they remind us that worship makes "hard contact" with God's transcendence in acts of real participation in the life, death, and resurrection of Jesus Christ. In worship, God condescends to play with us, accepting our participation as we are, but at the same time engages us in a larger vision of who we could be. The developmental task of identity formation requires transcendence: we all choose our gods during adolescence—our "ideologies," as developmental psychologist Erik H. Erikson called them, systems of meaning by which the world makes sense.[22] After several false tries, we soon discover that not just any ideology will do; the object of our conversion matters. Only a transcendent God, one who sheds light on our selves from a point beyond the self, can both affirm who we are and invite us into something more.

Adolescents insist on playful worship—worship that is interactive, relational, self-forgetting, and which invites our participation in an expanded vision of reality. Playful worship is not synonymous with trivial, lighthearted, or even exciting worship; youth have their fill of frivolity elsewhere, and the church neither can nor should out-entertain the entertainment industry. What congregations can do, and what true worship does do, is invite youth's full participation instead of their passive assent in the practices of worship. The relational nature of play is critical to adolescents, whose developing sense of self requires the confirmation of others. The existential surrender associated with play engenders the kind of authenticity that adolescents prize, for when we play, our defenses melt. The active give-and-take, relational nature of play is inherent in prayer, praise, proclamation, sacrifice, sacrament, almsgiving—vehicles God "hot-wires" to enter our world again and again as the life, death, and resurrection of Jesus Christ reverberate in the "now."

Practicing Self-Abandonment: Worshiping the Ecstatic God

Closely related to practices of play are practices of ecstasy. If God uses practices of play to condescend to us and "meet us where we are," God employs practices of ecstasy to transport us into a state of being in which we glimpse ourselves and others, however briefly, as new creations in Jesus Christ. True ecstatic ritual seeks an altered state of consciousness, in which the worshiper experiences something extraordinary, something different, something to be identified with the divine reality.[23] These experiences are short-lived, but profoundly liberating. Practices of ecstasy issue in a range of affective experiences, from a pleasant sense of release to trances and glossolalia. They free us to fall into the embrace of the Divine Lover, whose ecstatic love for us overflows into all creation.

Like cautious parents overseeing their child's first serious crush, mainline Protestants historically have viewed ecstatic worship askance. Ecstatic ritual, according to anthropological research, "is often practiced by the lowly and the oppressed for whom participation produces a temporary respite from the pressures of life. People whose lives are given little structure because they have been denied participation in well-defined, socially acknowledged roles seem to be especially prone to experiences of trance and possession."[24] Given the marginalized role youth assume in American culture, their interest in ecstatic ritual is hardly surprising.

But adolescents are drawn to ecstatic experience for developmental reasons as well as sociological ones. In his theory of adolescent identity formation, Erikson observed what he called the adolescent craving for "locomotion."[25] Locomotion is both a physical and an existential need of adolescents, whose primary criterion for excellence is "Did it move me?" Adolescents evaluate every experience according to the heights and the depths, the ecstasy or the anguish, it inspires. With the onset of formal operational thought, or the newfound cognitive capacity for abstract thinking, adolescents can think reflectively, express themselves extravagantly, and experience both wonder and dread in new, expansive ways. Teenagers look for a "high," quite simply, because for the first time they are cognitively capable of it.[26]

Theoretically, at least, worship offers a form of locomotion. Worship "moves" us, physically and existentially, toward the awesome nearness of God as well as to a profound sense of belonging to a larger whole: the body of Christ. Practicing abandonment means relinquishing control to God, who transports us into a new reality. In many traditions, expressive worship provides catharsis for worshipers in the same way mosh pits offer adolescents a safe space to "get primal." In some Pentecostal churches—where membership among the young is on the rise—practices of self-abandonment include glossolalia, being "slain in the Spirit," and "quaking" (a form of dance permitted because feet do not leave the floor). On the other end of the liturgical spectrum, young adults converting to Eastern Orthodoxy (also increasing in numbers) report a similar appreciation for ecstatic ritual, facilitated by a liturgy that assaults the senses with visual, aural, aromatic, gustatory, and tactile experience making worship almost trancelike.

By far the most common form of ecstatic ritual among adolescents (and probably the most valued) is music. Whether worshiping through music involves singing, dancing, or even moshing (yes, Christian concerts have mosh pits too), adolescents insist that worshiping involve opportunities to lose themselves in song. The "universal language" of music is often cited as a boundary-breaking medium, another example of the borderless nature of global culture. The explosion of the Christian contemporary music industry since the 1970s suggests an important place for explicitly religious music, but since music is a purely subjective medium, lyrics often play a secondary role to a song's beat, tone, or "texture" in determining a song's sacred significance for teenagers. As a result, youth frequently find secular music as worshipful as Christian music, ancient chants as moving as hip-hop, as they seek a language of praise that transcends verbal discourse.

Practicing Passion: Worshiping the Suffering God

Despite our truncated use of the term to describe the trials of Jesus during Holy Week, passion does not validate divine suffering, but rather underscores divine love—a love so profound it willingly suffers on behalf of the beloved. Nobody wants to be passionately in love more than a teenager. "The single desire that dominated my search for delight," Augustine wrote of his own adolescence, "was simply to love and be loved."[27] The sign of true love, as any die-hard *Titanic* fan will tell you, is love that is worth dying for. For adolescents, the authenticity of Jesus is told on the cross. He suffered for his beloved; ergo, his love was true.

Erikson called this search for "fidelity"—the strength of having something "to die for"—the most passionate striving of adolescence. In general, mainline Christianity (like mainstream American culture) expects fidelity of young people, but only reluctantly challenges them with investments worthy of the "little deaths" of self-denial. At the same time, we ignore the fact that contemporary youth are intimately acquainted with suffering. Widespread cultural denial of lifestyle-inflicted wounds caused by poverty, divorce, violence, and hopelessness only magnifies their senselessness. The deluge of data dumped on adolescents by the information age has analyzed their pain but not eradicated it. Technology has enabled them to process information quickly, but has failed to offer hope. At root, suffering is a mystery. But unlike most adults, who tend to view mystery as a source of fear, contemporary adolescents view mystery as a source of possibility. "The truth is out there," proclaims Fox TV's *The X-Files*, an affirmation of faith celebrated by millions of youthful viewers every week. Mystery—despite its undeniable discomfort—is good.

The suffering God is a mystery. Despite the advice of church growth experts to remove crosses from sanctuaries ("seekers" might be offended), the cross stands at the center of adolescent worship, which addresses a quintessential "seeker" crowd. The cross is not rational. The suffering of Jesus cannot be made logical, domesticated, or explained away. It is a mystery—and because it is a mystery, it contains the seeds of hope and redemption. As "Generation X" theologian Tom Beaudoin observes, images of a suffering Jesus have a personal meaning for this generation that these images don't have for their elders.[28]

The passion of Christ, a doctrine much overlooked by twentieth-century mainline Christianity, stands to be reclaimed for worship with adolescents in global postmodernity. While mainstream theologies since Scholasticism have favored the rational methods acceptable to the modern university, passion never lost its subjective foothold in the practices of popular piety or popular culture. Even today, a quick read through the lyrics of mainline Protestant hymnals reveals enough "blood" theology and passionate verbiage to make most of us look twice. At the same time, atonement imagery figures prominently in popular music, video channels, and movies. The point is not that adolescents want to suffer; the point is that they want desperately to love something worthy of suffering, and to be so loved.

Like all philosophical reactions, the "postmodern" swing back toward the gut overshoots its mark, leaving in its wake New Age theologies, angel lore, and a deification of personal experience that no careful reading of Christian theology can fully sanction. On the other hand, as Walter Brueggemann has demonstrated, the biblical tradition "consistently claims that the impossibilities of *passion* will eventually prevail over the more disciplined *perspective* [of reason]."[29] Christians have thus always approached passion with two minds. On the one hand, passion is linked with "natural" impulses that place us in conflict with God and other human beings and therefore must be curbed. At the same time, passion is an attribute of God, whose love is capable of both boundless delight and unspeakable suffering, and therefore provides our own human experience with a means for self-transcendence.[30]

Worship that hopes to address the cultural context of adolescence must take into account the immediacy of the cross as a sign of God's fidelity and passion for us. Rather than recoiling from divine mystery, adolescents embrace it, especially in sacramental acts that embody the mystery of Jesus' suffering love. Sacraments invoke God's immediacy in mysterious, direct, and brazen ways. In the experience of the Eucharist, for example, "The distance between the human and the divine disappears."[31] God's unfailing promise to meet us in sacramental practice transforms these ordinary means of grace into extraordinary vessels of hope, offering the immediate possibility of divine-human contact. In these sacramental practices adolescents receive the grace necessary for the otherwise impossible task of fidelity, the strength of love that is "to die for."

Moshing to Zion

It is too simple to reduce worship in the cultural context of adolescence to marketing. What will appeal to the youth? How will we get them to come? What should we avoid so they won't leave once they get there? Hundreds of resources are produced each year to answer such questions, all of them obsolete within a week. Frankly, media-saturated, information-overloaded, advertising-savvy adolescents don't really care what we do to attract them, or how we do it. They care that, when they worship, God is present, and that something "happens" because God is there.

Experiencing God's immediacy, therefore, is crucial for adolescent worship, regardless of the form worship takes. Despite impressive statistics suggesting otherwise, God's presence during worship—even bad worship—is never in question. Our ability to perceive God's presence, however, is seriously in question. Adolescent worship is no mere tip of the hat toward "the church of tomorrow." Adolescent worship offers the mainline church a chance to tune up our divine perceptual skills, clean our God-lenses, sharpen our spiritual hearing, in order to apprehend the God who is with us in spite of ourselves. After several centuries of estrangement, reacquainting ourselves with "religious affections" in worship represents an important beginning. Practices of play, ecstasy, and sacrament represent God-initiated forms of divine-human encounter, but they also guarantee that "something happens" during worship: we apprehend God's immediacy—if not at the altar, then in the mosh pit, where the subjective experiences of transcendence, abandonment, and mystery are the name of the game.

9

Amplified Versions

Worship Wars Come Down to Music and a Power Plug

Andy Crouch

A seasoned worship leader, Andy Crouch questions what it means to participate in so-called contemporary worship and then explains in a second article how he learned to appreciate contemporary worship for its simple aesthetic.

If I could nominate one phrase to be left in the dust of the twentieth century, it would be the one that launched a thousand committee meetings: *contemporary worship*. The truth is that any worship practiced by contemporary people, no matter how ancient its form, is contemporary. And any worship, no matter how simple its structure, draws on tradition, such as the American tradition of prayer-and-song services that goes back to the revivals of the early-nineteenth century.

No, the real distinction between "contemporary" and "traditional" worship comes down to music and a power plug. The genres of music that we now call "contemporary" are dependent on amplification for their very existence. Neither bone-crushing electric guitar solos nor intimately breathy love songs could exist without electrically powered support systems. While Pavarotti sometimes uses a discreet microphone, and pop stars sometimes go "unplugged," the essence of contemporary music is electric.

A vocal minority of North American Christians is fiercely opposed to amplified music in worship. I am not one of them, even as a musician trained in the Western classical tradition. After all, I studied Latin and Greek in college, too, but they are not my native language. Amplified music is the mother tongue of our day, and I'm never quite as at home as when I'm immersed in its cornucopia of rhythmic and melodic delights. And if amplified worship conjures up painful memories of amateur, three-chord guitarists banging out repetitive choruses, unamplified worship has caused plenty of pain itself. Shaky amateur choirs, repetitive anthems, musically numb organists—need I go on?

The truth is that amplified worship's most celebrated practitioners bring an astonishing level of excellence to their electric guitars and 28-piece drum sets. They are even reintroducing the art of improvisation to worship at a level that hasn't been heard for centuries—in white churches, anyway. At its best, amplified music is to sound what a cathedral is to stone: an expression of the timeless longing to build something greater than ourselves, pointing to Someone greater still.

But I am troubled by many amplified worship services. Next time you're in one of these settings, watch and listen to the congregation. Get ready for the sound of silence. If the sheer volume of amplified worship is like a sonic cathedral, it can also trump the most forbidding medieval liturgy in its capacity to stun churchgoers into a passive stupor.

Cynics compare these services to rock concerts, but rock concert audiences participate with a fervor that would put most congregations to shame. They dance with abandon, they scream, they hold up lighters, they even bring offerings—homemade signs, flowers, undergarments. In the face of amplified worship, most congregations don't do much more than clap, close their eyes, and sway a little. Especially among self-styled "postmodern" churches, which like to turn down the lights and turn up the sound, two-thirds of the people could keel over and the band would play on. When you can't hear yourself singing, why even try?

Singing used to flourish in Protestant churches for a theological reason. Protestants believed and taught the priesthood of all believers. But today we are witnessing the rise of a new priesthood—the ones with the (literal) power. Armed with microphones and amps, gleaming in the multi-hued brilliance of spotlights, the amplified people do for us what we cannot do for ourselves: make music, offer prayers, approach the unapproachable.

It's not surprising that many churches have reverted to this pre-Reformation state. Most believers never wanted to be priests. "Meet your Maker" is a euphemism for death; why do we think that people will be eager to do it on Sunday night? Much better to let a priest do the dirty, dangerous work of relating directly to God through sacrifice and prayer. Even singing, that original music that rises from the center of the body, makes us self-conscious. With recorded music so omnipresent and music education so scarce—it was cut from public schools when today's young adults were children—the idea of making one's own music is as foreign to a contemporary American as the idea of a personal relationship with the gods was to a pagan.

To their credit, many of the amplified priests are troubled, as faithful priests have always been, by the lassitude of their people. But what are they to do? When they turn up the volume, when they play more brilliantly, the crowds grow. The crowds, meanwhile, go home satisfied. They have seen a great show. And unlike a rock concert, it didn't cost them a thing.

A Humbling Experience

Contemporary Worship's Simple Aesthetic

Andy Crouch

Okay, first the full disclosure. I spend a good part of my life leading worship through contemporary music in decidedly non-liturgical settings. From InterVarsity's Urbana student mission convention—where since a dramatic transition in 1990 "worship" has run the gamut from gospel to salsa to MTV-style videos to United Methodist charismatic gatherings in cavernous assembly halls with troops of dancers and banner-carriers interpreting the lyrics of pop praise music. I've seen and led a lot of worship that is coming to very few churches near you. And I love it.

On the other hand, on Sunday mornings my wife and I sit, stand, and kneel in the brownstone beauty of St. James's Episcopal Church, where we are led in a weekly Eucharistic liturgy that would make terrible radio and worse television. The sound system is tinny and used only for speaking, never for music. Our multimedia consists of stained glass windows, carved woodwork, organ music, and the elevation of the Host at the Feast. I love that, too.

Reprinted from *re:generation quarterly* 3, no. 1 (Winter 1997): 11–13. © 1997 by Andy Crouch. All rights reserved. Used by permission.

So, when I'm asked to write about the current outpouring of innovation in worship, I confess a certain ambivalence. The truth is that when I'm among the innovators, I'm often pressing for tradition—hymns, silence, a bit of mystery to counteract our media-fed busyness. Among the conservators, though, I'm constantly restraining my impulse to cut loose. A good bass player and some reggae could do wonders for St. James's.

That I have this problem at all is a sign of the revolution that has taken place in North American church life in the last ten years. The contemporary worship movement, spurred by factors from church growth anxiety to seeker sensitivity to a (baby) boom of pastors who had garage bands in their youth, has shaken up the way many of us see worship. While the range of expressions is very broad, contemporary worship has two distinctives: a near-total lack of conventional liturgical forms and an enthusiastic embrace of contemporary culture, especially pop and rock music.

Contemporary worship has enormous appeal to people who thought the church had gotten stuck in 1950. But it has also attracted criticism, including criticism from people who were not even born in 1950. In its pop-culture forms especially they see the "dumbing down" of the Christian faith as churches condescend to, rather than challenge, believers. A lively embrace of tradition seems like a much better option than a sell-out to innovation.

Yet even our most "traditional" worship was contemporary at some point. Not that long ago, the pipe organ was a dubious innovation, tolerated by the early Swiss Calvinists only because it improved the otherwise horrendous singing of untutored congregations. Latin, Greek, and (with some caveats) King James English were at one time simply the common language, no more religiously or aesthetically privileged than are Spanish, Chinese, or English today. Attempts to squelch innovation in worship are about as likely to succeed as the Académie Française's war against "le camping." It is a historical truism that worship, like all aspects of human culture, is constantly developing and innovating as far back as we can see.

At any rate, much of the enthusiasm for "traditional" liturgy and music—among Protestants at least—amounts to little more than social climbing. To illustrate from my own tradition, you can go to nearly any county seat in the country and see a church built around the turn of the century by newly prosperous Methodists. Its architecture, nine times out of ten, is a painstaking imitation of Presbyterian or Episcopalian churches back East. Formal liturgy and classical music, robes and elevated pulpits, periodic sentences and seminary degrees were all ways of asserting a new class identity, leaving behind our vaguely scandalous frontier roots. Such motives may be inevitable, even forgivable, but they're not the stuff of which Christian choices are made.

Not that the purveyors of contemporary worship lack economic motives. Take Hosanna! Integrity—please. This publicly traded company (*nasdaq: itgr*—call your broker!), while providing an outlet for some very creative and committed artists and pastors, has done more than anyone else to turn contemporary worship into a consumer product. With new tapes and CDs coming out every month, Integrity Music embraces Frito-Lay's neat definition of the consumer ethic: "You can't eat just one." Like potato chips, these tasty little morsels go down easy, contain just a hint of nutrition, and leave you hungry for more.

There's also enough priestly mediation in Integrity's products to make a latter-day Luther nail Ninety-Five Theses to their door. On one particularly remarkable tape jacket, we are told that extended instrumental solos featuring world-class studio players "showcase the inspiring worship of these talented musicians." Wow. Who needs a priest when you have Justo Almario? Just put on the headphones and let the leader, band, and audio-air-brushed congregation worship for you.

So what keeps me coming back to—and indeed leading—contemporary worship? This may surprise you, but I have become convinced that my heart needs it. At its best, contemporary worship embraces simplicity and abandons sophistication, takes the ordinary languages of our time (spoken, musical, and visual) and consecrates them—and in so doing models an aesthetic that comes from the heart of the gospel. To persuade you of this, let me introduce some words of Paul from Philippians 4:8:

> Finally, brethren, whatever is true, whatever is honorable, whatever is just, whatever is pure, whatever is pleasing, whatever is commendable, if there is any excellence, if there is anything worthy of praise, think about these things.

This is one of a surprisingly small number of New Testament passages that make explicit contact with Greek philosophical ideas of the true, the good, and the beautiful. Jesus' words in John 8:32 are another: "You will know the truth, and the truth will make you free." Modern readers have been quick to lift these passages from their context and turn them into generalized philosophical encouragements—Philippians 4:8 and John 8:32 grace more than one university shield.

But like John 8:32, Philippians 4:8 is not about truth, beauty, or excellence in general. This sentence comes, rather, at the end of Paul's very specific attempt to redefine the true and the beautiful in light of Christ Jesus, who "did not count equality with God a thing to be grasped, but emptied himself, taking the form of a servant," and humbled himself "even [to] death on a cross" (Phil. 2:6–7 RSV). For Paul, it is this humility that is "worthy of praise." In stark contrast to sublime conceptions of beauty that envision it as a move to something higher, closer to God, Paul sees that "excellence" is found in the move lower, closer to the poor.

And Paul's aesthetic intuitions, subordinated as they are to the gospel, prove themselves in the Christian life. Those of us who have gained some sophistication in European culture need to admit that no one has ever been saved by attending the symphony. No—every Christian who has learned to "discern what is best" has learned this by moving lower, drawing closer to the poor and the poor in spirit.

When I look beyond the middle-class pop that dominates the local Christian bookstore, I remember that the poor have always had contemporary worship—simple songs and culturally relevant visuals that make the elite blush. Spend some time in a storefront church, go to Mexico on El Día de los Muertos, join in the evangelistic crusade of a tree-planting Pentecostal missionary in Africa, and you will encounter truly contemporary worship—intimately, even shockingly, tied to the ordinary present. Whatever is happening in the cathedral, the poor are busy bridging the gap between the impossible transcendence of religion and the nearness of their hopes and fears. Lacking a history or any certain hope for the future, the poor have no choice but to create worship that is contemporary.

It is no accident that the poor have embraced Pentecostalism, that most urgently immediate of Christian traditions. While surely not what the Catholic cardinals of Medellín had in mind when they coined the phrase, Pentecostalism embodies (not just proclaims) "God's preferential option for the poor." The worship and prayer lives of Pentecostals—exuberant, loud, wholehearted—model for the rest of us just how "contemporary" worship can be. Pentecostals experience God's contemporary, immediate presence because, lacking the promises of transcendence offered by economic or cultural achievement, they are willing to become poor in spirit.

God's closeness to the poor and their worship is hinted at in Isaiah 57:15: "I dwell in the high and holy place, *and also* with him who is of a contrite and humble spirit" (RSV). This truth is fully revealed at Christmas, when we celebrate the decisive triumph of contrition and humility—a manger, a teenage mother, a baby—over all the high and holy places—temples, liturgies, and oratorios—ever constructed.

At its best, contemporary worship has this humility that I, neither poor nor Pentecostal, desperately need. When it is performed without pretension, pop music has a simplicity that reflects its sources in European-American folk music and African-American jazz and blues. These musical forms find their roots and authenticity among the poor and suffering. The bare stages of contemporary churches, the edgy guitar sounds, the simple lyrics all say: he is here, he is close. You do not need to dress up for him: he laid aside his own dress, even down to his last piece of clothing, for you. You do not need to learn his language: he has learned your language. You can come to him as a child—indeed, you must.

My more traditional friends lament the fact that the contemporary worship movement is not producing, so far as we know, a J. S. Bach, and they wonder if artistic excellence is being irretrievably lost in the church. But from the perspective of heaven, all of us—from Bach to Salieri to a guitarist banging out those tired old I-vi-IV-V chords like she invented them—are four-year-olds making finger paintings of the sun, the house, and Mommy and Daddy. Does God treasure these pictures for their artistic merit? No—our art is treasured in heaven simply because Abba loves his children. Should we not, then, strive for artistic excellence? Of course we should—watch a four-year-old draw and you will see single-mindedness and attention that adult artists take up Zen to recapture. It's just that our best artistry is more suited for the heavenly refrigerator than the Trinity's ballroom. It's child's play. And that's just as it should be.

The great advantage the poor have, with their "contemporary" worship, is that they understand this: the only way to the high and holy place, for us, is through contrition and humility. As I have learned from the worship of those who are not privileged, and as I have sought to draw that worship into my own life and the life of the well-educated congregations I serve, I have discovered a beauty that transcends even the subtle excellence of jazz chording, the blues form, or Latin polyrhythms. The beauty there is the beauty of the servant Jesus, my Lord and my example.

Ultimately, the most pressing questions in worship are not about liturgical or musical style, but matters of the heart. How thoroughly has the gospel shaped us? How much have we identified, not with the highest aspirations of humankind but with our humblest beginnings and our saddest endings? Are we, in the words of Isaac Watts's ever-contemporary hymn, "like a child at home" in the presence of God? If these questions reveal in you, as they do in me, a heart of wealth, self-sufficiency, and grown-up unfaith, I offer a possible cure for the soul. Relax your grip on sophistication. Take up the fingerpaints and—with all the skill and abandon you can muster—draw the house, the sun, the family. Through such small things we may come to know an excellence that is at once smaller and greater than any other—the holy love of God.

10

New Approaches to Worship

Mike Riddell, Mark Pierson, Cathy Kirkpatrick

*Writing from within the global alt.worship movement, this
team of authors examines closely the relationship between
popular culture and corporate worship and suggests a new
paradigm for worship leadership.*

Worship as Art

The entrance to the art gallery had become a dressing room. My daughter
and I were each fitted with a clear plastic body suit (stapled to fit around
our contours), plastic bags were tied over our shoes, surgeon's rubber
gloves put on our hands, and the outfit topped off with a white hardhat
with full clear visor. Looking like we were ready for a DIY [do-it-yourself]

Originally published in a slightly different form in *The Prodigal Project: Journey into the
Emerging Church* (London: Society for Promoting Christian Knowledge, 2000), 61–81.
© 2000 by Mike Riddell, Mark Pierson, Cathy Kirkpatrick. Reprinted with changes by
permission of the publisher.

tour of Chernobyl, we were ushered through a décor of hanging plastic strips into a huge white space. Floor of white polyethylene. Wall and ceiling painted white. Large floor-to-ceiling flexible mirrors along the walls distorted our movements.

A dozen or so big circular children's paddling pools were spread around the space. Each of the pools had a fountain—spurting paint. The pools were each filled with a different colored paint. Occasionally paint sprayed down at random intervals from shower heads hidden in the ceiling. The space and audience were splattered in paint! It was confusing—not what I expected in an art gallery—and wonderful—we were part of the installation. Participants, not just spectators.

I have no idea now what the installation was meant to be about. I don't think I did back then! Something about "forcing a confrontation between audience anticipation and participation," according to the gallery notes. All I could think about as we slipped around the paint-splashed floor between the fountains and pools, and stood under paint drips and sprays in our child's-play version of space suits, was: "Wouldn't it be great if we could do worship in a setting like this!" Active participation with open-ended interpretation. Room to move physically and cognitively. Creative context and content. Andy Warhol goes to church! If I could find some way of providing this kind of context and setting for theologically sound Christian worship, then maybe I'd have something that my old school friends could relate to. Maybe even a setting in which they could begin to understand something of how the gospel might be good news for them. Another journey of discovery had begun for me . . . .

Church too easily becomes a place where you cannot be yourself; worship an activity that is imposed on you with a set response expected regardless of how you feel or what's been happening in the previous days. Worship always communicates. The problem is that much of what is communicated isn't helpful . . . .

I began thinking about the possibilities of art as worship, and more significantly, of worship as an art. In particular of worship preparation as an art. What would happen to the worship I prepared if I looked at it differently? What if I saw the task not as a mechanical, logical, modernist one of putting stuff in the right order so that it "progressed" through a form to give a predetermined message with an anticipated outcome, but instead saw myself more like a curator of an art gallery? A curator who considers the space and environment as well as the content of worship and who takes these elements and puts them in a particular arrangement, considering juxtaposition, style, distance, light, shade, and so on. A maker of a context for worship rather than a presenter of content. A provider of a frame inside which the elements are arranged and rearranged to convey a particular message for a particular purpose.

A message that may or may not be overtly obvious, may or may not be similar to the message perceived by another worshiper.

So instead of Worship Leader, or Worship Planner, I become an artist, a framer, a reframer, a recontextor, a curator of worship. I provide contexts, experiences for others to participate in. . . .

What Is Worship?

Worship preparation is *primarily* about providing a *context* rather than a *content*. The context being an environment in which heart, soul, mind, and strength have opportunity to respond to God. This is not to deny content (although the gospel *is* primarily about a relationship rather than propositions), but to emphasize that the content can be understood in a variety of ways according to the context it's placed in. As an example, the reenactment of Jesus' last meal with his disciples could emphasize forgiveness, community transformation, relationship, or salvation, depending on the context it is presented in. Worship has generally majored on content, with little or no appreciation of what the context is doing to that content. For example, what does it mean to talk about loving one another in a building where we sit and look at the back of each other's heads, or to listen to teaching on the priesthood of all believers and "body ministry" when the service is led entirely from the front by elderly white males?

If the worship producer sees herself as a curator or artist, then context becomes very important. The curator of an art or museum exhibition will arrange the elements of the exhibition in a carefully thought-through context, designing for a particular effect or response, and aware that juxtaposition, distance, light, shade, color, texture, proximity, background, temperature, space, interaction, and words will all affect how people respond. So the worship curator needs to consider all these elements of context (and more) in preparing worship for others. She is providing a frame for the existing elements, a frame that conveys a particular message; a message beyond that of the individual elements. This provides a boundary within which a certain worship content or experience is provided. The same elements arranged in a different way would provide a different context and be capable of conveying a different message.

This is the scary part. Any context always allows for a variety of interpretations. Worship leaders have known this but not talked about it, and worshipers who leave the service without being able to remember the three points of the sermon have often been left feeling inadequate or "out of touch with God" because they were unmoved by the specific content. They didn't "get the point." By contrast the worship curator encourages a variety of interpretations and outcomes from the worship event. As the context of worship allows for and encourages an open-endedness—the main outcome is that worshipers have met with God in some way—a variety of outcomes is not only acceptable, it is desirable. The purpose of the curator is to enable people to respond to God with all their being, and the huge range in people types, personal experiences, time on the journey of faith, learning styles, faith stages, and so on, needs not only to be allowed for, but catered for.

As an artist would encourage a variety of interpretations of her art (each equally valid), so the worship curator will encourage a variety of responses to God. In worship this is more important than ensuring a specific content is conveyed. The content is a platform, a starting point that gains meaning and relevance, and perhaps even value, when it is given a context in worship. In my view, worship is not primarily content that we accept or reject, neither is it something that is done to us or imposed on us, or even provided for us, but rather it is a context in which we interact with God in whatever ways are appropriate for us at the time. The alternative can easily be a content-laden, directed, linear, and narrow approach to worship that generally appeals to a select group who can understand it and interpret it. It becomes like "high art"—accessible only to those with the right education and training who can "understand" what it's about.

A Risky Business

This raises questions about whether all interpretations have equal validity, and if it is possible for an interpretation to be wrong; for worshipers to misread the worship. Perhaps this is where the analogy of worship as art begins to break down. It's unlikely that misunderstanding the artist's intention with a piece of art will be of any great consequence, but the same outcome in a worship setting may mean that historic Christian faith is misrepresented. The quick response to this challenge would be, "Well what's so different to what goes on in churches every Sunday now," but that's hardly satisfactory. I think the main safeguard must be that our worship needs to be based around the biblical tradition. These stories of God's involvement with people through history and in particular of Jesus' dealings with people, are the core of Christian faith, and if we use them as the core of our worship we shouldn't wander too far from the center (providing we are resisting the temptation to "explain" too often what the stories mean rather than letting them speak for themselves).

Also important here is the integrity of the worship curator. She must have the skills, understandings, insights, and trust required to bring parable and punter[1] together in an appropriate as well as a meaningful way. Beyond that it is a matter of trusting each other, of depending on the Spirit to lead us into truth, and the consistent-over-time retelling of the stories of Jesus to shape us. In practice the worship we provide will rarely be as open-ended and non-directive as I may have implied. As soon as the first Scripture passage is read or appears on a screen, guidance is being given and a way of interpreting the context suggested. Perhaps someone needs to formulate a "hermeneutic of context"; a reflection on the way in which the worship environment influences the interpretation of what is happening.

If you think that adopting the model of worship producer as artist/curator is an easy way out, think again! If our goal is to work with people to provide contexts in which we can worship God (or maybe the best we can hope for is a context in which people *may* worship God?), then we will need to be able to do much more than just shuffle songs and link them by key. We'll need a deep understanding of who's at worship—who our community is, what's going on for them individually and corporately this week. We'll need to understand something of the breadth and depth of Christian history and of the various traditions of worship. We'll need to know about the power of symbols and ritual and be able to use both wisely. The need to know the stories of Jesus and of God's dealings with people through history is greater, not less. More skills and understanding are required than previously, not less . . . .

Approaching worship preparation as an art is risky. There is the risk of failure, of being misunderstood, of being labeled "trendy" or "new age," or "not Christian," or "lacking in content." If you've read this far you're probably already familiar with that territory. There's also the risk that you and your friends might end up with worship that enables you to encounter God in a way you haven't for a very long time. As I said, it's a risky venture, worship. . . .

Getting It Together

When it comes to getting together to "do worship" in a new way, whether it be with a few friends, or a sizeable group, there are some important concepts to keep in mind if you want to avoid becoming that which you have moved away from. One of the most significant characteristics of the emerging culture is the desire for hands-on participation, at all levels. Not the kind of youth service participation where the youth leader puts the service together and then invites participants to do one of the bits he or she has prepared, but rather participation and ownership of the worship event because it is "our" worship. I believe that worship should be firmly rooted in the lifestyles, hopes, dreams, music, rituals, fears, and aspirations of the people who are worshiping. It should reflect who they are. As Cathy noted in this book, the moment we try to "do worship" for a mythical third person who may walk in off the street at any moment, we have lost the plot and are doomed to enduring mediocre worship that satisfies no one. Participation and involvement are first principles. This doesn't mean that everyone has to agree on every aspect of every service. It does mean that generally the worship relates to the subculture of those who are worshiping, and that at least from time to time everyone involved is able to make specific connection at depth. . . .

Worship must be culturally relevant. This participation is what gives worship authenticity and builds community. It makes worship accessible by rejecting the cultural accretions the gospel has picked up over time and allowing the heart of the gospel to connect with the reality of life for the worshipers.

> The first thing to realize is that worship is not a means to evangelism. It is not something Christians do in order that some good, however it is defined, will happen to other people. Worship is our way to God and at the same time our celebration of the love of God. The key to authentic worship is the presence of authentic worshippers. They transform the most routine liturgies into encounters with the love and glory of God. So our question is not how to make worship more appealing to people outside of the churches in order to attract them to our midst. The question is how Christians worship together authentically. If we do, we can be assured that our partners and friends may also experience God in some way in and through our service of worship.[2]

Writing about the American church Sally Morgenthaler agrees, "our failure to impact contemporary culture (with the gospel) is not because we have not been relevant enough, but because we have not been real enough."[3] Perhaps you've experienced that for yourself.

A commitment to real participation also means that the worship will not be led by a single figurehead, either in preparation or in production. Leadership moves around the group and the space. The "front" may be as difficult to determine as the leader.

Everything is considered for possible use in new worship. Nothing is too old or too new, too traditional or too postmodern, too secular or too sacred to be considered for the mix. The only elements rejected will be those that don't achieve the ultimate goals of bringing together experience and understanding; materials and methods that promote a body/mind/soul split; themes that aren't aware of our relationship to the earth, and those exclusive in language of acceptance.

There may be little obvious logical progression to the worship. Multimedia images may be juxtaposed with ancient chants and techno music. Or even concurrent with them. The worship arises from within a local community of people who know what they relate to in music, ritual, image, and symbol, and who know how far they can go with those elements and still connect the gospel with their lives. They realize they're not perfect and they expect to evolve and change as time goes by, and as God works within their lives and their community. But they are also accepting and tolerant of groups who choose to worship differently, even strikingly differently, to them. They just ask for this same tolerance to be extended to them.

New worship groups will be as concerned about creating a space for worship as they will about creating the worship. The space will reflect who they are and what they hope for from their worship. It may be a lounge or a bar, a hall or a mall, a church or a nightclub. Wherever, it will almost certainly involve the creative contribution of artists making it "our space," visually attractive, recognizing and honoring the contributions of creative people, looking for ways to involve all the senses in worship, and helping the body contribute to the worship experience rather than fight against it. Providing opportunity for a variety of responses, and always expecting God's Spirit to turn up and being constantly surprised when he does. . . .

Ambiguity

As Graham Cray, Principal of Ridley Hall, Cambridge, said, "This is a mission exercise to a culture that's in transition, it's full of risk, full of experiment, full of mistakes, full of other Christians not liking it and thinking you're selling the Parson, that the gospel has been undermined, and so on. If you want to be popular in the traditional church don't get into this stuff. It's not a comfortable place to be."[4]

There are few hard-and-fast rules when it comes to reframing, but there are some important things to be aware of. It's not done to be trendy, to shock, for novelty, for the sake of change, to show how much more you know than the rest of your group. The purpose of reframing is to make stronger, clearer, deeper, more meaningful connections between people's lives and the gospel story. Secondly, reframing requires that you understand the essence and heart of the truth you're reframing. If you have no idea what Good Friday is about, you'll happily sing "Up from the grave he arose" on that day; if you don't understand what the Last

Supper is about, you won't be able to help others to connect with God in that experience regardless of what elements you use. . . .

Making Room for God

My goal in preparing worship is always to provide an experience that gives room for God to speak to those present and for them to respond to God—heart, soul, mind, and strength. I keep that in mind as I curate the elements of a service and constantly question how any of the elements and their combinations contribute to that end. Good worship connects the lives of the worshipers with the life of God. "We're here to seek and to be sought by God," is a fitting call to worship.

Although I have long since lost track of the source of this quote it expresses rather well the participation and integration that is vital to good worship. "Life is neither the candle nor the wick, but the burning. Even so, worship is neither the gathering of the people present nor what they say and do, but the sharing of an experience of the presence of God, and a celebration of that experience."

If you're working on worship with a larger group—say fifteen or more—you could use a process that we've often used. Divide the group into seven subgroups and assign one part of the running order to each subgroup.

1. Call to worship—bring us in, prepare for worship
2. Prayer of confession and words of forgiveness
3. Celebration—of God, of life
4. The Word
5. Responding to the Word
6. Prayers for others
7. Blessing to send us out

Decide on a Scripture text and give the groups 30–45 minutes to come up with their two to three minute segment. We usually do this at the end of our intensive courses that have included a variety of techniques in using video, making slides, etc., and so restrict the groups to using the overhead projector or slide projector only. No video and no music. The service progresses without announcement and we play a track of music of our choosing behind it all, for example Peter Gabriel's "The Passion" or Sue Wallace's "Prayers for the Digital Orthodox,"[5] raising and lowering the volume as necessary.

I am constantly amazed by the creative responses groups come up with under the pressure of these tight parameters. Once we stood in a circle while a large wooden cross was laid on the floor in the center. As an act of confession we were asked to turn our backs on the cross while words were spoken that picked up the things we might have done that this movement symbolized. Then as we stood in silence someone came and stood behind us one at a time and said "Christ has forgiven you, turn toward home" and grasping both shoulders gently turned us back toward the center, each other, and the cross. Stunning stuff. For the celebration we lay on the floor with our head on the stomach of the person next to us and had a communal laugh. The Word was chanted over a body percussion created by drumming on our knees and slapping our thighs. Simple, creative, very memorable and moving. ". . . the sharing of an experience of the presence of God, and a celebration of that experience." It's called worship.

You need to start with a clean state, a group of like-minded people. (Who wants to face criticism or have to justify what you do at this stage of the process?) This is worship for the group gathered, and no one else. And you need to take a risk.

Room for All

This might be as far as you go, getting together from time to time to worship. If your group attracts more like-minded pilgrims, or if you have a much larger group to begin with, you will need to constantly battle against the slide toward institutionalism—becoming what you have left behind. Two major contributors to that slide will be trying to please everyone every time you meet, and the pressure to keep up the "program" even when most of the group no longer want it, or have moved in a different direction. The influence of these factors will depend greatly on whether the worship you are running is an independent group or attached to an existing church structure in some way. The spectrum ranges from two or three friends getting together in their lounge and "doing worship," through groups who do a monthly or bimonthly "alt.worship" service as part of the program of their church, to those groups that function as ongoing Christian communities (i.e., churches), while exhibiting most of the characteristics of alt.worship. The middle group is the most common and the latter quite rare. So what makes these services and groups different to the mainstream church that their participants have moved away from?[6]

Some of the underlying principles at work in these groups and in most groups who describe themselves as doing "alt.worship" or "new worship" would be a commitment to the following:[7]

Participation: People are encouraged, but not forced, to participate in the worship. The worship event provides numerous points and ways for people to be involved, with their body, mind, and emotions. The desire for hands-on participation is one of the most significant characteristics of the emerging culture. This need goes beyond "getting Mary to read a prayer" and means involvement in the planning and preparing of the worship at all stages and levels. This is worship of the people by the people for the people. There is a high level of ownership by those worshiping.

Community Based: This relates to participation but reminds us that worship should be firmly anchored in the lives of the worshiping group. It is not imposed on the group by any outside force but grows up from within the life of that community, expresses who they are, and builds them up. So worship is prepared with the needs of the community that will worship in mind. As mentioned earlier the moment you try to do worship for a mythical third person who may walk in off the street at any time, you have lost your way. I don't know what sort of music church worship leader Tommy Walker produces but the sentiment he expresses is right on. "People are constantly coming to me and asking, 'How do you do this hip music?' . . . I'm not doing hip music because it's hip. I'm doing it because that's how I worship God."[8] Worship must reflect who you are and connect with who you are if it is ever going to be authentic and meaningful for anyone else.

This call to worship expresses it very aptly . . .

> God is here. His Spirit is with us. This is not a performance. This is our worship. This is not a rave or a disco. This is our worship. This is not a special event for young people. This is our worship. We invite each other to use the environment, the visuals, the music, and the words, to stimulate our thoughts and draw our hearts to wonder at the goodness of God. Invite God to meet us as we seek to meet God. This is our worship. God is here.[9]

Culturally Relevant: Worship will reflect the culture or subculture of the worshipers. It will reject cultural barriers that are not part of the gospel. The motifs and symbols, music and language will be meaningful to those worshiping. They may not be as meaningful for, or understood by, those outside the subculture.

No Prima Donnas: The service usually moves through without any particular leader being obvious. Elements of worship flow from one to another without announcement and people involved in leading segments will do so from various places around the space. It doesn't all happen at the front.

Wholeness: Worship will involve the whole person. Body, soul, mind, and spirit. Deliberate efforts will be made to engage the whole person in the worship. Related to this is the belief that both understanding *and* experience are essential in worship, and opportunities will be created for both.

Eclectic: All of life and history and experience are in the grab bag of elements that may be used in worship. Any source of ideas, music, words, images, is considered from any religious or non-religious tradition. The alt.worship curator and worshiper reject any notion of a split between sacred and secular. They are willing to use ideas, materials, and forms from the secular world in worship.

> We're sensing a longing for the old and the familiar even as time hurtles on the threshold of a new millennium. That's why we need AncientFuture Faith. Faith that's filled with new-old thinking, that re-appropriates the traditional into contemporary, faith that mingles the old-fashioned with the newfangled, faith that understands the times in which we live in order to claim the era in which God has placed us for Jesus Christ.[10]

Leonard Sweet's coining of the term AncientFuture Faith sums up the eclecticism of new worship well.

Multimedia: All forms of media are available to be used in worship—to communicate and to create atmosphere. Not only technological media like slide and video projectors but also all forms of the arts—visual, fine, and performing. Use of media may not be linear or discrete. Non-linearity and concurrency are common, as is juxtaposition of otherwise unrelated items. So two readers may be alternately reading the verses of a Psalm at the same time as unrelated video images and slide texts are projected onto screens around four walls and a drum'n'bass track is played in the background. The whole is more than the sum of the parts.

Provisional: No one involved in alt.worship or new worship experiences thinks they have arrived. One of the given understandings is that we're on a journey from the modern to . . . who knows what? We are living in the interim between the "then" and the "not yet." This is one of the reasons that worship experimentation is so vital. The "not yet" will be shaped by the trials and experiments going on now. Anything we do is provisional, open to further change and evolution. The need for constant experimentation has never been greater.

At the same time there is no sense of exclusivity. New worshipers need to be marked by their tolerance of other forms of worship, recognizing that they are valid for other people and subcultures.

11

Missing God at Church?

Gary M. Burge

In this chapter Gary Burge invites the reader to consider
corporate worship that is a divine encounter led by pastors
with priestly skills using language that is liturgically rich,
rather than a time for only receiving ethical exhortations.

Sing a hymn. Pray.
Sing a hymn. Pray.
Hear the sermon. Pray.
Sing a hymn. Pray.

Say "liturgy" and my evangelical college students have a reflex akin to an invitation to take a quiz. Say "mysticism" and they

Originally published as "Are Evangelicals Missing God at Church? Why So Many Are Re-discovering Worship in Other Traditions," *Christianity Today* 41, no. 11 (October 6, 1997): 20–28. © 1997 by Gary M. Burge. All rights reserved. Used by permission.

are drawn, fascinated, eager to see what I mean. They want spontaneity yet drift toward the Episcopal church. They carry *NIV Study Bibles* but are intrigued by experiments in prayer, Christian meditation, spiritual disciplines honed in the medieval world, and candlelit sanctuaries. Some play the Chant CD endlessly. Os Guinness, Saint Teresa of Avila, and Richard Foster might all inhabit the same book bag.

Karen is typical of these students. She grew up in a large, independent Bible church in the Midwest where she attended every youth camp and mission trip her family could find. Her role models came from the glossy pages of *Campus Life*. When she came to Wheaton College, she attended a large, influential, conservative evangelical church. But after a year, her mind began to wander. "There was no imagination, no mystery, no beauty. It was all preaching and books and application," she told me. Now a senior, Karen is attending an Episcopal church nearby with a sizable group of her best friends.

Ask her if she likes liturgy and her eyes narrow: "Liturgical? Like in robes and candles and that sort of thing? Of course not." But I press, asking what she likes about the Episcopal church. "I truly worship there. It's the wonder, the beauty I love. I feel closer to God."

In reading my semester exams, I discovered that one particularly insightful student, Amy, wrote about worship:

> I think that much of modern society has lost a sense of divine, holy space. This becomes obvious to me in our church architecture. The splendor and holiness of cathedrals which created the ultimate feeling of divine space has been replaced by gymnasiums and impermanent buildings. A sanctuary should be a place that is completely separate—that radiates the holiness of God. Plastic cups and folding chairs aren't enough. There has to be an environment that communicates God's holiness to my senses and to my spirit.

What is going on? What deficit, what paucity of experience in their world is not being met? What drives this irony, this rejection of "liturgy" and this embrace of things that undergird every liturgy? What leads countless students to attend a breakaway Episcopal church (The Church of the Resurrection) where waving banners, the Book of Common Prayer, dance, guitars, ornate liturgical decor, and healing all work together? One Wheaton colleague who attends there commented, "At last a place where I can find intelligent charismatic worship—with dignity."

A new Greek Orthodox church opened in Wheaton just last year. Already a sizable number of our students are passionately committed members. Chrismation is a new word on campus. Some of us are predicting a small migration there, with icons soon to follow in Fischer dormitory.

And I just received a copy of *Rediscovering the Rich Heritage of Orthodoxy* (Light & Life, 1994). What amazed me is that it was written by an old friend, Charles Bell, with whom I studied at Fuller Seminary. "I have finally come home," he penned on the inside cover. And in the book he describes how this centuries-old, high liturgical church attracted a classical Pentecostal like him—a former chaplain at Oral Roberts University who holds a Ph.D. in theology from the University of Aberdeen, Scotland, and was ordained by the Vineyard Fellowship.

My pilgrimage is less dramatic but shares a common thread. I grew up in the former Lutheran Church in America, chiefly through the inspiration of my Swedish-Lutheran family. I still remember serving as a young acolyte, tending the mysteries of candle and altar and Communion table. My Catholic high school friends wore "Saint Christopher" chains, but I had my own "I am a Lutheran" medallion.

But when I entered the University of California I met the "Jesus movement," a spiritual counterpart to the 1960s counterculture. I followed them to Calvary Chapel in Costa Mesa, California, and witnessed something no Lutheran boy could imagine. It was a world of rock 'n' roll healing services in Hawaiian shirts, leather Bibles, and speaking in tongues by the thousands. I began to question my liturgical Lutheranism. When I entered Fuller Theological Seminary in 1974, the charismatic renewal was in full swing, and again, the diversity of the church and non-liturgical emphases on personal decision, power encounter, and healing swept me into their orbit.

It has been a long journey, but along the way I left the Lutheran church behind. Calvary Chapel, too. I even keep my hair cut. And now I swim in the mainstream of evangelicalism. Soul-winning, hard-hitting sermons, and revival hymns have become a staple of my diet. And deep inside I know that something is terribly wrong. Something is missing. My friends bravely announce the certainty of evangelical orthodoxy, but somewhere the mystery of God has been lost.

Evangelicalism is not a monolithic environment. I have been many places where the profundity of spiritual life and the numinous character of worship are celebrated. My Pentecostal/Holiness friends will be quick to point out that in their sanctuaries the sermon is secondary to a holy encounter with God.

Still, I suspect that there is a growing dissatisfaction in evangelical ranks, and nowhere is this pain felt more deeply than in the context of worship.

These migrations and impulses among my friends and students have forced me to ask new questions about what we are doing when we worship. In our zeal to be practical and relevant, perhaps we have missed something. We are participatory—including testimonies and prayers and choruses from the congregation—and yet some are saying their experiences seem hollow. They are not participating. We engineer "worship experiences," and yet heartfelt needs still go wanting. As a friend recently said, "I'm tired of sitting on my hands during worship."

So what is worship? Worship, I believe, is a divine encounter that touches many dimensions of my personhood. It is an encounter in which God's glory, Word, and grace are unveiled, and we respond, in songs and prayers of celebration. Worshipers seek an encounter with the glory of God, the transcendent power and numinous mystery of the divine—and in so doing, they recognize a Lord whose majesty evokes strong praise, petition, and transformation.

But my evangelical training has emptied Sunday's worship hour of God's majesty and mystery. Divine encounters seem few. Two factors have stood in our way.

First, we have been taught that the sermon must exposit the biblical texts, and that immediate and timely application should follow every message. While all of this is true, nothing has been left to our imaginations. Little has been left to our hearts except post-sermon feelings of conviction and exhortation. We leave the hour heavy, thinking more about what we must do than wondering about the mystery of God and his doings on our behalf. Therefore we have evolved an experience that is at best intellectual, a worship that studies the Bible. Homilies evolve into thirty-minute teaching sessions. And when it touches our emotions, it weighs us down, convicting us of wrongdoing and inadequacy.

To reinforce this we have created our own liturgy, a friend once told me, and its rhythm goes like this: we sing, pray, sing, pray, preach, pray, sing, pray. Before long the monotony of its cadence leaves us numb, wondering if there is no new form, no new dance that can be written for us. Even benedictions have become nothing more than reminders of the sermon's three points. These observations have forced me to question our role as ministers and worship leaders; to question the function of the sanctuary, the aesthetics of our music, and the content of our prayers.

There is a second barrier. Paul suggests that worship includes the mundane affairs of living, that we should "present [our] bodies as a living sacrifice, holy and acceptable to God, which is [our] spiritual worship" (Rom. 12:1). Some of us have used this verse to distort the principal meaning of worship. Rather than encountering God, our worship has become ethical.

Good Christian behavior has become the expression of true, spiritual worship. Sunday worship hour has become an equipping/training station for the world. Rather than being an "otherworldly" encounter reminding us of our heavenly identity, it has become "worldly" in the sense that its focus is horizontal, sharpening our discipleship in the world.

I see this horizontal emphasis symbolically in our use of the sacraments. In what sense is the Lord's Supper a unique meal with Christ? What has become of the church's historic interest in "divine presence" in these elements? Does this meal emphasize fellowship and confession (namely, our efforts), or does it represent communion and encounter (God's efforts)? I see liturgical routines that speak paragraphs of this "horizontal" theology, routines that gradually shape worshipers who have never known Eucharist as encounter. The same is true with infant baptisms and child dedications that become platforms for talking about better parenting. I have actually left such baptism services despairing over being an inadequate parent rather than contemplating the wonder of my childlike dependence on the generous mercy of God.

Thus two handicaps stand in our way. We have reduced our worship service to intellectual exhortations and ethics. Don't get me wrong. Both of these are good. But they do not evoke the sort of divine encounter many of us yearn to find on Sunday morning at church.

I believe evangelicals are yearning to recapture worship that lifts us—as a medieval cathedral lifted the eyes of the fourteenth-century worshiper—to truly meet God. Some will object, saying that this yearning is gnostic ("such world-denying behavior!") or narcissistic ("such emphasis on personal gratification!"). But it is neither of these. Incarnational theology demands that we emphasize encounter.

The mystery of our faith is the eruption of God's divine presence in the commonplace things of this world. But if it is only the commonplace that we see, we may fail ever to see God at all. What will facilitate this eruption of divine encounters for me as I worship? And can evangelicals find merit in something that is neither intellectual nor ethical?

For a number of years I served on the staff of a Presbyterian church in Evanston, Illinois. Among my many excellent memories, worship stands out. Its splendor had to do with many things: the architecture of the building (towering stained glass that paraded the heroes of the Bible; woodcarvings of angels and saints adorning wall and pillar), the music (instruments, organ, voice), the dignity of its liturgists (their dress, speech, and demeanor), theologically informed liturgies (crafting space for confession, silence, Word, and response alike), and the attitudes of the congregation (expectant, responsive, hushed as worship unfolded). Even our lighting was intentional, aimed at enhancing visual stimuli that would direct men and women to God. Our organist worked hard to build artful transitions between events in the worship service.

I recall sitting in the sanctuary next to our (then) nine-year-old daughter. Each Sunday we would pick a window and tell the story of who was represented there and what the symbols meant. They were beautiful and powerful and instructive. And they were densely theological, using eye-gate as vehicle for inspiration. The effect was disarming when one Sunday I asked her to stand and turn to count how many "stained glass" people were watching us in the pew. She realized that we were surrounded by a "host of witnesses" who had been faithful to God despite their circumstances (Heb. 12:1). On another Sunday our talk of a window was interrupted by bells. The bell choir had surrounded the sanctuary, and from every wall, complex and delightful notes swelled, calling us to worship. It was unworldly. Heavenly, perhaps. And it was intentionally theological.

I tell this story only to suggest that many worshipers come looking for more than fellowship, exposition, and exhortation. They seek an experience of "the holy." They come looking for awe and reverence, mystery and transcendence. Furthermore, many of their sensory faculties need to be engaged: Their senses of sight, sound, touch, and smell are powerful avenues of communication. One glance at the Old Testament directions for orchestrating temple worship will remove all doubt that this is our task. Fire, incense, tapestry, and gold joined with ritual activities that reminded worshipers of the reverent awe demanded of them. Bells and breastplates provided a visual feast evoking images of God's presence. Even the temple's architecture did this. One climbed higher as steps led "up" to the Holy Place.

Evangelicals need to reclaim their Old Testament heritage. We need to unburden ourselves of those reflexes forged during the Reformation and Enlightenment that shunned the pageantry and visual media of medieval Catholicism. But as we head down this road, we must hear a warning that speaks to us out of the centuries. Spiritual transcendence does not occur simply through aesthetic techniques. Bells and glass and pageantry will not in themselves bring the spiritual reality we seek. Mysticism is not a magic act. It is an outgrowth of a genuine and vibrant relation with God. Gourmet recipes should always be served on expensive china; but exquisite china in itself can never supply a meal.

My evangelical roots have reminded me in no uncertain terms that the pastor is "one" with the people. We uphold Martin Luther's "priesthood of all believers." In Presbyterian parlance the pastor is one of the elders—a teaching elder—alongside so many other elders. And so our demeanor, our dress, our participatory leadership style have evolved to communicate that there is no hierarchy in our congregations.

I now disagree with this model. I am not suggesting that pastors have privileges in the grace of God or the economy of the church unavailable to others. But I am suggesting that in worship, the pastor must become priest. The pastor plays a role—a significant role—in the divine encounter offered in worship. The pastor assumes the role of mediator, incarnating God to the people, forging an atmosphere and image that men and women will absorb when they contemplate divine things.

When I go to my kitchen hungry, I often take the food that is most easily within reach. When we go to worship empty, we assimilate those images that are most accessible. I have seen this at work again and again. One pastor I have watched is serious and severe. One seems to be "going through the motions." Another exudes grace radiantly and powerfully. As they conduct worship, they set patterns in place that form the image of God in worshipers' minds.

I remember when one of our daughters was baptized. She stood near the baptismal font as our pastor bent over, asking her questions of faith. His dignity, his well-prepared words, his touch, and his gaze all entered the archive of her experience. Later she said, "I remember Pastor coming near, and I was covered and lost in his long, black robes, and he baptized me." Responses from a standing congregation and a thundering hymn cemented images that have never gone away.

If it is true that we forge images for our people, that we are priests and mediators of God's encounter with his people, that congregants look to us and pattern their mental images of God from us, we must be intentional about everything we do as we lead worship. In a word, we must be leaders, strong leaders. We must be architects of worship because it is through our craft that we will be able to enrich and build the spiritual lives of our people. Through our craft, we will facilitate worship.

In our evangelical tradition we are comfortable saying that our words must be true because as we preach, we speak for God. Now more is required. Our total leadership, our complete conduct must be true because (like it or not) all that we do speaks paragraphs about God and his desires.

But there are no gimmicks. Priestly leadership is not a set of learned theatrical skills. As pastor-priest, we bring to the congregation the glory of our encounter with God. Having spent long, enduring time in the Lord's presence, we speak to our congregations out of those encounters. As I think carefully how I translate the elements of this encounter to my people, I create forms that express where I have been. A friend described to me his experience worshiping at All Souls Church in London when John Stott was preaching. For the entire service until the sermon, Stott was on his knees in prayer. And then when he spoke, he brought to his leadership the freshness of being in God's presence.

Evangelical exhortation and ethics now demand a supplement through worship that facilitates divine encounter. It must evoke deeper mysteries. It must lift us. And as we worship, liturgists and leaders become a priesthood, mediating God, showing the depth of their own experiences, radiating God's glory, pointing weary souls heavenward.

But I think there is another element to this worship experience that cannot be missed. Our evangelical tradition has taught us to champion spontaneity and to make a virtue out of informality. Some of us are sure that God cannot hear written prayers. Corporately spoken creeds, prayers, and liturgies stifle us and the Lord, or so the argument runs.

Here I have again changed my mind. Yes, there are liturgies that are memorized and meaningless. But what I have in mind are repetitive speech-forms that accompany every service. That is, when I introduce worship, when I offer the Eucharist, when I baptize, even when I bury, I employ familiar, dignified forms that evoke a history and an importance among my listeners.

I have noticed, for instance, that both the marginally churched and the faithful Christian want to hear the Twenty-third Psalm recited at a funeral and 1 Corinthians 13 at a wedding and the hymn "Amazing Grace" sung at thresholds of crisis. There is something reassuring in this recitation of old things, something that links us with history and tradition. It is like holding a book well worn by your grandparents' fingers. In some mysterious way, we feel strengthened.

I recall a pastor who created his own liturgy for every infant baptism. He would hold the child aloft and introduce him or her to the congregation, saying, "This is your new family." But then he would begin to recite an artful, dignified paragraph about this child's vulnerability and God's love. He spoke about how God loves us before we are even able to know him, before we can see beyond our own fingers. He recited this verbatim for every baptism, and each time it sounded as if it was his first time. Imagine the wedding of imagery and theology here! People looked forward to these baptisms, for they spoke not just of cute babies, but of us, our vulnerability and our near-sightedness, and God's redeeming, forgiving love.

The same is true for benedictions. Recitation is a reminder of what is profound and important. Recitation assures us that we are where we should be. Recitation carries us with familiarity when sometimes we cannot carry ourselves.

I started a tradition in one of my theology classes that now won't die. I learned that our students had never heard of Israel's great Shema Yisreal: "Hear, O Israel: The LORD our God is one LORD. You shall love the LORD your God with all your heart and with all your soul and with all your might" (Deut. 6:4–5). So we began reciting it in Hebrew at the start of each class period. At first they thought it was odd. Then they knew that they had inherited it. And then they would not let me begin class without it. Was it novelty? Not by the twelfth week. It set the rhythm, it moored us theologically, it centered us in a tradition as old as Moses.

I also see it on the faces of students when I lead them on trips to Israel. When we stand near the Sea of Galilee and recite the Beatitudes near where Jesus said them, I am anchoring them. I am giving them a treasure, a gift of vision and sound to which they may turn in memory for many years. I also prepare them in advance. Perhaps I will have them memorize the Twenty-third Psalm and then hold it in abeyance until they enter the desert, only there to recite it alone as biblical shepherds often did. To sit in the desert, to feel the jeopardy of a sheep in the wilderness, and to recite an ancient hymn of God's provision is to cultivate divine words that will serve for life.

Therefore, my plea is for worship that becomes familiar but not trite, that employs dignified language but is not stilted, language that is planned but is not mechanical. As a child, I grew up in a Lutheran tradition that still stays with me today. After forty years I can still recall the melodies of the liturgies, the cadence of the Nicene Creed, even portions of the set Eucharistic prayers. When I have little else to fall back on, these deep-set foundations become my security. Evangelical worship must begin building immovable foundations.

All of this—worship that is a divine encounter, pastors with priestly skills, language that is liturgically rich—means that we build a service that is centered on God rather than the human community. This sort of worship does not merely tell people about God, it invites them to meet and engage God in his presence. This worship makes us less aware of the people sitting nearby and more aware of God who is above. Above all, this worship is creative as it permits men, women, and children to express themselves through their giftedness. And it employs numerous avenues of expression: from creative use of sound to expressive uses of color and movement. But the aim is never to entertain or inspire the congregation. The aim is worship with abandon, worship that solicits no spectators.

My students and colleagues are looking for worship that weds dignity and spontaneity, worship that is theologically informed and liturgically intentional. My students and friends are migrating to new spiritual homes. They are looking for pastors who can be priests, liturgists who can evoke the divine Word and vision, worship services that do not push them into the world merely to be better Christians, but services that become a divine refuge—a divine encounter that lifts their lives and souls to an entirely new plateau. And to that I say amen.

12

Art for Faith's Sake

Clayton J. Schmit

Explaining that in corporate worship we often express that
which is too deep for words, Clayton Schmit encourages
the church to intelligently and appropriately incorporate art
into our worship services for faith's sake.

Worship has always been an artistic enterprise. We know that ancient Jewish worship was centered in the Temple, an architectural masterpiece, and that it was musically elaborate and replete with ritualistic art. The religious environment of Rome during the earliest days of Christianity, as Larry Hurtado has recently shown, was rich with architecture, statuary, and painted imagery: artistic artifacts created for worship of pagan idols. In this Roman setting, Christianity emerged, borrowing heavily from Jewish, but also pagan culture.[1] From the Jewish synagogue, Christian worship borrowed numerous artistic elements: readings from the Prophets and other Hebrew writers, the singing of

Reprinted from *Theology, News and Notes* 48, no. 2 (Fall 2001). © 2001 by Fuller Theological Seminary. All rights reserved. Used by permission.

psalms and spiritual songs, traditions of ritualistic prayer, and ritual furnishings. Images of God were not allowed in Jewish worship, however, so when painted and sculpted images of Jesus began to appear in Christian worship, in this particular aspect, Christian worship resembled Roman pagan worship, where images of deities were common.

Since its emergence, Christian worship has continued to find expression through artistic means. In large measure, the histories of Western art and music run parallel to the history of the Christian church. And today, regardless of denominational or liturgical tradition, Christian worship is made up of artistic forms. In most traditions, music holds central place as, to use Martin Luther's term, "the handmaid of the gospel." Whether Christians sing hymns, settings of the psalms, spiritual songs, anthems, or praise choruses, music is the principal artistic form that shapes Christian worship. But many others are involved. We gather in architectural structures; we enter rooms sunlit cobalt and ruby through stained-glass filtered light; we sit in well-fashioned furniture; we listen to the literature of the Scriptures; we hear aesthetically crafted messages; we move in processions; and we view images of the symbols and historic figures associated with our faith. When we gather for worship art is all around us, and even within us. We even claim that worship is an art in itself. Just as in opera, which is made up of dance, orchestral music, vocal music, literature, and visual art, worship is a distinct form of art that combines many elemental forms.

Clearly, the forms of art that relate to worship function in the public interest. When people gather for public worship, art draws them together, instructs them, unites them, enlightens them, and provides the means for personal expression and transformation. The numerous artists and artisans that create opportunities for Christian worship do their work for the sake of the people of God who gather to have an encounter with their Creator and Redeemer. Worship art is created for a clear purpose.

Art for Art's Sake

Throughout its history, art has regularly been used as a tool for accomplishing particular purposes. In medieval churches, stained-glass pictures of biblical narratives were presented in order that the illiterate public might know the stories of their faith. Pictures have long been painted to commemorate historic occasions or to reinterpret significant events. Statues of great persons have been erected to serve the purposes of honoring a memory or creating solidarity for a nation's populace. Using art as a means of meeting public needs was, in fact, a typical reason for creating art up until the mid-nineteenth century. Christopher Witcombe has summarized the prevailing attitude:

> The so-called academic painters of the nineteenth century believed themselves to be doing their part to improve the world in presenting images that contain or reflect good conservative moral values, examples of virtuous behavior, of inspiring Christian sentiment, and of the sort of righteous conduct and noble sacrifice that would serve as an appropriate model . . . to emulate.[2]

But in that era, as the moon of progressive thought rose, its light began to reveal an emerging reaction against the way that art had been used.

The use of art for public purpose began to change as artists started to exercise a sense of artistic freedom. Rebelling against the conservative notion that the purpose of art was to safeguard tradition, a wave of "avant-garde" modernists began to encourage artists to educate the public in a new way, by depicting political and social problems. Art still served a public purpose, but its function was not to uphold the status quo or preserve tradition. It was to raise to public view the plight of humanity and to illuminate exploitation. (A characteristic example of this use of art can be seen in the novels of Charles Dickens, wherein the deplorable social conditions of Victorian England are vividly depicted.) But, even this noble purpose was soon abandoned as artists exercised greater freedom. They began to seek release not only from academic art, but also from any demands of the public. Before long, artists claimed that their work should be produced not for the sake of public enlightenment, but for the sake of the art itself. The watchword of this movement was "art for art's sake." It stood for an artist's freedom from the tyranny of purpose.

Since that time, artists have enjoyed the freedom to express themselves in ways that explore and stretch form without regard for inherent meaning or purpose. Still, some forms of art have continued to function in public service. Among these are forms such as film, as it has been used to present news or to propagandize. Painting and photography are, and have long been used, for the purposes of advertising and amusement. And music can be used for many things, such as the expression of nationalism (as in "La Marseillaise" or "The Star-Spangled Banner"), social commentary (as in the sixties' folk music or modern rap), or lament (as in settings of certain psalms or the moaning of country western singers).

One of the settings where art has continued to serve a public function is in Christian worship. Worship consists of art that is not created for its own sake. It is created and brought into liturgical use precisely because it serves a good public purpose. It gives expression to people's experience. It teaches the faith. It serves as a vehicle of the Spirit and a means of communication with God. Why is it that worship consists of artistic forms that serve such particular functions? The answer is a theological one.

The Wellspring of Worship

God's people assemble for worship to enter into a communion and a communication that runs along vertical and horizontal axes. Vertically, there is the encounter between God and God's people. The lines of communication run both ways. God speaks to us when the Bible is read and when the Word is proclaimed by the preacher and the choir. God speaks to us also as we wait upon the Lord and listen for the stillness within. God's word comes to us in Scripture, sermon, song, and silence. And the communication runs in the opposite direction when God's people pray. Heavenward flow our pleas and petitions, our praise and thanksgivings, our confessions and confusions, the emptying of our deepest reservoirs of human concern.

By what measure can we determine whether this communication and encounter is effective? It would be impossible to invent an empirical means by which to measure the quality of such a highly subjective experience. But, we do know that when God speaks to us, it is about matters of the soul. Worship is not concerned merely with our minds and moods. It is not about education or entertainment. We do not go to worship to learn math or science or how to spell *Ecclesiastes*. And we do not worship in order to be made to laugh or cry or be moved by music. God's people worship because we long for an encounter with the God of the universe. We seek a deep sense of meaning and belonging and to enter into a dialogue with the one who knows us better than we know ourselves. The communion of worship is no shallow stream, but a deep river into which our souls dive to find comfort and contentment. This cannot be measured, but it can be known and felt.

The horizontal aspect of worship is also deeply enriching. We assemble not only for communion with God, but also to be with God's people. They are the body to which we belong. To worship together means that we meet God together and that we share God's love with one another. Again, this is no trifling encounter. It has greater potential for intimacy and depth than the average PTA or Rotary meeting. Worship is not only the place where we experience God's love, but also the moment where it finds immediate expression. Here, we pray for one another, sing in solidarity with one another, share the kiss of peace, and open ourselves to one another through the transforming power of Word, water, and wine. To calculate the success of such an experience is also beyond science. But, the soul knows when it has been reached.

Worship, when it is effective as vertical and horizontal communion, is about matters that are soul-deep. The psalmist knew this, who said, "As a deer longs for flowing streams, so my soul longs for you, O God. My soul thirsts for God, for the living God. . . . Deep calls to deep at the thunder of your [waterfalls]; all your waves and your billows have gone over me" (Ps. 42:1, 2, 7). Worship is a wellspring from which we draw and dispense living water.

The Function of Art

But the question remains, Why art in worship? We use art in worship because worship is about the deep issues of faith and life. In fact, we need to use art in worship for precisely that reason. How else could we reach the depths of human experience than through art? This is what art is uniquely able to do. To calculate the function or meaning of art is another mercurial task. It may mean and do many things. Artists themselves find it difficult to point to precise meanings in their own work. What it means to them may be far from what it means to or how it affects the percipient. But, they do know that art has something to do with their emotions and their experience with the world. They observe human experience, filter it through their own, and find symbols of expression that present those feelings and experiences to the world through artistic creations. Somehow, in the process, something deep is said. Deeper, in fact, than can be put into words. Ask a painter what a work means. She will likely tell you to look at the painting. That is what it means. Words cannot better describe what she has to say. They can only capture a fraction of what the art is about.

Words fail, unless your artistic medium is the use of words. And even then, a poem means what it says and not what one might describe it to mean. Poems create images that describe real things better than pages of detailed, accurate reporting can. For example, imagine trying to describe a flower. How could you improve on this: "If you're not familiar with the trillium, imagine the flower that would come from a flute if a flute could make a flower. That is the trillium, a work of God from a theme by Mozart."[3] We are used to using words in worship, but not in a technical way. Words in worship are poems. What does it mean to say that "my soul longs for you, O God," as a "deer longs for flowing streams"? It means so much more than you can say in more precise, less poetic language. The range of emotion and faith indicated by these words cannot be calculated. The meanings for author and reader cannot be reduced to so many digits or word units on a page. The key to art is that it speaks of many things, deeply held things, deeply personal things, and richly true things. Art speaks of human emotion and experience on a stratum that other more discursive media cannot reach.

Why do we need art in worship? Because faith resides on that soul-deep level of human experience. To reach that depth in human or divine communication, or to unleash the secrets of the heart in prayer, we need symbols that get us to that level. Mere words will not suffice. We need music, the flow of aural symbols that set us upon "the river whose streams make glad the city of God" (Ps. 46:4). We need the narratives of biblical life which are the aesthetic analogs to our own lives. We need the poetry of sermon and prayer which are the metaphors for our experience and concern. We need imagery that draws our imagination into the sphere of revelation. We need movement and dance, so that our soul's deepest held yearnings can find physical expression and release. In worship, we need art that has a purpose. Without it, we are mute. When we attend worship that does not work, we do not realize the failure empirically. It comes to us as an unkept promise. Something wells up that finds no expression: a volcano that cannot erupt; a stroke victim who has much to say but cannot find speech. That kind of worship is frustrating on the deepest level. What it needs is the art. Therein lies our voice, our fluency, our exclamation, our eruption of praise.

Art's Liturgical Purpose

Not all art today is made for a particular purpose. In many cases art is still made simply for its own sake. But, the art that we use in worship is made for liturgical purpose. It is the expression of things deeply felt. Art that has this kind of purpose does not correspond to the notion of "art for art's sake." But, it does correspond to another apt phrase. It was coined by art collector and church musician Jerry Evenrud. He refers to art in worship as "art for faith's sake."[4] Precisely. That is what we need: worship that is art-filled for the sake of the faith of the people of God who gather for communion with God and with one another.

This means, of course, that preachers and worship leaders are artists. Or, they should be. This also means that there is an aesthetic responsibility that worship leaders bear. Imbedded within that responsibility is the understanding that worship artists will comport themselves as all successful artists do: They will observe the world honestly and report it truthfully. They will practice so as to be prepared to present their art in the best way. They will coordinate their work with that of other artists so that as an integrated experience, worship will emerge as an art form in itself. And, they will seek excellence in performance not for the sake of themselves or their art, but for the sake of those who perceive it. There may be many reasons for an artist to create a form of art. But when it is made available for use in worship, a clear public purpose prevails. When it functions effectively, art that is used in worship is never more, but nothing less than art for faith's sake.

13

Beyond Style

Rethinking the Role of Music in Worship

John D. Witvliet

In asking six questions of local congregations, John Wit-
vliet exhorts local congregations to be imaginative and per-
sistent in the work of corporate worship.

Arguably no other religion in recorded history features such a daz-
zling variety of liturgical music as does Christianity. For twenty
centuries, Christians at worship have sung everything from contemplative Byzantine chants to exuberant Methodist frontier songs, from the
trancelike music of Taizé refrains to the precise rhetoric of Isaac Watts
and Charles Wesley, from songs with the Dionysian ecstasy of African-
American gospel anthems to those with the Apollonian reserve of a
Presbyterian metrical psalm, from the serene beauty of a Palestrina
motet to the rugged earthiness of an Appalachian folk tune, and from

Reprinted from *The Conviction of Things Not Seen: Worship and Ministry in the 21st Cen-*
tury, ed. Todd E. Johnson (Grand Rapids: Brazos Press, 2002), 67–81, 220–21. © 2002 by
Brazos Press, a division of Baker Book House Company. Used by permission.

the enforced silence of Quaker corporate mysticism to the sustained exuberance of an African-American ring-shout sermon.

These forms of music are not just adornments to Christian experience. They are the pulse of faith, integral to the different ways in which Christians have experienced worship and God's presence for over two thousand years. For many Christians, it would be difficult to imagine worship without music. In some churches the music starts when the community gathers and doesn't stop until the service ends. Even in congregations where music is subservient to preaching or other acts of worship, often it is the music that has the staying power to stick with people all week long. It is the music of worship that echoes in our minds during sleepless nights and that we whistle on the way to work.

Correspondingly, music is a source of Christian identity. One of the ways to tell what kind of Christian you are—what "species" of the Christian "genus" you belong to—is to think about the kind of liturgical music that has shaped your soul. Music identifies us as belonging to a particular denomination, tradition, ethnic group, or generation. One of the most reliable methods for grasping the inner pulse of a given community—whether from centuries ago or miles away—is to understand that community's music.

This is nowhere more evident than in today's North American church climate. Today, people gravitate to a given congregation more for the music that is sung than for the doctrine that is taught. A given congregation is as likely to advertise its identity by reference to its music as it is by reference to its denominational affiliation. Indeed, omnipresent stylistic terms like "traditional," "contemporary," and "blended" are generally understood to refer primarily (if not exclusively) to music, despite the fact that liturgical "style" is just as variable in other dimensions of worship, including preaching, liturgical leadership, and prayer.[1]

The centrality of music both in Christian experience and in congregational identity is part of the reason why Christians spend so much time fighting about it. Ninety-nine times out of a hundred, the worship wars of the past decades (although frankly, when hasn't there been a worship war?) are about nothing more than music—what music will be sung, what style will it be, who will lead it, what instruments will be used, and how loud will it be.

All of this recent bickering is also explained by how significantly Christian liturgical music has changed in the last few decades.[2] Some churches are singing from the wealth of hymnody generated by the late-twentieth-century hymn renaissance (more hymns in traditional forms have perhaps been written in the last thirty years than in any period except during Charles Wesley's lifetime).[3] Others are packing up their hymnals and singing an exclusive diet of recently written praise songs. Some churches are reclaiming ancient patterns for worship, including the Christian year, lectionaries, and traditional structures of the eucharistic prayer. Indeed, this liturgical movement has led Methodists and Presbyterians to sing their eucharistic prayers, evangelicals to light Advent candles, Roman Catholics and Episcopalians to nurture congregational participation in psalmody, and some Mennonites, Brethren, and Nazarenes to form lectionary study groups. At the same time, other congregations are becoming more market driven. Church growth theorists—of both mainline and evangelical stripes—invite us to purchase subscriptions to *Net Results* and to buy books with such titles as *Entertainment Evangelism*. There is a great concern for a congregation's market niche and the way that music can function as a tool to appeal to a wide spectrum of people. These competing impulses have put enormous pressure on musicians in congregations to meet competing demands and expectations. They have also fueled intense debates and even divides within countless congregations.

Problematic Discussions

Frequently the deep emotions that well up inside us over these matters confuse our ability to think straight. Critics of "contemporary music" lament the simplistic repetition of words in most praise songs, neglecting the fact that cyclic form and textual repetition has a storied and time-honored history in Judeo-Christian worship. (One congregational music committee recently spent most of its meeting bashing textual repetition, only to end its meeting by selecting Handel's "Hallelujah Chorus" for an upcoming Easter service.) Meanwhile, proponents of "contemporary" music argue that most praise songs are straight from Scripture, while neglecting to note that the overwhelming majority of praise songs set only a small portion of certain kinds of scriptural texts to music.

Some of our arguments in these matters are just plain vague. We tolerate abstract and nebulous arguments that call for a "better hymnody" that embodies "higher musical quality" without specifying what that means. Who determines what that looks like? On what standards is it based? Such statements often conceal our unwitting reliance on aesthetic sensibilities geared toward other forms of musical expression, such as concert music of either classical or popular forms—sensibilities that may not be particularly helpful for assessing liturgical music.

Among the most tendentious arguments are those that involve the use of history. Proponents of contemporary music based on the pop forms claim that since Luther and Wesley used musical tunes from the barrooms, so should we.[4] Others respond by holding up the meticulous craftsmanship of Bach or Buxtehude, seemingly unaware of their concern for congregational song. Almost everyone discusses such historical precedents on the basis of which argument they want to advance in the contemporary situation, with a striking disregard for historical facts.

History is not the only form of propaganda. Contemporary cultural judgments function in the same way. So, there are some who have never seen a Gallup poll they didn't like. They argue that if a plurality of Americans like music of a certain style, then that's what we ought to use in church. By this way of thinking, a given congregation's music ought to sound a lot like the music that most worshipers have preset on their car stereos, whether or nor music in worship has a different function in our life. On the other hand, there are others who either refuse to be aware of the musical dimensions of ambient culture or refuse to find anything of value there. By this way of thinking, every musical innovation is dismissed as a part of our "individualistic, materialistic, hedonistic" culture without a moment's consideration. The bewildered observer, sensing that most cultures are an ambiguous mixture of good and bad, is rightfully frustrated with either side.

Beyond the Fight

Fighting about music—especially with such jumbled arguments—is not a body-of-Christ way to solve our problems. These kinds of arguments simplify complex issues, cut off discerning communication, and fail to embody the virtues that are part of the grateful Christian life.

Consider a different vision. Near the opening of the book of Philippians, Paul records his prayer for the Philippian Christians: "And this is my prayer, that your love may overflow more and more with knowledge and full insight to help you to *determine* what is best, so that in the day of Christ you may be pure and blameless, having produced the harvest of righteousness that comes through Jesus Christ for the glory and praise of God" (Phil. 1:9–11, emphasis mine). At the heart of this prayer is Paul's desire that his readers will exercise the virtue of discernment. He wants them to be able to make good choices, to "determine what is best."

What does it mean to discern? Discernment is what Solomon asked for when he asked for "an understanding mind . . . to discern good from evil." Augustine defined it as "love making a right distinction between what helps us move toward God and what might hinder us."[5] Discernment requires making choices, saying "yes" to some things and "no" to others.

Paul gives us a short recipe for discernment. Knowledge and insight are two key ingredients. They provide a measuring stick by which to judge a given innovation or practice. To make good choices, we need to ask probing questions and search for penetrating insight into truth. We need the mind of Christ.

Another ingredient is love—not a sentimental love that baptizes every fad but a deep, pastoral love that nurtures long-term spiritual health. Such pastoral love requires a community. Psalm 19:12 asks, "Who can detect their errors?" reminding us that none of us by ourselves alone has the perspective to see the whole picture. That's why Paul prays for "you all" (second person *plural*) to determine what is best.

Finally, discernment, like every virtue, is less an accomplishment to achieve than a gift to receive. The chief ally and agent in any communal discernment process is none less than the Spirit of God. Discernment is a Pentecost virtue, a gift of the Spirit, and so, something for which we should pray.

Toward Criteria for Music in Christian Worship

Robert Webber knows about the criteria for music in Christian worship. Robert Webber has recognized music's power. He has also entered into the middle of the worship wars, serving as a witness to the importance of theological reflection in the middle of contemporary discussions. As he has traveled all over North America teaching and lecturing, he has addressed countless questions about the practice of music. Along the way, he has articulated in common, accessible language the kinds of criteria that don't merely perpetuate the problem but actually can lead toward resolution. In this chapter, I will expand on Webber's work and place his work in conversation with other recent writers. The goal of this chapter is to propose categories for thinking about the valid and healthy use of music in the context of Christian worship, categories that are accessible enough to function well in the next worship committee meeting in most North American congregations. I will introduce these categories by means of six overarching questions that every congregation and every church musician might profitably address. These questions are designed to help congregations "determine what is best."

Question 1, a theological question: *Do we have the imagination and resolve to speak and make music in a way that both celebrates and limits the role of music as a conduit for experiencing God?*

At a conference some time ago, a pastor stood to advertise a search for a church musician. When asked what kind of person was needed, the pastor replied in a stammering, stuttering way—the kind of speech that tells you the person is probably saying what he or she really thinks rather than giving an edited, politically correct version of the same. The

answer came back: "Some one who can make God present in my congregation." Now this, to put it mildly, is a rather loaded expectation![6]

Yet, language like this is increasingly present in want ads for parish musicians. Churches are looking for people whose creativity and
charismatic personality can turn an ordinary moment into a holy
moment. This tendency is not limited to charismatics. Churches with
names not only like Community Church of the Happy Valley but also
Tall Steeple Presbyterian Church want to hire musicians who aspire
to make holy moments. One attempts to do this on a pipe organ with
a loud trumpet stop and one attempts it with microphone and drum
set, but both are striving to make God *present*, in some true, if elusive,
sense. In congregations today, our strongest sacramental language is
often not used to speak about what happens at the pulpit, font, and
table, but rather what comes from our conga drums, synthesizers,
and swell box. Even the architecture of many worship spaces (which
rarely lies about what is most important) conveys the "sacramental-
ization" of music. The front-and-center space formerly reserved for
pulpit, font, and table or altar is now reserved for worship bands or
towering pipe organs.

Certainly, this concern for attending to holy moments is important.
Arguably, most Christian musicians (in every style) are drawn to music
because of a transformative musical experience. Yet no one, no matter
how charismatic, can make a moment holy by his or her own creativity, ingenuity, or effort. Scripture records a long line of those who tried:
the prophets of Baal at Carmel (1 Kings 18), old Uzzah, the servant
who wanted to help along the cause of God by rescuing the ark of the
covenant from the shaking ox cart that was carrying it (2 Samuel 6;
1 Chronicles 13), and Simon, the magician, who longed for the divine
power of healing to reside in his hands (Acts 8).

To avoid a similar temptation, some years ago choral conductor Westin
Noble selected an anthem on the Pauline text "God does nor dwell in
temples made of human hands" for (of all things) a chapel consecration
service. The choir proclaimed the Word of the Lord through music that
day echoing Paul's sermon in Acts 17:24–25: "The God who made the
world and everything in it, he who is Lord of heaven and earth, does
not live in shrines made by human hands, nor is he served by human
hands, as though he needed anything, since he himself gives to all
mortals life and breath and all things." This word guarded against the
assumption that a certain kind of building could enshrine or produce
God's presence. It served as a powerful reminder that God's presence
is to be received as a gift, that it cannot be engineered, produced, or
embodied automatically (though one does wonder how the building
committee felt about that statement).

Westin Noble's choice reflects a well-established Christian instinct about the arts in worship. Augustine was nervous about sung alleluias that distract our attention from the God who gave us voices and was worried when "the music itself was more moving than the truth it conveys."[7] John Wesley advised, "Above all, sing spiritually. Have an eye to God in every word you sing. Aim at pleasing him more than yourself, or any other creature. In order to do this *attend strictly to the sense of what you sing, and see that your heart is not carried away with the sound, but offered to God continually;* so shall your singing be such as the Lord will approve here, and reward you when he cometh in the clouds of heaven."[8] More recently, Thomas Long has warned, "If one desires an intimate encounter with the holy at every service, then go to the Temple of Baal. Yahweh, the true and living God, sometimes withdraws from present experience. In sum, God does not always move us, and everything that moves us is not God."[9]

There is no doubt that music has great significance in the divine-human encounter of worship. In spoken prayer, word mediates divine-human interpersonal encounter. In sung prayer, music does this multivalently. Augustine is right: "To sing is to pray twice." Pipe organ music, an African drum, unified unaccompanied voices, all of these and many more forms of music do function to inspire praise, evoke wonder, reveal new insight, and generate qualitatively different religious experiences.

But can we safely take the next step and believe that music generates an experience of *God?* By no means. That places far too much power in music itself. Music is not God, nor is music an automatic tool for generating God's presence. Rather, in Robert Webber's words, music "*witnesses* to the transcendence of God . . . it elicits the sense of awe and mystery that accompanies a meeting with God."[10] Music is an instrument by which the Holy Spirit draws us to God, a tool by which we enact our relationship with God. It is not a magical medium for conjuring up God's presence.

Imagine a church musician agreeing to take a new position in a congregation, provided that she or he would be able to lead one service without music at all. Most congregations would be perplexed at the thought of an entire service without music. Yet this would be a prophetic demonstration that while music was incredibly important, it is also not absolutely *necessary*. Rhetorically, musicians gain credibility when they are willing to both promote and limit their statements about the power and beauty and universal significance of pipe organ music. Spiritually, we gain great freedom in Christ when we celebrate the fact that a divine-human encounter is not finally dependent on our musical achievement, but is a Spirit-given gift.

Question 2, a liturgical question: *Do we have the imagination and persistence to develop and play music that enables and enacts the primary actions of Christian worship?*

Some time ago, I asked a group of elementary students—always one of the best barometers of the "living theology" of a congregation—to talk with me about the meaning of worship. We took out a bulletin, and I asked them to tell me what was going on at every point of the service. When I pointed to the "prayers of the people," they told me, "Well, there we are talking to God." When I pointed to the Scripture reading, they told me, "Well, there God is talking to us." So far, so good. But when I pointed to the opening hymn, they told me, "Well, there we are singing." They told me this even though the first hymn was a prayer.

In other words, when it came to the music, they had no theological explanation of what was happening. They could only refer to what we were doing on the surface. This response is very instructive. So often we experience music in worship not as a means of praying or proclaiming the Christian gospel but as an end in itself. This is not only a problem for children in worship but also for adults—and for the musicians that lead them in worship.

This is precisely the worry of philosopher Nicholas Wolterstorff. "It is," Wolterstorff writes,

> habitual for musicians trained within our institutions of high art to approach the music of the liturgy by insisting that it be good music, and to justify that insistence by saying that God wants us to present our very best to Him—all the while judging good music not by reference to the purposes of the liturgy but by reference to the purpose of aesthetic contemplation.[11]

This concern applies equally to forms of church music derived from popular culture chosen for its emotional or entertainment value. In contrast, Wolterstorff calls for liturgical artworks that "serve effectively the actions of the liturgy . . . without distraction, awkwardness, and difficulty."[12]

The primary elements of worship are those that express and enact our relationship with God: God speaks to us through Scripture, God nourishes us at the table; we thank God, we confess our sins to God, and we declare our faith to each other before God's face. Music always serves to accomplish one of these actions. Some music helps us confess sins. Some helps us express thanks. Some of it is the means by which we proclaim God's words. Music is always a means to a greater spiritual end, a means for enacting our relationship with God.

Thus, Robert Webber speaks of music as "the wheel upon which the Word and Eucharist ride" and the arts as "the means by which Christ is encountered."[13] Music must support—in unique and invaluable ways—the primary actions of worship rather than serving as an end itself. As Webber concludes, "Worship is never to be arts-driven, but arts-enhanced. What should be prominent is the celebration of God's great deed of salvation in Jesus Christ. When the arts serve that message, they serve and assist our worship."[14]

This functional view of music has direct implications for congregational practice. For congregations with an established pattern or liturgy, it means that musicians must select music that enables the congregation to truly do what the liturgy requires. A piece of music that accompanies a penitential prayer must actually allow the people of the congregation to confess their sins. Having an orthodox text set to a memorable melody is not enough; music must also enable the action it accompanies. For congregations without an established pattern, the challenge is greater. In this case, a worship leader must lead the congregation in such a way that the deep purposes of a given song or hymn are clear. A lament text introduced as simply "another good song for us to learn" will likely not be experienced by most worshipers as a lament—even if the text is clear. Music—in any style—becomes problematic when we don't experience it as helping us to accomplish the primary tasks of worship, when we respond to a piece of music by saying, "Wow, that was impressive," rather than, "That music really helped me pray more honestly."

Question 3, an ecclesial question: *Do we have the imagination and persistence to make music that truly serves the gathered congregation, rather than the musician, composer, or marketing company that promotes it?*

Nearly every tradition agrees that Christian worship is the work of God's people, a corporate activity in which the sum is greater than the parts, in which our being together as liturgical agents is primary. Music has a significant role in making this corporate dimension of worship palpable. Whether at a Bobby McFerrin, U2, or B. B. King concert, a Columbine memorial service, or a Notre Dame football game, music forges first-person-plural experiences.

As communal song, congregational song differs from many of the genres and institutions of high art in Western culture. In concert music, we value the proficiency of the solo artist. In worship, the pinnacle of musical virtue is to find an entire congregation singing well—honestly, musically, imaginatively, prayerfully, beautifully. In his book *Holy Things*, Gordon Lathrop makes this point as follows:

In current European-American culture, certain kinds of art will be misplaced in the meeting: art that is primarily focused on the self-expression of the alienated artist or performer; art that is a self-contained performance; art that cannot open itself to sing around a people hearing the word and holding a meal; art that is merely religious in the sense of dealing with a religious theme or enabling individual and personal meditation but not communal engagement; art that is realistic rather than iconic; art, in other words, that directly and uncritically expresses the values of our current culture.[15]

In liturgical art, no pride of place is offered to the autonomous, solitary, artistic genius. Instead, the liturgical artist is called to take the role of servant, giving worshipers a voice they never knew they had to sing praise and offer prayer to God.

Thus service as pastoral musician-liturgists requires not only theological and artistic conviction but also hospitality. The fourth-century "Constitutions of the Holy Apostles" advised bishops: "When you call together an assembly of the Church, it is as if you were the commander of a great ship. Set up the enterprise to be accomplished with all possible skill, charging the deacons as mariners to prepare places for the congregation as for passengers, with all due care and decency."[16] The craft and coordination and "performance" in the work of the church musician finds its ultimate goal and purpose in welcoming the people of God to experience the power and joy of profound and communal liturgical participation. As Alice Parker reminds us, "There are churches in all denominations in this country where congregations do sing well, and it is always because there is at least one person who is actively expecting it."[17]

This raises several significant questions: Whom do we welcome to our musical feasts? Do we actually welcome a community? Do our texts have a breadth of viewpoint? Are our tunes more communal than soloistic? Do we welcome children? Do we welcome persons who speak other musical languages?

But if we do these things, the response typically goes, there will be no time for really good music. Good music, however, is partly a matter of what we say it is, what standard we use to judge it, what virtues we aspire to. All composition (and music making) is in part the ability to create works of integrity and imagination within a set of constraints. The organ stop list is one set of constraints. So is the liturgical pattern used by your community. So is the musical skill of your congregation. It may be true that one ultimate test for the pinnacle of achievement in worship music led by a contemporary worship band is to see how supple and powerful a sound can be created with $200,000 worth of

sound equipment, or how seamlessly a group of twelve instrumentalists can improvise off music charts, or how hot a combination of new
guitar and percussion riffs a band can generate. It may be true that one
ultimate test for the pinnacle of achievement in worship music led by
an organist is to see what an organist and builder can do with a $2 mil-
lion dollar budget for building a new instrument; another is how well
an organist can play a featured recital at an American Guild of Organists convention. A more important test, however—which also needs to
be recognized, celebrated, affirmed, and credentialed—is to see how
effectively, honestly, and knowingly a worship band or organist can get
a congregation to sing well together. Music in worship is not primarily
about individual choice, participation, or preferences, but about the
entire congregation.

And many voices would extend this reasoning one step further to
argue that music in worship is not only about individual congregations
but also about the whole body of Christ, the whole catholic church.
In his description of liturgical music, Dietrich Bonhoffer explores this
catholic impulse:

> It is the voice of the *Church* that is heard in singing together. It is not you
> that sings, it is the Church that is singing, and you, as a member of the
> Church, may share in its song. Thus all singing together . . . serves to widen
> our spiritual horizon, make us see our little company as a member of the
> great Christian Church on earth, and help us willingly and gladly to join
> our singing, be it feeble or good, to the song of the Church.[18]

In a culture that celebrates individual choices and preferences, this vision calls us to a new way of experiencing music. This vision invites us
not to ask, "Did I like that music?" but rather, "Did that music give me a
powerful sense of joining with Christians in other times and places?"

Question 4, a question about aesthetic attitudes: *Do we have
the persistence and imagination to develop and then practice a rich
understanding of "aesthetic virtue"?*

Most conversations about music in the church center on the music
itself—whether it is relevant, authentic, well crafted, well chosen, or
interesting. These concerns are important but incomplete. Equally important are the attitudes toward the arts that we cultivate and tolerate
in the Christian community. In a winsome chapter in his book *Religious
Aesthetics*, Frank Burch Brown identifies four distinct attitudinal problems about the arts—let's call them "aesthetic sins"—that persist like
viruses in the church.

First, there is the *Aesthete*, "the person whose chief goal is not glorifying
and enjoying God but glorying in the aesthetic delights of creation." This

may be the person in the church who loves to hear their Bach straight and couldn't care less if that music enables liturgical action. Or it may be the contemporary worship fan who is more a connoisseur of sound systems than of expressing gratitude to God.

Second, there is the *Philistine*, the one who "does not highly value or personally appreciate anything artistic and aesthetic that cannot be translated into practical, moral, or specifically religious terms." This is the sin, Burch Brown notes, that is exposed in Alice Walker's *The Color Purple*, where Shug says to Celie: "I think it pisses God off if you walk by the color purple in a field somewhere and don't notice it." The Philistine is the person who refuses to devote any energy to reveling in the God-given ability to create or who refuses to appreciate the creative work of others. This is the person (perhaps even a musician) who treats music like a commodity, simply a tool to attract people or increase revenue.

Third, there is the *Intolerant*, the one who "is keenly aware of aesthetic standards of appraisal, but elevates his or her own standards to the level of absolutes." This, notes Burch Brown, is "the aesthetic equivalent of the sin of pride . . . it severs human ties and does violence to the freedom, integrity, and self-hood of others." This is the sin of those in the church who don't perceive how their own critique of another musical style applies equally to their own stylistic preferences. This is the sin of those who caricature music they don't like.

Fourth, there is the *Indiscriminate*, the one who embraces "radical aesthetic relativism . . . [who] indiscriminately [embraces] all aesthetic phenomena." Indiscriminate people are those who "cannot distinguish between what in their own experience has relatively lasting value and what is just superficially appealing."[19] This is the person in our congregations who has never heard a praise song or choral anthem he or she didn't like, or the musician who simply wants to please everybody and will never admit that some music is actually inferior.

Burch Brown's way of thinking is striking, in part because it speaks of aesthetic experiences in *moral* categories (evoking the coupling of moral and aesthetic categories, which has a long history in the Christian tradition). The use of such categories is helpful, because it gives names to complexities we often fail to acknowledge. A lot of energy in the church is spent working against only one form of aesthetic sin, rather than all four. Thus some musicians are tempted to fight only philistinism, thinking of their life's work as a sustained attack on poor aesthetic sensibilities. Likewise, some pastors spend a lot of energy working against intolerance, especially when two competing groups in a congregation seem to embody this vice in equal measure. In most communities, it remains stubbornly tempting to fight philistinism with aestheticism and to fight intolerance with indiscriminancy.

Burch Brown's vision challenges us to work for the *simultaneous* reduction of intolerance, aestheticism, indiscrimancy, and philistinism not just in our congregations, but also in ourselves. All of us have a different prayer of confession to offer: some of us work against the sin of indiscriminancy, others the sin of intolerance. These vices cohabit in our individual souls and in our congregations. We need to name and work against all four simultaneously.

The positive side is that such vices suggest corresponding virtues. Moments of liturgical aesthetic *virtue* happen, too. Perhaps a musician will willingly embrace a piece of music in a style she doesn't prefer but at the same time help the enthusiast for that music to become more discriminating. Perhaps someone will express delight in his discovery of a canticle, psalm, or hymn that conveys his own prayers better than he could have himself. Another time, someone in your congregation may have a chest cold and, because she is not able to sing, will for the first time listen to the sounds of corporate singing around her and be moved by the power of this common expression. Yet again, someone will sing a text, be struck with the power of the thought expressed, and later add it as a quote as part of his email signature. Another time, your congregation may pull off the unthinkable: they will sing a meditative prayer text softly, without singing weakly. In many musical styles, these are virtuous moments to celebrate.

Question 5, a cultural question: *Do we have a sufficiently complex understanding of the relationship between worship, music, and culture to account for how worship is at once transcultural, contextual, countercultural, and cross-cultural?*

One of the many contributions of Vatican II to twentieth-century Christian worship was its insistence that liturgical expression reflect the particular cultural context of local congregations. This insistence calls to mind John Calvin's admonition that matters in worship for which we lack explicit biblical teaching that are not necessary for salvation ought "for the upbuilding of the church . . . to be variously accommodated to the customs of each nation and age."[20] Since Vatican II, a small cadre of liturgists have attempted to be conscious of how this accommodation—variously termed contextualization, indigenization, inculturation—can best take place. Spurred on in part by the postmodern concern for cultural particularity, this project has been approached enthusiastically by many ecclesiastical traditions. The Roman Catholic Church has produced a much-discussed "indigenous rite" for Zaire. Protestants have eagerly encouraged the development of indigenous musical repertoires in Africa, South America, and Southeast Asia. And many traditions are exploring the stunning variety of cultural expressions that contribute immeasurably to the liturgies of the world church.[21]

Significantly, the recent move toward inculturation has both *promoted* and *limited* indigenous forms of expression. It has encouraged the development of indigenous forms only insofar as they complement the historic structure of Christian worship. Generally speaking, this movement has argued that Christian worship should arise naturally out of its cultural environment but that it should also critique aspects of the culture that run against central tenets of the Christian faith. The movement has argued that worship should avoid *both* "cultural capitulation" and "cultural irrelevancy."[22]

One of the mature statements to come out of this movement, the "Nairobi Statement on Worship and Culture," has been produced by the Lutheran World Federation. This statement argues that healthy congregations should have worship that is self-consciously transcultural, contextual, countercultural, and cross-cultural—all at the same time.[23]

First, all Christian worship should be *transcultural*, embracing the universal dimensions of the Christian gospel and of Christian liturgy. Thus all worship should feature the centrality of the Word, honest prayers offered in the name of Jesus, the proclamation of the full gospel of Christ, the rich celebration of baptism and the Lord's Supper. Correspondingly, we should lament forms of worship that do not embody the nonnegotiable and universal components of Christian liturgy.

Second, all Christian worship should be *contextual*, reflecting the unique genius of the culture in which it is placed, speaking directly to that culture, and arising naturally from people of that culture. When the transcultured elements of worship are practiced, they will be done in vernacular languages, with forms of rhetoric, dress, gestures, postures, and symbols that enable local congregations to celebrate them in deep and rich ways. Correspondingly, we should lament worship that feels disembodied, that seems disconnected from the real living, breathing people who live and work in a given community.

Third, all Christian worship should be *countercultural*, resisting those aspects of culture that detract from deep, gospel-centered celebrations. When technology, material wealth, constant noise, or individualism threaten to erode a community's authentic faith, then worship forms should protest rather than embody these cultural traits. Correspondingly, we should lament worship that simply baptizes everything in culture that comes along.

Fourth, all Christian worship should be *cross-cultural*, incorporating elements, prayers, and music that a given community receives as gifts from Christians in other times and places. In music, this happens when even ethnically *homogenous* congregations attempt to become musically *multilingual* and sing songs and hymns from a variety of cultures. Correspondingly, we should lament worship that is insular, that gives the impression that a given congregation has no need for other parts of the body of Christ.

Like Burch Brown's work on aesthetic sins and virtues, the "Nairobi Statement on Worship and Culture" affirms four virtues that must be cultivated simultaneously. Here is a theory of inculturation that is not governed by an implicit either/or rhetoric. Rather efficiently, this document properly complicates our thinking about the proper relationship between music and culture.

Here again, each Christian leader and each community needs a different prayer of confession. Some of us need to confess our imperialism, some our cultural retrenchment, some our indiscriminate use of elements of our culture.

In most congregational discussions, the discussion of worship and culture is remarkably simplistic. Most congregations and their leaders are more excited about one of these four adjectives than the others. In one congregation, one group argues that the pipe organ should be locked up because it is irrelevant, while another group asserts that the pipe organ is necessary because it is countercultural. In another congregation, a congregation adds $200,000 per year to its budget for video production to have music videos call the congregation to worship each week, based on the idea that worship should reflect local culture.

Imagine congregational musical life in which musicians constantly pursue balance in these matters. So a worship band that was working on a hard-driving new ballad—the height of perceived contextuality—might also work on learning a Taizé refrain as a countercultural protest against overly noisy and technologized forms of music.

Question 6, an economic question: *Do we have the imagination and persistence to overcome deep divisions in the Christian church along the lines of socioeconomic class?*

Finally, we come to a troubling area that resists easy answers and challenges nearly every community to reconsider common practices. In the last generation, the church has worked at bridging barriers of color, race, ethnicity, and gender. But we have not done well with socioeconomic class. This may turn out to be the most vexing division of all.

The question before us is simply this: In a culture that is so obsessed with making and spending money, how can we promote excellent worship music but not promote the idea that it takes hundreds of thousands of dollars to worship God well? How can we celebrate the gift of music that is possible at a cathedral or megachurch (the cathedrals of Free Church Protestantism), with all their resources, without implying that that worship is somehow better than the worship offered at the small congregation eight blocks from the cathedral or two suburbs over from the megachurch, but across the tracks?

In 1853, *Presbyterian Magazine* extolled the virtues of Cincinnati's new Seventh Presbyterian Church as having a belfry "not surpassed for richness and beauty," an interior "illuminated by a superb chandelier of original design and chaste workmanship," and a gallery of "the most costly and imaginate [*sic*] specimens of its kind." All of this gentrified language may be true, but the impression it creates is deeply troubling. One wonders how Christians in the next century may read the Internet-archived newspaper headlines about today's megachurches or cathedrals or tall-steeple campuses.

Of course, these vexing economic questions can be wrongly used in an utterly philistine way. Resources and the costly use of them in the service of God are not bad. What is bad is the persistent implication that it takes money to truly worship God.

Thoughtful consideration of the economic implications of our worship may lead congregations to very different strategies. What if our cathedrals and megachurches hosted a festival service in which the orchestras, sound systems, and organs were set aside for a time as a witness to the virtue of Christian simplicity? What if large distributions of funds for musical resources in worship were paired with equally large distributions of funds to communities with fewer resources? What if we designed a church culture in which the staffs of huge suburban churches and church-related colleges attended worship conferences at small, rural churches, eager to learn about the virtues of smallness and simplicity rather than just the other way around?

Multiple Themes and Congregational Practice

At first glance, the six questions above, and the criteria they suggest, might sound entirely impractical. What musician in a local congregation has the time to promote musical, aesthetic, liturgical, theological, economic, and pastoral integrity—all at the same time?

It is true that we must not be too optimistic about criteria like these. The little boat of thoughtful discourse they are designed to promote is easily swamped by the tidal wave of aggressive marketing and personal tastes that dominate the worship music scene. In many congregations, the most important forces shaping music are a tenacious attempt to hold on to traditional practices, or, conversely, a strong desire to stay on the cutting edge of new musical forms. There seems to be little interest in thinking more deeply about music's function.

At the same time, these questions may still prove to be useful. For one, they help us have better conversations about music. They help us perceive and avoid overly simplistic arguments. We are less apt to become enthralled with a popular piece of new music if we don't perceive how that music will enable our congregation to pray more honestly next week. We are less apt to follow a simplistic cultural argument once we realize how complex the church's relationship to culture is. Our efforts toward musical integrity will bear richer fruit once we have a clearer sense of the aesthetic and liturgical virtues toward which we are aiming.

Asking these questions can also result in tangible differences in music in your congregation. Asking theological questions about music's role in mediating God's presence can lead a worship leader to change how he or she introduces a song. Asking questions about music's liturgical function can lead musicians to choose very different music for worship than if they simply were trying to please everyone. Asking questions about culture can lead musicians to choose a balanced diet of both contextual and countercultural music for next Sunday.

Sound, tangible changes are not inevitable, however. Such discernible changes require yet one more thing, signaled by the single word that has repeatedly appeared in the six questions: the word *imagination*. Most often, the ultimate constraint on our musical life together in congregations is not the lack of money, the lack of books or articles about the subject, or the lack of consultants who will come to help us. The ultimate constraint is our lack of imagination.

We need imagination to see what is really going on under the surface of our warlike conversations about music. We need imagination to see how the weekly practice of worship music embodies different aesthetic and cultural virtues and vices. We need imagination to perceive how our practice of music can, at the same time, be made more accessible and authentic, more relevant and profound. This kind of imagination that is forged by both knowledge and love will allow us together to "determine what is best."

14

A Matter of Taste?

Frank Burch Brown

In this chapter Frank Burch Brown adeptly highlights the narrow musical scope of much "contemporary worship" and encourages widening the musical horizons for corporate worship today.

The cover of the August 1996 *Atlantic Monthly* announced a Christian cultural revolution: "Giant 'full-service' churches are winning millions of 'customers' with [their] pop-culture packaging. They may also be building an important new form of community." Author Charles Trueheart described what he calls the "Next Church": No spires. No crosses. No robes. No clerical collars. No hard pews. No kneelers. No biblical gobbledygook. No prayer rote. No fire, no brimstone. No pipe

Originally published in a slightly different form in *Good Taste, Bad Taste, and Christian Taste: Aesthetics in Religious Life* (New York: Oxford University Press, 2000). Reprinted from "Religious Meanings and Musical Styles: A Matter of Taste," *The Christian Century* 117, no. 25 (September 13, 2000): 904–11. © 2003 by Christian Century Foundation. Used by permission.

organs. No dreary eighteenth-century hymns. No forced solemnity. No Sunday finery. No collection plates.

The list has asterisks and exceptions, but its meaning is clear. Centuries of European tradition and Christian habit are deliberately being abandoned to clear the way for new, contemporary forms of worship and belonging. The Next Church and its many smaller, typically suburban relatives are held up as models of the options available to Christians who want to "catch the next wave."

Music provides the clearest indication of the revolutionary change. The musical idioms of the Next Church are contemporary (nothing dating from before 1990 in many cases). One twenty-four-year-old pastor characterized the predominantly rock music of his university-related church as "a cross between Pearl Jam and Hootie and the Blowfish"—in other words, somewhere between angst-ridden "grunge" and upbeat pop.

Yet in many of these churches, the spectrum of styles offered is actually quite narrow—as it has been in most churches throughout history. Country music is usually out of the question, as is religious jazz in the style of either Duke Ellington (in his "Sacred Concerts") or Wynton Marsalis (*In This House on This Morning*). Nor is there music like that of Sister Marie Keyrouz, a Lebanese nun who has begun singing the chants of her tradition in an appealing, "secular" style that utilizes colorful instrumental accompaniments. The typical Next Music sound is club-style soft rock.

It would be unusual to hear anything in these churches so morally daring as certain songs of the Grammy-Award-winning Indigo Girls, or anything so ironically and astutely probing as a song on ecological spirituality by James Taylor ("Gaia," from *Hourglass*), or music as alert to alternative spiritualities—African and South-American—as Paul Simon's *Graceland* and *The Rhythm of the Saints,* or as achingly yearning in overall effect as k. d. Lang's "Constant Craving" (*Ingenue*) or U2's "I Still Haven't Found What I'm Looking For" (*Joshua Tree*). These are only a smattering of widely accessible, white and mostly middle-class alternatives.

The more ritualized yet contemporary music from Taizé (composed by Jacques Berthier) and the newly composed yet folk-based songs of the Iona Community in Scotland apparently smack too much of traditional religion to find wide acceptance in the Next Church.

And little of what is currently heard in the megachurch or suburban church with contemporary worship resembles contemporary classical "spiritual minimalism." Nothing in those settings sounds much like Arvo Pärt, Philip Glass, John Tavener, John Adams, Giya Kancheli, or (more Romantic in idiom) Einojuhani Rautavaara. Nor would such churches, which often make use of recordings, be tempted to venture into the recorded repertoire of more avant-garde classical composers such as Igor Stravinsky (by now virtually a classical icon), Olivier Messiaen, Krzysztof Penderecki, Sofia Gubaidulina, or James MacMillan—all certifiably contemporary and almost shockingly spiritual, and frequently explicitly theological.

The current selectivity in church music, because it is more the rule than the exception, would be unremarkable except for the claim made by the Next Church and its contemporary Christian relatives: that theirs is the truly contemporary alternative for Christian music today.

In his book *Dancing with Dinosaurs: Ministry in a Hostile and Hurting World*, William Easum makes this very claim about worship and music. A former United Methodist pastor, Easum works as a consultant with congregations and religious organizations. He describes major changes in worship as the "second stage" of the Reformation. "The shift in the style of worship is the most obvious and divisive [of the changes]. This divisiveness is over the style of worship rather than doctrine or theology."

Easum insists that the generations that are most vital to church growth, the midlife baby boomers and the baby busters (born after 1964), do not want to be reverent or quiet during worship. He singles out music as the "major vehicle for celebration and communication." Few movies, he observes, make a profit without a solid sound track. So what sort of sound track should a church choose, given the variety of options? Easum claims that the right method for arriving at a suitable style is to determine which radio stations most of the "worship guests" listen to. "Soft rock," he declares, is usually the answer.

For Easum, classical music—and traditional church music in general—is a relic of a dying past. "Classical music was rooted in the native folk music of the time," he says. "That world is gone." He quotes John Bisagno, pastor of the First Baptist Church in Houston:

> Long-haired music, funeral-dirge anthems and stiff-collared song leaders will kill the church faster than anything in the world. . . . There are no great, vibrant, soul-winning churches reaching great numbers of people, baptizing hundreds of converts, reaching masses, that have stiff music, seven-fold amens and a steady diet of classical anthems. None. That's not a few. That's none, none, none.

If you want life and growth, Easum suggests, make use of music, art, and media that are "culturally relevant." He repeatedly emphasizes the importance of "quality music"—music produced not by choirs and organs, but by praise teams, soloists, and a variety of instrumentalists and small ensembles that use synthesizers, drums, and electric guitars. Quality music, especially in the context of youth evangelism, needs to be entertaining. What about cultivating some sort of developed and mature taste for quality in worship music? Easum says, "Worship is not the place to teach music appreciation." The only question that worship communities need to ask about music is: "Does it bring people closer to God?" Music is never the message. "No form is inherently better than another. Music is good if it conveys the gospel; it is bad if it does not." Easum is willing to cite historical precedents if he thinks they serve his purpose:

> Spiritual giants such as Martin Luther and Charles Wesley showed us the importance of culturally relevant music [by] taking the tunes out of bars, putting words to them and singing the songs in worship. They accommodated the people in order to reach them with the message that would change their lives. They did not conform the message, just the *package.*

Christians should be able to sympathize with most of Easum's pastoral and musical concerns. Importing Vivaldi or Brahms or William Mathias into a church community whose native musical languages are closer to those of Madonna, Jimmy Buffett, or John Tesh is like missionaries imposing European or North American religious styles on drastically different cultures. (Not that converts do not sometimes need and welcome a sharp alternative to their native cultural vocabulary. Chinese Christians have treasured the gospel hymns brought to them by nineteenth-century missionaries, choosing them over songs using Chinese folk tunes or composed later by Chinese Christians and in a Chinese idiom.)

Easum makes a valid point, moreover, in claiming that music that was originally secular has repeatedly found its way into church. The boundary between sacred and secular has repeatedly been blurred or transgressed. No one style is unalterably sacred or unalterably secular. And Easum is probably correct that much of the soft rock or pop music that he advocates for worship has become a kind of generic musical product, with no set of specifically worldly associations that would prevent its use in worship. One could make a similar observation regarding the baroque and early classical musical styles of the seventeenth and early-eighteenth centuries (roughly from Handel to Haydn), which crossed rather freely from the operatic stage and concert hall to the church and back again.

Again, matching religious words with neutral or nonspecific popular music can bring out a suitable range of meanings that the music might not have on its own. Amy Grant, Petra, and countless others adopt and adapt rock as a Christian musical style that their listeners find entirely consonant with their sense of Christian life and proclamation.

Finally, we can agree with Easum's implicit claim that church music has sometimes been unduly limited by traditional suspicions of pulsing or lively rhythms, "irreverent" instruments, and entertainment. (Religious music would be in trouble in much of the world if it could never be rhythmic or animated.)

Despite the merits of some of Easum's claims, he makes several highly questionable assumptions:

- that religious quality and musical quality are both reliably indicated by numerical success
- that liking a certain kind of music for light entertainment is the same as liking that music for all the purposes of worship
- that the key to musical quality, religiously and aesthetically, is immediate accessibility
- that religious music is never, therefore, a medium one might expect to grow into and grow through as a part of Christian formation and development

We also question other Easum claims: that worship music must always be upbeat and animated if it is to be "culturally relevant"; that classical music in general is stodgy and fossilized; that religious words guarantee genuinely religious music as long as the music is likable; and that music can be treated simply as a "package" that contains the gospel message instead of as an art that embodies and interprets the gospel message by its structure and by the very way it sounds. Finally, Easum assumes that he is competent to make judgments about the viability of particular kinds of music without engaging in genuine dialogue with musicians trained in those traditions. Thus, far from exhibiting ecumenical taste, he takes a selective and dogmatic position disguised as an obedience to a gospel imperative to spread the Good News.

In fairness, it must be said that the musicians Easum has dealt with might not have been open to much dialogue. Traditional and classical musicians in the employment of churches have all too often dismissed pastoral and worship concerns as irrelevant to their music-making. Faced with the narrowly musical mind-set and unchristian arrogance of certain professional "classical" church musicians, Easum has taken matters into his own hands. He has discerned and reacted to congregational restlessness and dissatisfaction, something that more traditional musicians have been slow to notice and reluctant to treat as relevant to their work. That does not mean, however, that Easum and others taking his approach exhibit the sort of taste and informed judgment that would make them reliable guides to Christian growth (or even church growth) in the sphere of music and the arts.

Consider the current status of classical music—and of certain other "minority" styles—in church and out, and the use of "secular" musical styles in church, and hence the relationship between medium and message in worship. The argument that traditional church music, particularly classical, is either extinct or well on the way toward extinction may seem to be of relatively minor theological consequence. Yet it is highly charged from the perspective of those Christians whose faith is significantly shaped through such music. It has a direct bearing on the question of assessing "cultural relevance." The way the argument is usually deployed (whether true or not) reflects a highly questionable understanding of the range of art needed for the whole of the Christian life.

Easum predicts, for example, the quick death of all symphony orchestras that do not soon begin to feature a significant amount of pop and rock music. A number of observations counter his suppositions and provide the sort of evidence regarding "cultural relevance" that Easum would have every reason to regard as pertinent.

First, opera has experienced a tremendous revival of late, and not only among the senior generations. Opera houses in many parts of the world (including the United States) are filled to capacity and are adding series. The number of people in North America who say they very much like classical music stands at a substantial 14 to 20 percent across the generations, a more consistently favorable cross-generational response than for most other styles. Although the sale of classical recordings is a relatively small percentage of total audio sales, that can partly be explained by the fact that classical music is much less oriented toward the currently fashionable and the new, which quickly becomes unfashionable and is therefore replaced. As Mark C. Taylor remarks, fashion—being "forever committed to the new"—speaks only in the "present tense." That hardly argues against incorporating classical styles in many church settings, but instead cautions us that riding each successive wave of fashion may be neither desirable nor even possible.

Other music, known as "early music" (roughly European "classical" music before the eighteenth-century classical period), has attracted a significant and ardent audience that augments the already considerable following of baroque music such as Pachelbel's "Canon in D," Bach's *Brandenburg Concerti*, and Handel's *Messiah*. A concert by the women's medieval quartet Anonymous 4, the Monteverdi Consort, or the Tallis Scholars is normally packed, whether they sing in Rome, London, or Indianapolis.

And recent years have seen a surge in the popularity of chant. The widespread introduction of religious services using music from the religious community at Taizé, France, fits with this trend, since much of it tends to be rather contemplative and in harmony with the moods if not modes of chant. The attraction of such "boring" ritual music challenges Easum's notion that "culturally relevant" music must be lively and entertaining.

Still another trend—and this one should have caught Easum's attention, given his interest in "sound tracks"—is the use of music that draws on classical idioms in the composition of musical scores for films of high drama, serious feeling, or intense introspection. An array of recent movies use music indebted to classical traditions. The music that John Williams has composed for the *Star Wars* series often sounds like something one might expect from Sergei Prokofiev or Gustav Holst. The film *Shine* features the Rachmaninov *Third Piano Concerto*. One can also cite John Corigliano's largely classical score for *The Red Violin*, the contemporary classical music for Terrence Malick's war movie *The Thin Red Line*, the fascinating and contemporary sound tracks for the morally complex films of Krzysztof Kieslowski, Ennio Morricone's score for *The Mission*, and music for "period" films such as *Shakespeare in Love*.

These examples suggest that "classical" music is not only very much alive, though evolving, but also enormously varied—more varied than one would guess on the basis of the "classical music" one typically hears in churches.

Before judging which kinds of music are culturally relevant and relevant to the transformation of values appropriate to Christian culture and growth, it is important to attain a theologically adequate and aesthetically informed picture of the musical options. I would argue that out of many legitimate options, the Euro-American classical tradition remains one of the most varied, profound, and adaptable traditions—in ways churches have yet to imagine.

If churches interested in survival and growth follow the advice of those pushing hardest for "cultural relevance"—and many churches are doing just that—Christian churches will be put in the ironic position of refusing to make use of music as serious (or exalted) as what one hears on a regular basis in the movie theater, on television and radio, in the opera house, symphony hall, and local restaurant. And that would be because the churches have misunderstood their cultural situation and defined their mission in terms of misplaced marketing values—values that can seriously undervalue the spiritually transformative potential of challenging artistry (both "classical" and vernacular). The same values would have had Jesus popularize his image and simplify his message before it was too late.

Similar misunderstandings can be found in common assumptions about the viability of simply "packaging" a sacred message in an appealing secular style. Protestants and other Christians have made wide use of secular sources for their hymn tunes and religious music. J. S. Bach borrowed from his secular cantatas and harpsichord concerti when composing his sacred works, including his *B Minor Mass*. Martin Luther has been credited with saying he did not want the devil to have all the good tunes. Yet secular and popular music was not the only sort that Luther wanted to raid. He was openly jealous of "the fine music and songs" and "precious melodies" that the Catholics got to use at masses for the dead, and thought it would "be a pity to let them perish." He said that the pope's followers in general possess "a lot of splendid, beautiful songs and music, especially in cathedral and parish churches," which ought to be divested of "idolatrous, lifeless and foolish texts" and reused for the sake of their beauty. He was hardly the advocate of strictly casual and vernacular styles.

John Calvin was extremely cautious about the music he sanctioned for use in worship, which he thought should exhibit moderation, gravity, and majesty. Luther and John Wesley could both be very particular about the tunes they wanted to use with hymn texts. Wesley designated the ones he judged to be suitable; Luther would not sanction the free use of music from bars and brothels.

Why would any Christian theologian, pastor, or musician want to make such discriminations? It is doubtful that they would if they thought that music provides nothing more than a "package" for the gospel message, and one that is adequate as long as it is appealing. That is not what any of the major Reformers thought, even though they were sure that some secular music could legitimately be borrowed and adapted for religious purposes.

Christians today need to be thinking more carefully and deeply about sacred and secular in the realm of music. Art, and certainly musical art, may have a special religious calling, because it tends to come from the heart and go to the heart—to paraphrase what Beethoven said of his *Missa Solemnis*. But perhaps not all art is meant to touch the heart, let alone the soul; and perhaps even the music that touches the heart does so in quite different ways. A clever piano sonata that Mozart composed in his head is not likely to be perceived as religious or "spiritual." However justified Karl Barth's conviction may have been that Mozart's ostensibly secular music is possibly even more significant, religiously, than his masses, a lover of Mozart's music may "adore" Cherubino's adolescent and flirtatious songs in the *Marriage of Figaro* without needing to regard them as even remotely religious, let alone as generally well suited for worship. As for the masses, clergy and musicians from Mozart's time to the present have expressed reservations about their more operatic traits—the religious admiration of Barth and Hans Küng notwithstanding.

One does not have to believe that certain styles of music are inherently religious in order to be convinced that some kinds of music are generally more suitable for worship than are other kinds. Pianist and musicologist Charles Rosen has articulated a number of cogent reasons for regarding the classical style of Haydn, Mozart, and Beethoven as peculiarly handicapped in the realm of sacred music. In Rosen's view, those composers wisely departed from the more strictly "classical" conventions to become more "archaic" in style (modal, contrapuntal) when writing their most serious church music—Haydn's oratorio *The Creation*, for instance, or Mozart's *Requiem and Mass in C Minor*, or Beethoven's *Missa Solemnis*.

And some musical styles are more flexible than others. Both baroque music and African-American gospel music have roots within the churches as well as within secular settings, permitting composers and performers in these idioms to make relatively minor stylistic adjustments that will readily put into play the appropriate range of associations, thoughts, and feelings.

Other music is designed and adapted primarily to do such things as create cerebral conundrums (some avant-garde classical works) or energize sporting events, entertain at parties, reduce stress, or enhance bedroom desires. As Martha Bayles argues in *Hole in Our Soul: The Loss of Beauty and Meaning in American Popular Music*, early rock 'n' roll, for all its undeniable sexual energy, originated out of a milieu deeply influenced by a white Pentecostalism that borrowed African-American rhythm-and-blues styles while remaining defensively segregated. Elvis Presley, Jerry Lee Lewis, and Little Richard all grew up in Pentecostal churches and sometimes made highly conflicted, guilt-ridden alterations of their churches' music. But, Bayles goes on, a multitude of influences—including the impulses of artistic modernism—conspired to push moral and religious associations and tensions out of much subsequent popular music. Her claim may be overstated, but it finds a certain amount of agreement among popular musicians themselves.

Some musical styles, instead of being flexible or neutral, seem quite specialized in character—something made exceptionally clear by novelist Robertson Davies in *The Cunning Man*, in which the narrator describes his first encounter with plainsong:

> At first I did not know what it was. At intervals the eight men in the chancel choir, or sometimes Dwyer alone, would utter what sounded like speech of a special eloquence, every word clearly to be heard, but observing a discipline that was musical, in that there was no hint of anything that was colloquial, but not like any music I had met with in my, by this

time, fairly good acquaintance with music. My idea of church music at its highest was Bach, but Bach at his most reverent is still intended for performance. This was music addressed to God, not as performance, but as the most intimate and devout communication. It was a form of speech fit for the ear of the Highest.

Gregorian chant would serve poorly for purposes of inebriated celebration; by the same token, the latest Ricky Martin hit would serve poorly for purposes of meditative prayer.

Thus, in response to any uncritical willingness to adopt for worship whatever music people favor in their radio listening, one might ask: Is it possible that musicians in our notably secular era have become especially adept at shaping music to specifically erotic, recreational, and commercial purposes? If so, might not bending those sorts of music to the ends of worship be like choosing to praise or thank God in the tone of voice one would use to order a pizza or to cheer a touchdown—or perhaps even to make the most casual sort of love?

No doubt part of the meaning we hear in a given kind of music is "socially constructed," which raises the possibility that an alteration in the construct will alter completely how the music sounds. Simon Frith makes such an argument when he proposes that it is "cultural ideology," rather than anything within the music or its beat, that produces most of the sexual and bodily associations of rock 'n' roll. But his elaborate and brilliant defense of that claim is too clever. Nothing one can do will convert Gregorian chant into a style as bodily and erotic in its center as various kinds of rock; nor can rock be made to sound as contemplative or as ethereal as chant, though it can indeed take on an aura of ecstasy.

The whole question of meaning in music is elusive, and in many ways a matter of intuitions that we cannot fully explain. Nonetheless, music, as literary and cultural critic George Steiner insists,

> is brimful of meanings which will not translate into logical structures or verbal expression . . . Music is at once cerebral in the highest degree—I repeat that the energies and form-relations in the playing of a quartet, in the interactions of voice and instrument are among the most complex events known to man—and it is at the same time somatic, carnal and a searching out of resonances in our bodies at levels deeper than will or consciousness.

Because of the virtually sacramental "real presence" of its meaning, music has "celebrated the mystery of intuitions of transcendence."

Particular sorts of music have a range of possible nonverbal meanings that verbal language and cultural context can then shape and construe in more specific ways. One can distinguish between religious music most appropriate for the inner sanctuary (both literally and figuratively), and that which is best for the nave of the church, or for the courtyard, recreational hall, or concert stage. One can fittingly choose to use religious music in any of these settings, but its character and purpose will shift accordingly, with convention playing a role in shaping those choices.

None of this means that worship services should never make use of rock, or even heavy metal and "grunge." Robert Walser argues that this notoriously "diabolical" genre of music can be converted into a credible and creative force with a Christian evangelistic message. According to Walser, the Christian heavy metal band Stryper communicates "experiences of power and transcendent freedom" in which a new sort of meaning emerges from the sounds and gestures, which begin to serve as religious metaphors: "The power is God's; the transcendent freedom represents the rewards of Christianity; the intensity is that of religious experience . . . . Stryper presents Christianity as an exciting, youth-oriented alternative."

But because religious meanings cannot simply be imposed on every sort of musical medium, regardless of its style, considerable musical and liturgical experimentation could be required to find out which forms of rock and pop permit or invite stretching for religious purposes. Christians probably need musical "laboratories," involving both clergy and musicians.

No doubt some of the worship services that now use popular and casual idioms were not awe-filled to begin with but awful: bland, stiff, and stifled. Nevertheless, if the medium of religious practice and expression is not only predominantly casual in style but also artistically "flimsy" (a complaint lodged by Kathleen Norris), or perhaps even kitsch, then one must ask: What sort of God are worshipers envisioning as they sing or look or move? To what sort of life and growth do they suppose they are being called? The possibility that a relatively casual and unchallenging style might be all there is to a community's worship life is bound to be deflating to those whose call to discipleship causes them to yearn for something more in aesthetic formation and development.

As for the uncritical adoption of "secular" styles, there is no denying that the act of giving ordinary, secular-sounding expression to extraordinary reality can transform the ordinary and secular into something sacred. But marrying gospel insights and liturgical actions to a musical medium that was originally secular in sound and purpose is an art. Carelessly done, it can inadvertently convert the sacred into something quite ordinary.

Testing Christian Taste: Twelve Guidelines

1. There are many kinds of good taste, and many kinds of good religious art and music. In view of cultural diversity, it would be extremely odd if that were not true.
2. Not all kinds of good art and music are equally good for worship, let alone for every tradition or faith community. In terms of worship, therefore, it is not enough that a work or style of art be likable; it must also be appropriate.
3. There are various appropriately Christian modes of mediating religious experience artistically—from radically transcendent to radically immanent in a sense of the holy; from exuberantly abundant to starkly minimal in means; from prophetic to pastoral in tone; from instructive to meditative in aim.
4. Every era and cultural context tends to develop new forms of good sacred music and art, which to begin with often seem secular.
5. Because every musical/aesthetic style calls for a particular kind of attunement, no one person can be competent to make equally discerning judgments about every kind of music. Yet almost everyone is inclined to assume or act otherwise. That impulse is related to the sin of pride.
6. It is an act of Christian love to learn to appreciate or at least respect what others value in a particular style or work that they cherish in worship or in the rest of life. That is different, however, from personally liking every form of commendable art, which is impossible and unnecessary.
7. Disagreements over taste in religious music (or any other art) can be healthy and productive; but they touch on sensitive matters and often reflect or embody religious differences as well as aesthetic ones.
8. The reasons why an aesthetic work or style is good or bad, weak or strong (and in what circumstances), can never be expressed fully in words; yet they can often be pointed out through comparative—and repeated—looking and listening.
9. Aesthetic judgments begin with, and owe special consideration to, the community or tradition to which a given style or work is indigenous or most familiar. But they seldom end there; and they cannot, if the style or work is to invite the attention of a wide range of people over a period of time.
10. The evaluation of art used in worship needs to be done jointly by clergy, congregation, and trained artists and musicians, taking into account not only the aesthetic qualities of the art itself but also

the larger requirements and contours of worship, which should at once respond to and orient the particular work of art or music.

11. While relative accessibility is imperative for most church art, the church also needs art—including "classic" art of various kinds—that continually challenges and solicits spiritual and theological growth in the aesthetic dimension. This is art that the Christian can grow into but seldom out of.

12. Almost every artistic style that has been enjoyed and valued by a particular group over a long period of time and for a wide range of purposes has religious potential. That is because life typically finds various and surprising ways of turning religious. As Augustine said, our hearts are restless until they rest in God.

Notes

Foreword

1. Alan Wolfe, *The Transformation of American Religion* (New York: Free Press, 2003), 36.

Introduction

1. Robb Redman, "What Worship Leaders Need to Know," *Worship Leader Magazine* (January/February 1998): 26–30.

2. Craig Douglas Erickson, *Participating in Worship: History, Theory, and Practice* (Louisville: Westminster/John Knox Press, 1989), 15.

3. James B. Torrance, *Worship, Community and the Triune God of Grace* (Downers Grove, IL: InterVarsity Press, 1996), 15.

4. Ibid., 14–15.

5. Ibid., 16.

6. D. A. Carson, ed., *Worship by the Book* (Grand Rapids: Zondervan, 2003), 45.

7. F. Russell Mitman, *Worship in the Shape of Scripture* (Cleveland: Pilgrim Press, 2001), 118.

8. Erickson, *Participating in Worship*, 16.

9. Ibid., 21.

10. Michael C. Hawn, *Gather into One: Singing and Praying Globally* (Grand Rapids: Eerdmans, 2003), 31.

Chapter 1: What Do We Mean by "Christian Worship"?

1. *The New Dictionary of Sacramental Worship*, ed. Peter E. Fink (Collegeville, MN: Liturgical Press, 1990), s.v. "Ritual" (by George Worgul).

2. Gordon W. Lathrop, *Holy Things: A Liturgical Theology* (Minneapolis: Fortress Press, 1993), 35–79.

3. Don E. Saliers, *Worship as Theology: Foretaste of Glory Divine* (Nashville: Abingdon Press, 1994), 166.

4. Martin Luther, *D. Martin Luthers Werke* (Weimar: H. Böhlau, 1913), [WA] 49:588.15–18, quoted in Peter Brunner, *Worship in the Name of Jesus*, trans. M. H. Bertram (St. Louis: Concordia Publishing House, 1968), 123.

5. *The Book of Concord; The Confessions of the Evangelical Lutheran Church*, trans. and ed. Theodore G. Tappert (Philadelphia: Fortress Press, 1959), 376.

6. John Calvin, *Institutes of the Christian Religion*, ed. John T. McNeill, trans. Ford Lewis Battles (Philadelphia: Westminster Press, 1960), 1192.

7. Commentary on Psalm 24:7, *Commentaries* 31:248. I owe this passage to Dr. John Witvliet.

193

8. "Of Ceremonies," *The First and Second Prayer Books of Edward V* (London: Dent, 1964), 326. Spelling modernized.

9. George Florovsky, "Worship and Every-Day Life: An Eastern Orthodox View," *Studia Liturgica* 2 (December 1963), 268.

10. Ibid., 269.

11. Nikos A. Nissiotis, "Worship, Eucharist, and 'Intercommunion': An Orthodox Reflection," *Studia Liturgica* 2 (September 1963), 201.

12. *Tra le sollecitudini*, in *The New Liturgy*, ed. R. Kevin Seasoltz (New York: Herder and Herder, 1966), 4.

13. Godfrey Diekmann, *Personal Prayer and the Liturgy* (London: Geoffrey Chapman, 1969), 57.

14. Odo Casel, *The Mystery of Christian Worship, and Other Writings*, ed. Burkhard Neunheuser (Westminster, MD: Newman Press, 1962), 141.

15. Evelyn Underhill, *Worship* (London: Nisbet and Co., 1936), 84–85.

Chapter 2: Worship as Adoration and Action

1. See Aristotle, *Nicomachean Ethics*, 1.177b.

2. On the relation between action and contemplation, see H. U. von Balthasar, "Aktion und Kontemplation," in *Verbum Caro*, Skizzen zur Theologie I (Einsiedeln: Johannes Verlag, 1960), 245–59.

3. Aquinas, *Summa Theologica*, II-II, Q.179, A.2 and Q.182, A.3, 4.

4. See Max Weber, *The Protestant Ethic and the Spirit of Capitalism*, trans. Talcott Parsons (New York: Charles Scribner's Sons, 1958), 80.

5. For a critique of Luther's vocational understanding of work, see Miroslav Volf, *Work in the Spirit: Toward a Theology of Work* (New York: Oxford University Press, 1991), 105ff.

6. James D. G. Dunn, *Romans 9–16*, Word Biblical Commentary 38B (Dallas: Word, 1988), 710.

7. See Ernst Käsemann, "Worship in Everyday Life: A Note on Romans 12," in *New Testament Questions of Today* (London: S.C.M. Press, 1969), 188–95.

8. See David Peterson, "Worship in the New Testament," in *Worship: Adoration and Action*, ed. D. A. Carson (Carlisle, PA: Paternoster, 1993), 51ff.

9. See Yoshiaki Hattori, "Worship in the Context of the Canonical Old Testament," 21 n. 1, 212.

10. According to the Atra-Hasis epic —and in this respect virtually all Mesopotamian myths of human creation agree —human beings were created in order to liberate the gods from strenuous labor. Creation of human beings was meant to solve the problem of lower gods refusing to do their work (see W. Zimmerli, "Mensch und Arbeit im Alten Testament," in *Recht auf Arbeit—Sinn der Arbeit*, ed. Jürgen Moltmann (Munich: Kaiser, 1979], 40–58, 52). In the Atra-Hasis epic, work is immediately related to the service of gods. In the Old Testament work is divorced from its immediate connection with cult and placed into service of culture. But as such, work is at the same time service to God.

11. See Hannah Arendt, *Vita Activa oder Vom tätigen Leben* (Munich: Piper, 1981), 281ff.

12. Os Guinness, "Mission in the Face of Modernity. Nine Checkpoints on Mission Without Worldliness in the Modern World" (paper presented at Lausanne II for the Plenary Session on the Impact of Modernization, Manila, Philippines, July 11–20, 1989), 5.

13. Ibid., 7.

14. José Porfirio Miranda, *Marx and the Bible. A Critique of the Philosophy of Oppression*, trans. John Eagleson (New York: Orbis Books, 1974), 35–76.

15. José Porfirio Miranda, "Is Marxism Essentially Atheistic?" in *Journal of Ecumenical Studies* 22 (1985): 509–15 (italics mine).

16. Ibid.

17. In a somewhat less radical way, Käsemann proclaims that worship and ethics fall into one and that ethics is the only "cult" that remains for Christians (Käsemann, "Worship in Everyday Life," in *New Testament Questions*, 191f).

18. See Yoshiaki Hattori, "Theology of Worship in the Old Testament," in *Worship*, 44.

19. See Peterson, "Worship in the New Testament," in *Worship*, 89.

20. In Eastern orthodox theology the summit of mystical life is sometimes perceived to consist "in the personal encounter with Christ who speaks in our hearts by the Holy Spirit" (P. Evdokimov, *L'Orthodoxie* [Paris: Desclée de Brouwer, 1979], 113).

21. "The Oxford Declaration on Christian Faith and Economics," *Transformation* 7, no. 2 (1990): 1–8, n. 30. For the background reflection on this formulation, see Volf, *Work in the Spirit*, 136ff.

22. On the presence of God in creation in relation to worship, see Alexander Schmemann, *Sacraments and Orthodoxy* (New York: Herder and Herder, 1965), 10ff.

23. See Peterson, "Worship in the New Testament," in *Worship*, 76.

24. See Paul Tillich, *Systematic Theology III: Life and the Spirit, History and the Kingdom of God* (Chicago: University of Chicago Press, 1963), 379f.

25. See Hattori, "Theology of Worship in the Old Testament," in *Worship*, 36; and see Peterson, "Worship in the New Testament," in *Worship*, 80.

26. Vladimir Lossky, *The Mystical Theology of the Eastern Church* (Crestwood, NY: St. Vladimir's Seminary Press, 1976), 9. For the same emphasis in the Catholic tradition, see Joseph Cardinal Ratzinger, *Schauen auf den Durchbohrten. Versuche zu einer spirituellen Christologie* (Einsiedeln: Johannes Verlag, 1984), 18.

27. See on that Volf, *Work in the Spirit*, 98ff; M. Hengel, "Die Arbeit in fruhen Christentum," in *Th Beit* (1986): 174–212, 180.

28. Though one should interpret the phrase as "God's we are, being fellow workers" rather than "we are labourers together *with* God" (so Gordon Fee, *The First Epistle to the Corinthians* [Grand Rapids: Eerdmans, 1987], 134), the agricultural imagery in the context suggests cooperation not only between Paul and Apollos but also of both of them with God: "I planted the seed, Apollos watered it, but God made

it grow" (1 Cor 3:6 NIV). The main point of the verse is, of course, that the work of both Paul and Apollos is useless unless God gives growth. But it implies also clearly that God cannot give growth to what Paul and Apollos (or some other human beings) have not planted and watered. The idea of apostles being co-workers with God is "consistent with Paul's thought in general" (see C. K. Barrett, *A Commentary on the First Epistle to the Corinthians* [London: Black, 1968], 86).

29. On contemplation as an activity, see von Balthasar, "Aktion und Kontemplation," in *Verbum Caro*, 245, 250.

30. Luther wrote: "ne *vita active* cum suis operibus et *vita contemplativa* cum suis speculationibus nos seducant" (WA 5, 85, 2f). On Luther's perspectives on *vita passiva* as distinct from *vita activa* and *vita contemplativa* in the context of a discussion about relation of theology to theory and practice, see O. Bayer, "Theologie und Philosophic in produktevim Konflikt," *Neue Zeitschrift für Systematische Theologie und Religionsphilosophie* 32 (1990), 226–36, 234.

Chapter 3: Liturgical Assembly as Locus of Mission

1. John Gordon Davies, *Worship and Mission* (London: S.C.M. Press, 1966), 9.

2. Ibid., 10.

3. For an introduction, see the chapter "Inculturation" in John R. K. Fenwick and Bryan D. Spinks, *Worship in Transition: The Liturgical Movement in the Twentieth Century* (New York: Continuum, 1995), 157–66. The Lutheran World Federation study on worship and culture has generated a significant body of literature on these issues in its Cartigny, Nairobi, and Chicago statements, together with their supporting papers and bibliographies; see S. Anita Stautter, ed., *Worship and Culture in Dialogue* (Geneva: Lutheran World Federation, 1994); *Christian Worship: Unity and Cultural Diversity* (Geneva: Lutheran World Federation, 1996); and *Baptism, Rites of Passage, and Culture* (Geneva: Lutheran World Federation, 1999).

4. In North America, this includes the debate surrounding so-called contemporary and traditional forms of worship as well as efforts to contextualize worship in the diverse cultures of North America. On the contemporary versus traditional discussion, compare, for example, Kennon T. Callahan, *Dynamic Worship: Mission, Grace, Praise, and Power* (San Francisco: HarperSanFrancisco, 1994) and Timothy Wright, *A Community of Joy: How to Create Contemporary Worship* (Nashville: Abingdon Press, 1994) to Frank C. Senn, *The Witness of the Worshiping Community: Liturgy and the Practice of Evangelism* (New York: Paulist Press, 1993) and the series Open Questions in Worship, 8 vols., ed. Gordon W. Lathrop (Minneapolis: Augsburg Fortress, 1994–96), especially vol. 1, *What Are the Essentials of Christian Worship?*, vol. 2, *What Is "Contemporary" Worship?*, vol. 3, *How Does Worship Evangelize?*, and vol. 6, *What Are the Ethical Implications of Worship?* On the matter of worship and the cultures of North America, see, for example, vol. 7 in the Open Questions series, *What Does Multicultural Worship Look Like?* See also the new ethnic liturgical resources prepared by the Evangelical Lutheran Church in America: the Spanish language worship book *Libro de Liturgia y Cántico* (Minneapolis: Augsburg Fortress, 1998) and *This Far by Faith: An African American Resource for Worship* (Minneapolis: Augsburg Fortress, 1999).

5. These schematic descriptions of what I have termed the conventional, contemporary, and radically traditional approaches to the relationship between worship and mission risk reducing some rather complex realities of church life and forcing them into clearly delineated models. Nonetheless, there is heuristic value—that is, we can learn something—in such descriptions, as long as we are clear that the understanding and practice of worship in relation to mission in its concrete actuality in congregational life will not conform neatly to any proposed model.

6. Davies, *Worship and Mission*, 7.

7. Darrell L. Guder, ed., *Missional Church: A Vision for the Sending of the Church in North America* (Grand Rapids: Eerdmans, 1998), 242.

8. Ibid., 243.

9. Rodney Clapp, *A Peculiar People: The Church as Culture in a Post-Christian Society* (Downer's Grove, IL: InterVarsity Press, 1996), 114–15.

10. Bruce D. Marshall, "The Disunity of the Church and the Credibility of the Gospel," *Theology Today* 50, no. 1 (April 1993), 81–82.

11. Senn, *The Witness of the Worshiping Community*, 5.

12. Gordon W. Lathrop, *Holy Things: A Liturgical Theology* (Minneapolis: Fortress Press, 1993), 207–10.

13. *The Use of the Means of Grace: A Statement on the Practice of Word and Sacrament*, adopted for guidance and practice [by the] Evangelical Lutheran Church in America (Minneapolis: Augsburg Fortress, 1997), principle 51 and application 51B.

14. Ibid., principle 51; the heading for principle 51 itself underscores the instrumental view: "The Means of Grace Lead the Church to Mission".

15. *Service Book and Hymnal* (Minneapolis: Augsburg Publishing House; Philadelphia: Board of Publications, Lutheran Church in America, 1958), I.

16. Ibid., 12.

17. The space was one designed by Sovik, Mathre, and Madson, Northfield, Minnesota, for Bethesda Lutheran Church, Ames, Iowa, and dedicated in 1964.

18. Contemporary Worship, 10 vols, (Minneapolis: Augsburg Publishing House; Philadelphia: Board of Publications, Lutheran Church in America; St. Louis: Concordia Publishing House, 1969–76).

19. *Lutheran Book of Worship* (Minneapolis: Augsburg Publishing House; Philadelphia: Board of Publications, Lutheran Church in America, 1978).

20. Ibid., 56.

21. Ibid., 70.

22. Wolfhart Pannenberg, *Christian Spirituality* (Philadelphia: Westminster Press, 1983).

23. Ibid., 17.

24. Ibid., 31–32.

25. Ibid., 31.

26. Ibid., 46.

27. Ibid., 36.

28. See *Prayers for the Eucharist: Early and Reformed*, 3rd ed., trans. and ed. R. D. C. Jasper and G. J. Cuming (New York: Pueblo Publishing Company, 1987), 119.

29. Alexander Schmemann, *For the Life of the World: Sacraments and Orthodoxy* (Crestwood, NY: St. Vladimir's Seminary Press, 1973).

30. It is worth noting that prior to his polemical writings about the mass, which presented the Lord's Supper as a testament or promise of forgiveness, Luther's theology of the Lord's Supper gave great weight to *koinonia* as the significance of the sacrament; see Martin Luther, "The Blessed Sacrament of the Holy and True Body of Christ, and the Brotherhoods, 1519," in *Luther's Works*, ed. Helmut T. Lehmann (Philadelphia: Fortress Press, 1960), 35:50–60. Although the centrality of this conception of the sacrament recedes in Luther's struggle against the sacrifice of the mass, it is never abandoned and should remain a part of any full account of Luther's understanding of the Lord's Supper. One could explore, for example, the connections of the communion concept of the sacrament to Luther's strong defense of the real presence against the views of other reformers; see "The Adoration of the Sacrament, 1523" in *Luther's Works*, 36:286–87; "The Sacrament of the Body and Blood of Christ—Against the Fanatics, 1526" in *Luther's Works*, 36:352–53; and "Against the Heavenly Prophets in the Matter of Images and Sacraments, 1525" in *Luther's Works*, 40:178. See Yngve Brilioth, *Eucharistic Faith and Practice: Evangelical and Catholic*, trans. A. G. Herbert (London: Society for Promoting Christian Knowledge, 1961), 95–98, 133–35; Pannenberg, *Christian Spirituality*, 38–41; and Thomas H. Schattauer, "The Reconstruction Rite: The Liturgical Legacy of Wilhelm Löhe," in *Rule of Prayer, Rule of Faith: Essays in Honor of Aidan Kavanagh, O.S.B.*, ed. Nathan Mitchell and John F. Baldovin (Collegeville, MN.: Liturgical Press, 1996), 275–76.

31. The reference is to Aidan Kavanagh, *On Liturgical Theology: The Hale Memorial Lectures of Seabury-Western Theological Seminary, 1981* (New York: Pueblo Publishing Company, 1984); see especially chapter 4, "Doing the World," 52–69.

32. Georges Florovsky, "Empire and Desert: Antinomies of Christian History," *Greek Orthodox Theological Review* 3 (Winter 1957): 133–59. Quoted in Rodney Clapp, *A Peculiar People: The Church as Culture in a Post-Christian Society* (Downers Grove, IL: InterVarsity Press, 1996), flyleaf.

33. *Lutheran Book of Worship*, Ministers Edition (Minneapolis: Augsburg Publishing House; Philadelphia: Board of Publications, Lutheran Church in America, 1978), 144.

34. See Pannenberg, *Christian Spirituality*, 35–58.

35. Nathan Mitchell, "The Amen Corner: 'Worship as Music,'" *Worship* 73, no. 4 (July 1999): 254. Mitchell is reflecting on and quoting from Catherine Pickstock, *After Writing: On the Liturgical Consummation of Philosophy* (Oxford: Blackwell Publishers, 1998), 196.

36. *Lutheran Book of Worship*, 70

37. Wilhelm Löhe, *Three Books about the Church*, trans. and ed. James L. Schaaf (Philadelphia: Fortress Press, 1969), 51.

38. Ibid., 50.

39. Ibid., 49.

40. Robert Jenson, "How the World Lost Its Story," *First Things* 36 (October 1993): 24.

41. Gregor T. Goethals, *The Electronic Golden Calf: Images, Religion, and the Making of Meaning* (Cambridge, MA: Cowley Publications, 1990). Today her study would need to include the impact of the computer and the dissemination of images through the Internet.

42. Ibid., 145.

43. Ibid., 150–51. The term "symbolic canopy" appears on page 163.

44. Ibid., 156.

45. Wilhelm Löhe, "Von den heiligen Personen, der heilgen Zeit, der heiligen Weise und dem heligen Orte" (1859), in *Gesammelte Werke*, vol. 3/I (Neuendettelsau: Freimund, 1951), 570.

Chapter 4: On Starting with People

1. Stephen Gardiner, *The Letters of Stephen Gardiner*, ed. James A. Muller (New York: Macmillan, 1933), 355. Spelling modernized.

2. Marshall McLuhan, *The Gutenberg Galaxy: The Making of Typographic Man* (Toronto: University of Toronto Press, 1962), 125.

3. Henry Barclay Swete, *Church Services and Service Books Before the Reformation* (New York: E. & B. Young & Co., 1896; London: Society for Promoting Christian Knowledge, 1930), 10.

4. Marshall McLuhan, *Understanding Media: The Extensions of Man* (New York: Signet Books, 1966), 87.

5. "The Preface" to 1549 *Book of Common Prayer, The First and Second Prayer Books of Edward VI* (London: J.M. Dent and Sons, 1952), 4.

6. Martin Luther, "Concerning the Order of Public Worship," in *Luther's Works*, ed. Helmut T. Lehmann (Philadelphia: Fortress Press, 1965), 53:11.

7. Marshall McLuhan, *Understanding Media*, 24.

8. Marshall McLuhan and Quentin Fiore, *War and Peace in the Global Village* (New York: McGraw-Hill, 1968).

9. B. F. Jackson, ed., *Communication-Learning for Churchmen* (Nashville: Abingdon Press, 1968), 72.

10. Walter M. Abbot, ed., *The Documents of Vatican II* (New York: Guild Press, America Press, and Association Press, 1966), 151.

11. Myron B. Bloy, *Multi-Media Worship: A Model and Nine Viewpoints*, ed. Myron B. Bloy, Jr. (New York: Seabury Press, 1969).

12. Rembert Weakland, *Worship in a Secular World*, *IDOC Papers* (Rome, January 20, 1968), 6.

Chapter 6: The Crisis of Evangelical Worship

1. Rudolf Otto, *The Idea of the Holy: An Inquiry into the Non-rational Factor in the Idea of the Divine and Its Relation to the Rational*, 2nd ed., trans. John W. Harvey (1950; repr., London: Oxford University Press, 1970), 193.

Chapter 7: A New Reformation

1. Rob Wilson, "Cyborg America: Policing the Social Sublime in Robocop and Robocop 2," in *The Administration of Aesthetics: Censorship, Political Criticism, and the Public Sphere*, ed. Richard Burt (Minneapolis: University of Minnesota Press, 1994), 290.

2. George Barna, "Teenagers and Their Relationships," *The Barna Report* (January–March 1999), 2.

3. Elaine Shepherd, *R. S. Thomas: Conceding an Absence; Images of God Explored* (New York: St. Martin's Press, 1996), 155.

4. Anna Muoio, "Sales School," *Fast Company* (November 1998): 108.

5. Michael J. Wolf, "The Pleasure Binge," *Wired* (March 1999): 86.

6. Spent annually on tourism worldwide: $1.9 trillion. See Peter Weber, "It Comes Down to the Coasts," *World Watch* (March/April 1994): 21.

7. Wolf, "The Pleasure Binge," 89.

8. Jane Miller, *Seductions: Studies in Reading and Culture* (Cambridge: Harvard University Press, 1991), 151.

9. Southern Baptist pastor Jim L. Wilson uses this phrase in his as yet unpublished article on the "cyber-pastor."

10. Wolf, "The Pleasure Binge," 90.

11. Pentecostalism boasts about twenty million new members a year, with especially large gains in Asia and Africa. Some Latin American countries are approaching Pentecostal majorities. Theologian Harvey Cox wrote his study of Pentecostalism not as an objective observer but as a participant. See Harvey Gallagher Cox, *Fire From Heaven: The Rise of Pentecostal Spirituality and the Reshaping of Religion in the Twenty-First Century* (Reading, MA: Addison-Wesley Publishing Company, 1995).

12. Quoted in D. J. Enright, *Interplay: A Kind of Commonplace Book* (Oxford: Oxford Press, 1995), 152.

13. George Lakoff and Mark Johnson, *Metaphors We Live By* (Chicago: University of Chicago Press, 1980), 236–37.

14. For more on this, see Leonard Sweet "Can You Hear the Double Ring?" *Vital Ministry* 2 (March/April 1999), 34–37.

15. James C. Collins and Jerry I. Porras, *Built to Last: Successful Habits of Visionary Companies* (New York: HarperBusiness, 1994), 212–18.

16. Tom Beaudoin, *Virtual Faith: The Irreverent Spiritual Quest of Generation X* (San Francisco: Jossey-Bass, 1998), 78.

17. George Barna, "Teenagers and Their Relationships," 3.

18. Stephen Crites, "The Narrative Quality of Experience," *The Journal of the American Academy of Religion* 39 (September 1971): 291–311.

19. *Times Literary Supplement,* issue 4938 (November 21, 1997), 9. Quoted in Mark Amory, "Elegy and Regret: Review of John Betjeman," *Coming Home: An Anthology of His Prose, 1920–1977* (London: Methuen, 1997).

20. Thomas E. Boomershine, *Story Journey: An Invitation to the Gospel as Storytelling* (Nashville: Abingdon Press, 1988), 18.

21. Ibid., 17.

22. Huston Smith, quoted in Marilyn Snell, "The World of Religion According to Huston Smith," *Mother Jones* (November/December 1997): 43.

23. Sir Karl Raimund Popper, *The Logic of Scientific Discovery* (1959; repr., New York: BasicBooks, 1961), 458.

24. Lorraine Code, "Who Cares? The Poverty of Objectivism for a Moral Epistemology," in "Rethinking Objectivity II," ed. Allan Megill, *Annals of Scholarship* 9, nos. 1–2 (1992): 7.

25. Fred Alan Wolf, *Taking the Quantum Leap: The New Physics for Nonscientists* (San Francisco: Harper and Row, 1981) and Fred Alan Wolf, *Parallel Universes: The Search for Other Worlds* (New York: Simon and Schuster, 1988). See also David Bohm, "Imagination, Fancy, Insight and Reason in the Process of Thought," in *Evolution of Consciousness: Studies in Polarity,* ed. Shir-

ley Sugerman (Middletown, CT: Wesleyan University Press, 1976), 51–68.

26. John Wheeler, "The Universe as Home for Man," *American Scientist* 62 (November 1974), 689.

27. Bryan Appleyard, *Understanding the Present: Science and the Soul of Modern Man* (1993; repr., New York: Doubleday, 1992), xvi.

28. Donald A. Norman, *Things That Make Us Smart: Defending Human Attributes in the Age of the Machine* (Reading, MA: Addison-Wesley Publishing Company, 1993), 250.

29. See Rodney Brooks, *Intelligence Without Reason* (Cambridge, MA: Massachusetts Institute of Technology Artificial Intelligence Laboratory, 1991). In Francisco J. Varela's words, "I am claiming that information—together with all of its closely related notions—has to be reinterpreted as codependent or constructive, in contradistinction to representational or instructive. This means, in other words, a shift from questions about semantic correspondence to questions about structural patterns." See Francisco J. Varela, *Principles of Biological Autonomy* (New York: North Holland, 1979), xv. In E. Neni K. Panourgia, *Fragments of Death, Fables of Identity: An Athenian Anthropography* (1996; repr., Madison: University of Wisconsin Press, 1996), Panourgia pioneers a new kind of anthropologist, the "communicative agent," that takes participant observation to the highest level and farthest limits.

30. Evelyn Fox Keller, *A Feeling for the Organism: The Life and Work of Barbara McClintock* (New York: W.H. Freeman, 1983), 203.

31. Humberto R. Maturana and Francisco J. Varela, *The Tree of Knowledge: The Biological Roots of Human Understanding* (Boston: New Science Library, 1987), 9, 23.

Chapter 8: Moshing for Jesus

1. Patricia Hersch, *A Tribe Apart: A Journey into the Heart of American Adolescence* (New York: Fawcett Columbine, 1998), 206–8.

2. Ibid., 207.

3. Personal conversation with Brent Benton, Brian Hughes, and Julie Kim, Princeton seminarians who reported on the reactions of their churches' youth to moshing, April 14, 1999.

4. Hersch, *A Tribe Apart*, 209.

5. George Barna, *Virtual America* (Ventura, CA: Regal Books, 1994), 58–59. Another 24 percent say they "rarely" or "sometimes" experience God's presence in worship, while 27 percent said they "always" experience God's presence in worship.

6. David Elkind and Sally Elkind, "Varieties of Religious Experience in Young Adolescents," *Scientific Study of Religion* 2 (1962), 102–12.

7. George H. Gallup, Jr., *The Spiritual Life of Young Americans: Approaching the Year 2000* (Princeton, NJ: George H. Gallup International Institute, 1999), 3.

8. Bill Moyers, "Of Myth and Men," *Time,* April 26, 1999, 94.

9. Bernhard Lang, *Sacred Games: A History of Christian Worship* (New Haven and London: Yale University Press, 1997), 1.

10. Steven Daly, "Britney Spears: Inside the Heart and Mind (and Bedroom) of America's New Teen Queen," *Rolling Stone,* April 15, 1999, 131. Quoted in *Youthworker Journal* (July/August 1999), 14.

11. See Matthew McAllister, *The Commercialization of American Culture: New Advertising, Control and Democracy* (London: Sage, 1996).

12. See Rex D. Matthews, "With the Eyes of Faith: Spiritual Experience and the Knowledge of God in the Theology of John Wesley," in *Wesleyan Theology Today: A Bicentennial Theological Consultation,* ed. Theodore Runyan (Nashville: United Methodist Publishing House, 1985), 406–15; Martin Luther, "Preface to the Romans," in *Martin Luther: Selections from His Writings,* ed. John Dillenberger (Chicago: Quadrangle Books, 1961), 24; Jonathan Edwards, "A Treatise Concerning Religious Affections," in *The Works of President Edwards,* vol. 4 (New York: Burt Franklin, 1968).

13. Joseph F. Kett, *Rites of Passage: Adolescence in America, 1790 to Present* (New York: Basic Books, 1977), 64ff.

14. I am indebted to Douglas Strong, professor of American church history, Wesley Theological Seminary, who pointed me to this thesis. See William McLaughlin, *Revivalism, Awakenings, and Reform* (Chicago and London: University of Chicago Press, 1978), and Richard Riss, *A Survey of 20th-Century Revival Movements in North America* (Peabody, MA: Hendrickson Publishers, 1988).

15. Jay R. Howard, *Apostles of Rock: The Splintered World of Contemporary Christian Music* (Lexington, KY: University Press of Kentucky, 1999). Quoted in Joshua Simon, "Hard Rockers, Holy Rollers," *Life* (July 1999), 81–82.

16. See Michael S. Hamilton, "The Triumph of the Praise Songs," *Christianity Today* 43, no. 8 (July 12, 1999), 29–35.

17. Among Christian youth in North America, "practices" of faith are proving a route to religious revival as teenagers take part in ancient Christian rituals (rosaries, contemplative prayer, fasting, service to the poor, sacraments, and singing, to name a few) that identify them with a community of faith defined by practices more than by territory.

18. Wade Clark Roof, "Today's Spiritual Quests," in *1997 Princeton Lectures on Youth, Church and Culture* (Princeton, NJ: Princeton Theological Seminary, 1998), 93–102. Roof cites current models of automobiles as evidence of the pervasiveness of the journey metaphor in North American culture. Advertisers promote cars named Trek, Voyager, Explorer, Quest, Pathfinder; Nissan recently advertised under the slogan: "Life is a journey. Enjoy the ride."

19. See Tom Beaudoin, *Virtual Faith: The Irreverent Spiritual Quest of Generation X* (San Francisco: Jossey Bass, 1998), and Kenda Creasy Dean, "X-Files and Unknown Gods," *American Baptist Quarterly* 24 (March 2000), 3–21.

20. See Johan Huizinga, *Homo Ludens: A Study of Play-Element in Culture* (1950; repr. Boston: Beacon Press, 1955; New York: J. & J. Harper Editions, 1970). The intrinsic relationality of play is described in D. W. Winnicott, *Playing and Reality* (London and

New York: Routledge and Kegan Paul, 1971), especially chapters 3 and 4, pages 38–64.

21. Wolfhart Pannenberg, *Anthropology in Theological Perspective*, trans. Matthew J. O'Connell (Philadelphia: Westminster Press, 1985), 332–33.

22. Erik H. Erikson, *Identity, Youth and Crisis* (New York: W. W. Norton, 1968), 189–91.

23. Lang, *Sacred Games*, 371.

24. Ibid., 369–70.

25. Erikson, *Identity, Youth, and Crisis*, 243.

26. Sharon Daloz Parks, "Becoming in a Complex World: New Powers, Perils, and Possibilities," in *1998 Princeton Lectures on Youth, Church, and Culture* (Princeton, NJ: Princeton Theological Seminary, 1999), 45.

27. Augustine, *Confessions*, trans. Henry Chadwick (Oxford: Oxford University Press, 1991), 24.

28. Beaudoin, *Virtual Faith*, 96–120.

29. Walter Brueggemann, "Passion and Perspective: Two Dimensions of Education in the Bible," *Theology Today* 42 (July 1985), 180 (italics original).

30. For a thorough treatment of the role of passion in Christian education, see Kenda Creasy Dean, "Youth Ministry as the Transformation of Passion" (Ph.D. diss., Princeton Theological Seminary, 1996).

31. Lang, *Sacred Games*, 431.

Chapter 10: New Approaches to Worship

1. *Punter* is a term used in alternative worship circles to describe worshipers. It is a positive and widely inclusive description.

2. Raymond Fung, *The Isaiah Vision: An Ecumenical Strategy for Congregational Evangelism* (Geneva: WCC, 1995), 13.

3. Sally Morgenthaler, *Worship Evangelism: Inviting Unbelievers into the Presence of God* (Grand Rapids: Zondervan, 1995), 30.

4. "Culture Shock" seminar, Greenhouse, London, February 1993.

5. See Paradox Music, http://www.abbess.demon.co.uk/paradox/, website now called Visions, http://www.abbess.demon.co.uk/visions/.

6. See ch. 6, "Growing Edges," for "The Story of Alt. Worship in Two Versions" in Mark Pierson, Cathy Kirkpatrick, Mike Riddell, *The Prodigal Project: Journey into the Emerging Church* (London: Society for Promoting Christian Knowledge, 2000).

7. I'm indebted to John Hoyland for a posting on June 5, 1995, that first attempted to define these elements.

8. Tommy Walker (music church worship leader), interviewed by Morgenthaler in *Worship Evangelism*, 41.

9. *Words from the Late Late Service* (Glasgow: Late Late Service, 1993), 2.

10. Leonard Sweet, "Knowing the Times," http://www.leonardsweet.com/sweetened/Editions/2-8-9/Index.htm (June 1999).

Chapter 12: Art for Faith's Sake

1. Larry W. Hurtado, *At the Origins of Christian Worship: The Context and Character of Earliest Christian Devotion* (Grand Rapids: Eerdmans, 2000), 19–26.

2. Christopher L. C. E. Witcombe, "Art and Artists: Art for Art's Sake," http://www.arthistory.sbc.edu/artartists/modartsake.html (Fall 1997), 1.

3. James Kilpatrick, *The Writer's Art* (Kansas City, MO: Andrews and McMeel, 1984), 1.

4. Jerry Evenrud, former director for music, worship, and the arts in the Evangelical Lutheran Church in America, describes himself as "a freelance advocate for music and art in worship." His lectures on the use of art and music in worship are given under the title, "Art for Faith's Sake."

Chapter 13: Beyond Style

1. The use of the term "blended worship" is frequently associated with the contribution of Robert Webber. Importantly, Webber's use of the term goes far beyond musical style to include all aspects of worship. Webber calls for worship leaders to look in a wide range of resources for texts, songs, gestures, and practices that will help a congregation celebrate Christ through the historic pattern of worship. Unfortunately,

many people seem more excited about the "wide range of resources" than the "historic pattern of Christian worship," resulting in services that are eclectic but not well grounded.

2. For a recent account of these changes, see Michael S. Hamilton, "A Generation Changes North American Hymnody," *The Hymn: A Journal of Congregational Song* 52, no. 3 (July 2001): 11–20; and Karen B. Westerfield Tucker, "Liturgical Perspectives on Changes in North American Hymnody in the Past Twenty-Five Years," *The Hymn: A Journal of Congregational Song* 52, no. 3 (July 2001): 22–27.

3. Since the mid-1970s, nearly every denomination has published a new hymnal. In the late 1990s and early 2000s, many have published hymnal supplements. More than ever before, these hymnals and supplements have been produced with cooperation among hymnals of various worship traditions. This ferment has led to a small industry of related efforts: the publication of dozens of single-author hymn collections, regular hymn-writing competitions, and conferences on hymn writing and hymn accompaniment. There has probably never been as many single-author hymn collections in print as there are today. In the journal *The Hymn*, the Hymn Society's book service is printed in a smaller and smaller type size with each issue in an attempt to cram all the new publications into these four pages.

4. See Paul Westermeyer, *The Church Musician*, rev. ed. (Minneapolis: Augsburg Fortress, 1997), 130–35. Here Westermeyer, in conversation with other leading voices regarding church music, dispels the myth that Martin Luther actually said the words, "Why should the devil have all the good tunes?" It is very difficult (perhaps impossible) to make an honest comparison between Luther and Wesley (who themselves lived in remarkably different contexts) and our own day. Such a comparison needs to do justice to all the implications of vernacularization, without confusing it with unrestrained popularization.

5. Augustine, "Of the Morals of the Catholic Church," 15.25 in *A Select Library*

of the Nicene and Post-Nicene Fathers of the Christian Church, ed. Philip Schaff, 1st ser. (Grand Rapids: Eerdmans, n.d.), 4:48.

6. See Lester Ruth, "A Rose by Any Other Name" in *The Conviction of Things Unseen: Worship and Ministry in the 21st Century*, ed. Todd E. Johnson (Grand Rapids: Brazos Press, 2002), 33–51.

7. Augustine, *Confessions*, trans. R. S. Pine-Coffin (Harmondsworth: Penguin Classics, 1961), 239.

8. From John Wesley, *Select Hymns*, 1761, quoted in preface of the *United Methodist Hymnal* (Nashville: United Methodist Publishing House, 1989), vii.

9. Thomas G. Long, *Beyond the Worship Wars: Building Vital and Faithful Worship* (Bethesda, MD: Alban Institute, 2001), 32. Long is reflecting on a passage by theologian Hendrikus Berkhof.

10. Robert E. Webber, *Worship Old and New: A Biblical, Historical, and Practical Introduction*, rev. ed. (Grand Rapids: Zondervan, 1994), 195. Emphasis mine.

11. Nicholas Wolterstorf, *Art in Action: Toward a Christian Aesthetic* (Grand Rapids: Eerdmans, 1980), 184.

12. Ibid., 185. This is one application of Wolterstoff's comprehensive theory of art: "I want to argue . . . that works of art are objects and instruments of action. They are all inextricably embedded in the fabric of human intention. They are objects and instruments of action whereby we carry out our intentions with respect to the world, our fellows, ourselves, and our gods. Understanding art requires understanding art in human life" (3). Wolterstorff sees this understanding of art as broader and more inclusive than other explanatory theories: "Over and over one comes across the claims to the effect that such and such is 'the essential function of art.' 'Art is mimesis.' 'Art is self expression.' 'Art is significant form.' All such formulae fall prey to the same dilemma. Either what is said to be characteristic of art is true of more than art, or, if true only of art, it is not true of all art. The universality of art corresponds only to a diversity and flux of purposes, not to some pervasive and unique purpose . . .

Seldom do we have before our mind's eye the whole broad sweep of the purposes of art" (18, 20).

13. Webber, *Worship Old and New*, 195; Robert E. Webber, *Signs of Wonder: The Phenomenon of Convergence in Modern Liturgical and Charismatic Churches* (Nashville: Abbott Martyn, 1992), 83; republished as *The Worship Phenomenon: A Dynamic New Awakening in Worship Is Reviving the Body of Christ* (Nashville: Star Song, 1994); republished as *Blended Worship: Achieving Substance and Relevance in Worship* (Peabody, MA: Hendrickson Publishers, 1996).

14. Webber, *Signs of Wonder*, 97.

15. Gordon W. Lathrop, *Holy Things: A Liturgical Theology* (Minneapolis: Fortress, 1993), 223.

16. "Constitutions of the Holy Apostles," 2.7.57 in *Ante-Nicene Fathers*, eds. Alexander Roberts and James Donaldson (Grand Rapids: Eerdmans, 1951), 7:421.

17. Alice Parker, *Melodious Accord* (Chicago: GIA, 1991), 6.

18. Dietrich Boenhoffer, *Life Together* (London: SCM Press, 1949), 51.

19. Frank Burch Brown, *Religious Aesthetics: A Theological Study of Making and Meaning* (Princeton, NJ: Princeton University Press, 1989), 152–54.

20. John Calvin, *Institutes of the Christian Religion*, ed. John T. McNeil, trans. Ford Lewis Battles (Philadelphia: Westminster Press, 1960), 4.10.30.

21. For example, see Anscar J. Chupungco, *Liturgies of the Future: The Process and Methods of Inculturation* (New York: Paulist Press, 1989), and *So We Believe, So We Pray: Toward Koinonia in Worship*, ed. Thomas F. Best and Dagmar Heller (Geneva: WCC Publications, 1995).

22. Kenneth Smits, "Liturgical Reform in a Cultural Perspective," *Worship* 50, no. 2 (March 1976): 98.

23. A summary of this statement is printed in Lathrop, *Holy People: A Liturgical Ecclesiology* (Minneapolis: Fortress, 1999) 233–36.

Contributors

Frank Burch Brown is Professor of Religion and the Arts at Christian Theological Seminary in Indianapolis where he directs a graduate program in church music.

Gary M. Burge is Professor of the New Testament at Wheaton College, Wheaton, Illinois.

Andy Crouch was most recently Editor in Chief of *re:generation quarterly*, a magazine that won the *Utne Reader*'s Alternative Press Award for spiritual coverage in 1999. He was formerly a campus minister with InterVarsity Christian Fellowship at Harvard University. He is also co-author of *The Worship Team Handbook*.

Kenda Creasy Dean is Assistant Professor of youth, church, and culture in the field of practical theology and Christian education at Princeton Theological Seminary.

Michael S. Hamilton is Associate Professor of History, Seattle Pacific University. Dr. Hamilton has published articles on several aspects of American evangelicalism in the twentieth century and is currently working on a book on the history of fundamentalism.

Cathy Kirkpatrick lives in inner-city Sydney, Australia.

Mark Pierson is Pastor at the diverse Cityside Baptist Church in Auckland, New Zealand.

Mike Riddell is Teaching Fellow in Applied Theology at the University of Otago, Dunedin, New Zealand.

Thomas H. Schattauer is Associate Professor of Liturgics and Dean of the Chapel at Wartburg Theological Seminary, Dubuque, Iowa.

Clayton J. Schmit is Arthur DeKruyter/Christ Church Oak Brook Associate Professor of Preaching at Fuller Theological Seminary and has been appointed the academic director of Fuller's Brehm Center for Worship, Theology, and the Arts. In addition to being a classically trained conductor, performer, and award-winning composer, Dr. Schmit brings extraordinary gifts to the art of effective preaching and is also a member of the Academy of Homiletics.

Leonard Sweet is Founder and President of SpiritVenture Ministries and the E. Stanley Jones Professor of Evangelism at Drew Theological School. He also serves as a Distinguished Visiting Professor at George Fox University and is the chief writer for preachingplus.com. He is a popular speaker and has written nineteen books.

Miroslav Volf is Henry B. Wright Professor of Systematic Theology, Yale Divinity School and Visiting Professor of Systematic Philosophy, Evangelical-Theological Faculty, Osijek, Croatia.

Robert E. Webber holds the William R. and Geraldyne B. Myers Chair of Ministry at Northern Baptist Theological Seminary, Lombard, Illinois. His essay was previously delivered to the summer 2000 conference of the Center for Catholic and Evangelical Theology, Collegeville, Minnesota.

James F. White holds the Bard Thompson Chair of Liturgical Studies at Drew University. He previously taught at the Perkins School of Theology for twenty-two years and was professor of liturgy at the University of Notre Dame until 1999. He has served as president of the North American Academy of Liturgy and received its Berakah Award. He also chaired the editorial committee of the Section on Worship of the Board of Discipleship of The United Methodist Church.

John D. Witvliet is Director of the Calvin Institute of Christian Worship at Calvin College and Calvin Theological Seminary in Grand Rapids, Michigan, where he has oversight of the Institute's practical and scholarly programs as well as being the project director of the Worship Renewal Grants Program, funded by the Lilly Endowment, Inc.

Tim A. Dearborn has served as a pastor and missionary for thirty years. His Ph.D. studies in systematic theology deepened his conviction that our calling in Christ is to participate by the Spirit in voicing creation's praise to the Triune God. Tim has served as professor of spirituality and mission for Seattle Pacific University, Fuller Theological Seminary, Regent College, the University of Aberdeen, and the French Evangelical Seminary. Currently, he serves as Associate Director for Faith and Development at World Vision International and has the privilege of participating with God's people in worship around the world. He lives in Seattle, Washington, with his wife, Kerry.

Scott Coil is Music Director and Liturgist at St. Alban's Episcopal Church in Edmonds, Washington. He has led numerous worship services for organizations and special events, including The Vine, the national conference for *Image: A Journal of the Arts and Religion*, and the 30th Anniversary Celebration of Evangelicals for Social Action. He currently lives in Seattle, Washington, with his wife, Emily.